LOGIC AND POLITICS

LOGIC AND POLITICS

Hegel's Philosophy of Right

PETER J. STEINBERGER , 1948 -

YALE UNIVERSITY PRESS
New Haven and London

Designed by Jill G. Breitbarth
and set in Times Roman type
by Rainsford Type, Ridgefield, Conn.
Printed in the United States of America by
Braun-Brumfield, Inc., Ann Arbor, Mich.

Library of Congress Cataloging-in-Publication Data
Steinberger, Peter J., 1948–
Logic and politics : Hegel's philosophy of right / Peter J.
Steinberger.
p. cm.
Includes index.
ISBN 0–300–03982–4 (alk. paper)
1. Law—Philosophy. 2. Hegel, Georg Wilhelm Friedrich, 1770–1831.
Grudlinien der Philosophie des Rechts. 3. Law—Methodology.
I. Title.
K230.H432S74 1988   87–21159
340′.1—dc19   CIP

The paper in this book meets the guidelines for permanence
and durability of the Committee on Production Guidelines
for Book Longevity of the Council on Library Resources.

10 9 8 7 6 5 4 3 2 1

Contents

Preface

During the past three decades there has been in the English-speaking world a substantial revival of interest in Hegel's philosophical system. Until quite recently this revival was almost entirely confined to those who studied philosophy in the "continental" way. I have no intention of subscribing here to a dichotomy—continental versus analytic—that I regard as fundamentally suspect; indeed, this book is specifically written against the philosophical pluralism that such a division implies. Nonetheless, the fact is that Hegel studies have generally been pursued by those who operate within marxist, phenomenological, or existentialist traditions; whereas those for whom philosophy owes more to Frege, Russell, Moore, and Wittgenstein tend to know little about, and have little interest in, the Hegelian system. It is a revealing fact that while Kant's First Critique has become a standard part of the Anglo-American philosophical curriculum, Hegel's refutation of it has not.

Such conclusions must now be qualified since the publication of three remarkable books by Charles Taylor, John Burbidge, and M. J. Inwood. Though different in quite profound ways, these books are similar in at least one crucial respect. All were written by individuals who are skilled in and, to a certain evident extent, committed to doing philosophy in a manner that many so-called analytic philosophers would approve of. In each case, the concern is to render Hegel's arguments in something like a logical form so that they can be evaluated in terms of the standard laws of thought and rational inference. The goal is less historical, literary, or even exegetical than discursive: it is to present Hegel's claims as clearly as possible, purging them of any peculiar terminological obscurities, and with a view toward taking them seriously as arguments that we might well adopt ourselves. It is unlikely, to be sure, that the publication of these three books will signal a sudden acceptance of Hegel into the canon of Anglo-American philosophy; it seems that no one has yet accomplished for Hegel what, say, P. F. Strawson did for Kant. Nevertheless, it is now far less necessary to defend an approach to Hegel that may, in some broad sense, be termed analytic.

With respect to the philosophy of Right, a rather different set of problems arises. Here the tradition of rendering Hegel's thought accessible and plausible is, in a sense, much more firmly established. It is rooted in the efforts of authors such as Knox, Kaufmann, Pelczynski, and Avineri to show that Hegelian political thought bears no internal relationship to twentieth-century fascism and that, on the contrary, the philosophy of Right is reflective of a quite moderate and rather liberal sensibility. These efforts have certainly made a great contribution in demonstrating beyond any doubt that traditional prejudices against Hegel, of the sort espoused by Karl Popper, have little if anything to do with what Hegel actually said and wrote. But in the process, a certain price has been paid. For what emerges is a kind of domesticated picture of Hegel that makes it extremely difficult to render intelligible many particular assertions of his which are, one would think, quite typically Hegelian—assertions pertaining to freedom, monarchy, the community as "Mind objectified," the nature of political philosophy, and the like.

In my view, the deficiencies of these studies stem from an unwillingness to read the philosophy of Right in the context of Hegel's larger philosophical system. The result is that while it is easy enough to see how Popper might be wrong, it is difficult to account for our strong intuition that Hegel's is not just another form of liberalism and that his political thought is somehow bolder and more radical than anything we find among the more orthodox defenders of constitutional government. There are, to be sure, a few studies which do indeed consider the relationship between Hegel's philosophy and his politics, notably, Judith Shklar's quite brilliant account of the political ideas of the *Phenomenology*. But even these tend to overlook the mature and definitive version of the Hegelian system as embodied in the *Science of Logic* and in the *Encyclopedia*.

The purpose of my book is to consider the philosophy of Right explicitly in light of the Logic, i.e., as governed by, and as an application of, Hegel's philosophical method. It seems clear that this is how Hegel himself intended the philosophy of Right to be approached; and it seems plausible to hypothesize that the nature of his political thought can only be apprehended if we come to grips with the kind of argumentation upon which it is based. In pursuing this hypothesis, I shall focus on a handful of claims which strike me as particularly revealing of Hegel's political thought in general. These claims are treated in Part Two, composed of chapters 3 through 6, which consider, respectively, issues pertaining to crime and punishment, the so-called moral standpoint, marriage, and the inwardly differentiated constitution of the rational state. My judgment is that each of these plays an important strategic role in the unfolding of the philosophy of Right such that an account of them, taken together, can provide a good introduction to the distinctive character of Hegel's political thought.

These four chapters are, in a sense, discrete, and each can stand on its own (though chapter 4 is best conceived as a set of transitional notes). On the other hand, they are connected in that each reflects the basic methodological principles established in Hegel's Logic. They are also connected in that they follow the general contour of the philosophy of Right, albeit selectively. Chapter 3 deals with a fundamental theme of Abstract Right, chapter 4 with Morality, and chapters 5 and 6 with Ethical Life. As in Hegel, the arguments are at once distinct and mutually dependent. My intention is that they build upon one another in such a way that each, though in some sense *selbständig*, can nonetheless be seen to presuppose its predecessors.

The intellectual contexts for these chapters are both political and methodological and are outlined in Part One. Chapter 1 provides an introduction to certain long-standing questions of political philosophy. The focus is on a handful of Hegel's more influential predecessors, and rather little mention is made of Hegel himself. The goal is to outline a set of fundamental issues in terms largely unaffected by the peculiarities of the Hegelian system. These issues may be thought to comprise the basis of an ongoing debate among political philosophers. I presuppose that Hegel was a self-conscious participant in this debate, and that its terms need to be clearly established if we are properly to evaluate the nature of his contribution to it.

Of course, to treat the philosophy of Right in terms of the larger system also requires some consideration of the Logic itself, and in chapter 2 I attempt to offer a brief account of Hegel's philosophical method. My intention in this regard is not to make an original contribution but rather, and more simply, to present my own understanding of Hegel's method preparatory to a discussion of his political thought. I certainly make no pretense that chapter 2 provides anything approaching a comprehensive account of "the logic of Hegel's Logic." My hope is only that it offers one plausible, provisionally acceptable account of Hegel's *method* or philosophical procedure, and that its errors and omissions are not fatal to my interpretation of the philosophy of Right.

Finally, I consider in an epilogue some of the more narrowly "political" implications of the philosophy of Right with respect to certain of Hegel's forebears and successors. If Hegel's political philosophy is shaped by his philosophical method, it is surely influenced also by the problems and perplexities of political life. Against certain emergent trends in the study of political theory, I do believe that at least some of these problems transcend the peculiarities of historical accident and raise perennial questions for philosophers of politics. At any rate, it is clear that Hegel thought this to be the case, despite his own emphasis on historical particularity, and that the philosophy of Right should indeed be read with the "tradition" of political philosophy in mind.

In the introduction to his fine study of Hegel, M. J. Inwood warns against those who would pursue "a bland 'rational reconstruction' of [Hegel's thought], which fits more or less loosely on his text and represents in any case only one of several directions in which his thought might be taken." I fear that this describes my own project all too accurately. I have tried to demonstrate the clarity and plausibility of Hegel's political thought, and it may be that any such effort leads necessarily to oversimplification and distortion. But if this is so, then we might well wonder about the philosophical value of studying Hegel at all; systems of thought that remain hopelessly murky and deeply implausible are unlikely to prove very edifying. I proceed, then, under the contingent proposition that an account such as the one offered here—if not the present one itself—must be tenable if we are to take Hegel seriously as a philosopher of politics.

Throughout I have relied on the main published version of the philosophy of Right, what we now call in English *The Philosophy of Right* of 1821. One must, of course, be mindful of the peculiar political situation in which this book was published and the sense in which its contents may have been influenced by questions of a nonphilosophical nature. The many volumes of lectures on the philosophy of Right collected and edited by Ilting, and more recently by Henrich and by Pöggeler, do indeed suggest certain discrepancies between what Hegel wrote and what he actually said to his students, and also between the positions he took before and after the imposition of the Carlsbad Decrees. The precise nature and importance of these discrepancies is, however, a matter of some substantial disagreement. Since my own purposes are not primarily historical or biographical, I am predisposed to work with the text that Hegel chose to leave behind, hence to assign priority to the published book on the philosophy of Right along with Gans's *Zusätze*, which have rightly been accorded a semiofficial status, as well as the correlative parts of the third section of the *Encyclopedia.*

Similarly, for Hegel's Logic I rely mainly on the first part of the *Encyclopedia*, the so-called Lesser Logic, rather than the Larger Logic, *The Science of Logic*. There is much debate regarding the relationship between these two versions, and it does indeed seem that they are curiously different in important ways. Such differences, however, pertain largely to claims of a substantive or metaphysical nature rather than to procedural or methodological claims, hence they do not generally affect the arguments made here. The Lesser Logic, though lacking much of the Larger Logic's explanatory material, has the virtue of concision and accessibility. As a book that went through two substantial revisions, the final one in 1830, its claims to being authoritative seem unassailable.

Unless otherwise indicated, parenthetic references in the text are to *Werke 7: Grundlinien der Philosophie des Rechts* (Frankfurt: Suhrkamp, 1970); this edition includes Gans's *Zusätze* (additions) and Hegel's own *Randbemerkungen* (marginal notes). Citations marked *EL* are to *Werke 8: Encyklopädie der Philosophischen*

Wissenschaften im Grundrisse, Erster Teil (Frankfurt: Suhrkamp, 1970), which includes Henning's *Zusätze*. In rendering passages from these texts in English, I have relied heavily on the well-known translations of Knox and Wallace, respectively; however, in most cases I have made numerous and sometimes quite major emendations. Also, citations marked *EG* refer to *Werke 10: Encyklopädie der Philosophischen Wissenschaften im Grundrisse, Dritter Teil* (Frankfurt: Suhrkamp, 1970); those marked *WL* refer to Lasson's edition of *Wissenschaft der Logik* (Hamburg: Felix Meiner Verlag, 1975).

In the interest of clarity, I have chosen to capitalize certain key words. There are, of course, good reasons for not doing so. There is little textual support for it, since all German nouns are capitalized. Further, there is the danger of mystifying Hegel's concepts, making them appear to be somehow less accessible than they really are; in fact, my explicit purposes are quite the opposite. Finally, there are many words that mean roughly the same to us as they do within the context of Hegel's technical system; here, it is not necessary to make a distinction. There are, however, some words for which the Hegelian meaning is very different from standard meanings, for example, "Right" (*Recht*) or "Understanding" (*Verstand*), to mention two. In such cases capitalization, though stylistically awkward, seems to be the simplest way of keeping things clear.

I am extremely grateful to George Armstrong Kelly and Allen Wood, both of whom read much of my work and responded to it at great length and from no conceivable motive other than pure generosity and a deep interest in the subject. Their willingness to devote time and attention to someone with whom they had no formal connection was matched only by the quite startling insight and erudition they brought to bear on my manuscripts; their professional dedication has been, for me, a source of genuine pleasure and an object lesson as well. Closer to home, though in different ways, I am also very much indebted to William Peck, Steven B. Smith, and Richard Wolin, all of whom read the entire text and provided especially useful comments and suggestions.

I am similarly grateful to my good friend Neil Thomason, who knows quite well how important our countless hours of debate, discussion, and hard work have been to me; and also to John Stanley, for helping me in so many ways with this and numerous other projects.

Of the many other people who read and commented on substantial sections of this manuscript, I especially wish to thank Steven DeLue, Arthur DiQuattro, Richard Flathman, Jeff Johnson, Joshua Miller, Robert Seaberg, and Charles Svitavsky. Also, Henry Kariel offered valuable aid and encouragement at a most propitious time. In general, this project has taught me that I, at least, am unable to function properly in isolation, and that an actively collaborative process may not only improve the quality of one's thought but also considerably add to the enjoyment of an endeavor that is already most enjoyable on its own account.

The project was undertaken with the generous support of Reed College and its Vollum Research Fund, which freed me of all teaching responsibilities during 1983–84; and also the National Endowment for the Humanities, which gave me a second year off during 1984–85. Chapter 3 originally appeared, in rather different form, as "Hegel on Crime and Punishment," *American Political Science Review* 77 (December 1983); chapter 5 is a revised version of "Hegel on Marriage and Politics," *Political Studies* 34 (December 1986); brief sections of chapter 1 were first published in "Hegel's Occasional Writings: State and Individual," *Review of Politics* 45 (April 1983), though I would now disavow much of what this last article says. I wish finally to express my appreciation to the community that is Reed College—students, colleagues, administrators, friends—for providing an atmosphere that encourages and honors the intellectual life.

PART ONE

*Contexts:
Politics and Logic*

1

Accommodationism and Perfectionism

The purpose of this book is to consider selected themes in Hegel's philosophy of Right with a view toward characterizing his political thought in general. Specifically, I hope to demonstrate the cogency and relevance of certain of Hegel's political arguments, to evaluate the plausibility of his overall position as embodied in the rational state, and to offer thereby an account of his political philosophy considered directly and explicitly as an application of the Hegelian philosophical method to issues of political, social, and moral concern.

My argument, however, is based on a number of premises that do not derive directly from Hegel's work, though they are fully consistent with it. These premises pertain to certain key issues of modern political theory and to the nature of political philosophy as a strategy of inquiry. I begin, therefore, with an effort to elucidate them and to offer an initial case for their plausibility. I do confess at the outset to a certain ambivalence regarding the pages that ensue. On the one hand, it may be that too much space is devoted to an exposition that might perhaps have been accomplished in a few brief sentences; on the other hand, I worry that the "initial case," even presented at such length, is somehow inadequate and that the reader will be insufficiently motivated to accept the premises, if only provisionally. My final judgment is that the account of Hegel offered in this book depends crucially upon these premises, hence the need to present them with some fullness and at some length, but that, further, in the light of my central task it is both sufficient and appropriate to treat them as premises rather than as complete and satisfying arguments.

From readers anxious to get on with Hegel, I can only ask patience and indulgence.

1

In the preface to the *Philosophy of Right*, Hegel writes of the importance "not only to dwell in what is substantive while still retaining subjective freedom, but also to possess subjective freedom while standing not in anything particular and accidental but in what exists absolutely."

Among other things, this passage alerts us, at the very beginning of the *Philosophy of Right*, to a central preoccupation of Hegelian political thought: the apparent tension between values or interests associated with the individual and those associated with society. In this particular formulation, the individual is defined in terms of "subjective freedom," i.e., the distinctively modern notion of the human person as an autonomous agent unconstrained in some important sense by imperatives external to himself. Society, on the other hand, is defined in terms of that which is "substantive", i.e., the classical notion that the structures of society reflect, or ought to reflect, behavioral injunctions—including substantive moral principles—which are objectively and demonstrably true and which are binding on the individual.

This theme emerges with perhaps greatest clarity when Hegel treats his predecessors in political philosophy. Thus, for example, in a famous passage he finds that Plato well understood the value of society as something substantive: "[He] displays the substance of ethical life in its ideal beauty and truth." But as the characteristic philosopher of classical politics, Plato also failed to acknowledge the individual qua free agent, i.e., failed to "cope with the principle of self-subsistent particularity." Plato saw, or at least sensed, that free individuality was "in opposition to . . . his purely substantial state" and thus excluded it from his state altogether. In Hegel's words: "The principle of the self-subsistent inherently infinite personality of the individual, the principle of subjective freedom, is denied its right in the purely substantial form which Plato gave to mind in its actuality"(185).

In more recent political philosophy, Hegel sees precisely the opposite defect. Of Rousseau, for example, he writes that "he reduces the union of individuals in the state to a contract and therefore to something based on their arbitrary wills, their opinion, and their capriciously given consent" (258). Rousseau, and other moderns such as Fichte and von Haller, fail to see the "absolute infinity and rationality in the state", hence do not understand the degree to which society is "substantive" or, again, a matter of objective and obligatory rules and injunctions.

In one sense, we might simply say that on such an account the ancients ignored the individual, properly understood, while the moderns ignore society, properly understood. Of course, much more is involved here. For Hegel, Plato's failure to understand the individual as a subject meant that his concept of society itself could not be philosophically satisfying. Similarly, by ignoring the sense in which the state must be substantive, Rousseau could not truly understand the nature of individuality and of individual freedom. Themes such as these will be treated more or less directly throughout this book. But for now, it is sufficient simply to note the sense in which this general problem was, for Hegel, absolutely central.

Of course, Hegel is hardly unique in this regard. Modern political philosophy is deeply concerned with the apparent opposition between individual and society. This may appear to be a not very controversial judgment, and surely it has been made time and again throughout much of the modern Western tradition. Still, the issue of individual and society is often thought to be so self-evident, so manifestly clear and straightforward, that we sometimes lose track of exactly what is involved in it. Thus, it may be useful briefly to reexamine the problem in broad outline and to specify once again certain of its particulars, if only for the purpose of clarifying our own ideas.

Virtually all modern political philosophers of any consequence place a great value on what may be called the "individuality of the individual." Of course, there are countless particular conceptions of human individuality, but all of them seem to share the view that the individual is, at least potentially, different and unique in some nonphysical or "spiritual" sense. That is, humans differ not simply in terms of physical traits (e.g., fingerprints) but, more importantly, in terms of spiritual or mental characteristics such as memories, experiences, neuroses, tastes, dispositions, choices, judgments, intellectual capacities, and the like. We may call this notion of spiritual distinctiveness the "bare-bones" concept of the individual. Particular conceptions of individuality vary largely in terms of what they add to the bare-bones concept.[1] That is, they vary in terms of which *kinds* of mental distinctiveness are predicable of humans and which of these are most crucial in differentiating one person from another. On some accounts, the individual is distinguished by a particular set of wants and impulses; for others, it is the autonomous functioning of a "rational will" that marks one person from another; and for still others, personal differences are rooted in different experiences and memories. But in all cases, the individuality of the individual is said to lie in some kind of thought-configuration that is unique to the individual and is embodied in actions which can thus somehow be identified as uniquely "his" or "hers."

It follows, then, that to the degree one values individuality, one also values such spiritual distinctiveness. We may restate this in terms of the following simple principle: *in moral and political discourse as we know it, the concept of the individual typically suggests, at the least, an interest in securing and expanding the opportunity of the person to be different in himself and to act in ways reflective of that difference.* I believe that all major political philosophers of the modern period would subscribe to this principle and hence share this commitment to individual spiritual difference, though again the particular implications of doing so vary greatly.

We should be clear as to what is not being claimed here. To value individuality is not necessarily to value individual liberty, though the two are frequently conflated. For individuality or spiritual distinctiveness can be associated with any number of other values such as attaining personal excellence, being well-adjusted, living in accordance with one's particular nature, and the like, none of which is related in any obvious way to being free. Moreover, to define individuality simply in terms of individual freedom runs the risk of lumping together the many different and incompatible senses of the word *liberty*. The principle I have described thus operates at a rather more general level. It simply says that to

---

1. I rely here on the now common distinction drawn between "concepts" and "conceptions." See John Rawls, *A Theory of Justice* (Cambridge, Mass.: Harvard University Press, 1971), p. 5.

value individuality necessarily commits one to preserving the person's opportunity or ability to be spiritually different in *some* manner and to act accordingly. This may or may not involve notions of freedom.

Indeed, the principle of the individual represents a formal requirement and is, as such, indifferent to an enormous range of philosophical controversies. We are led to ask a variety of questions: Which forms of spiritual distinctiveness are politically important? Which forms are trivial or, perhaps, undesirable? When should the individual abjure the opportunity to be different? But such questions typically involve considerations that go far beyond the conceptually necessary consequences of valuing individuality in the bare-bones sense. If we ask whether it is all right for a person to practice dialectic in the agora, in conformity with his *daemon* but in violation of the law, this presumably cannot be answered with reference only to the implications of bare-bones individuality. Valuing individuality—in the bare-bones sense, of itself and without qualification—commits one only to preserving the person's opportunity to be spiritually different in some way and to act accordingly. And to the degree that all those who value individuality necessarily share in the bare-bones concept, they necessarily share also this commitment to difference.

Already I have used the term "spiritual," and in a book on Hegel the implications of this are likely to be daunting. In fact, though, I am using the term only in the simplest sense to refer to the realm of thoughts, concepts, and consciousness—the mental realm—as distinct from the realm of purely physical things in the world. I believe that this use is entirely consistent, though not coterminous, with Hegel's concept of spirit. For Hegel, the word *Geist* does indeed refer to the realm of thoughts; however, it also includes a number of further considerations or implications involving, for example, the necessary interrelationships of all possible thoughts and, ultimately, the necessary structure of the world itself. Some of these considerations will be explored in chapter 2. But in either its narrow or broad sense, the word *Geist* does indeed refer to the realm of things mental and hence can be translated, I believe, as "spirit" or as "mind" with roughly equal accuracy.

Now while it is true that modern political philosophers value the individuality of the individual, it is if anything even more obvious that they also place a great value on the peculiar benefits conferred by society. As in the case of individuality, conceptions of society differ markedly. Society is essentially the expression of one or more material processes, especially economic, demographic, and ecological processes; or it is, rather, a question of shared meanings and conventions rooted in the structure of conscious human interaction; or, again, it is a matter of convenient and reciprocal exchanges between discrete and rational persons. Sociological theory, though less than two centuries old, provides a rich and extremely varied set of conceptions of society, the implications of which may be very important for political theory.

But again, there seems to be a certain common denominator. For in virtually any theoretical context, the word *society* connotes a system of rules according to which the activities of individuals are coordinated on the basis of identifiable patterns. These rules may be tacit or express, comprehensive or selective, fixed or negotiable. The source of such rules, and the precise effect they have on actual human activity, are difficult questions for professional social scientists. But that such rules exist, and that their putative purpose involves patterns of coordination among individuals, seems to be central to the concept of society as it appears in moral and political discourse.

We may call this the bare-bones concept of society; and it seems clear that in valuing society one values to that extent the implications of the bare-bones concept. Thus we have a second principle: *in political and moral discourse, the concept of society tends to suggest an interest in supporting and defending (some specified) systems of rules and (some specified) patterns of coordination.* Again, exactly which system and which pattern is desired will depend on how a variety of other empirical and philosophical problems are addressed. Nonetheless, all theorists of consequence will share, in some form, this commitment to rules and patterns.

While it is typical to think of the rules of society in terms of political laws promulgated by a sovereign legislative entity, the fact is that many other kinds of rules would qualify as well. These might include unwritten customs or mores, established ethical codes, cooperative agreements entered into by free and independent agents, and the like. The principle of society as such is indifferent to the distinctions between such rules. Like the principle of the individual, it operates at a more general level and demands only that we value some set of rules and patterns conceived in some identifiable manner.

Again, virtually all modern political philosophers value both individual and society; as a result, all share in roughly equal measure a certain basic problem. For it seems to be the case that the two principles we have outlined are somehow incompatible with one another. Specifically, the principle of society tends to turn against the principle of the individual inasmuch as the rules and patterns of the former are designed to constrain or prohibit the differences of thought and action sanctioned by the latter. That is to say, rule-governed patterns of interaction among individuals typically involve an unwillingness to tolerate individual deviations which threaten those patterns. Similarly, the opportunity to be different necessarily denies the force of certain rule-governed patterns. Again, the precise form of this problem will vary depending upon what has been added to the bare-bones concepts of individual and society. As will be shown below, Hobbes's account, for example, differs from Rousseau's at least in part because he understands individual and society in a rather different way. Still, inasmuch as they share the implications of the bare-bones concepts, both Hobbes and Rousseau necessarily confront certain common and fundamental features of the problem at hand.

In a sense, the problem is simply that there are two competing values which, in certain circumstances, cannot both be satisfied: to value individuality is sometimes to threaten social order, and vice versa. Such problems are common in moral life and they appear to be analyzable in terms of three kinds of elements: *general moral principles, empirical circumstances,* and *specific imperatives.* We can illustrate with the following case. Assume that I hold two moral principles or maxims: (1) things borrowed should be returned to their rightful owners, and (2) madmen should not possess weapons. Assume also the empirical circumstance that I have borrowed a weapon from George whom I now discover was and still is insane.[2] The juxtaposition of these principles and this circum-

2. I have altered the case from the *Republic*, book 1, in order to facilitate the argument. In Plato's version, "George" was not mad at the time of the loan; this considerably complicates the issue, but it does so in ways that are not germane to the present discussion.

stance produces two logically contradictory imperatives: I should return the weapon and I should not return the weapon. In the face of this dilemma, then, I need some strategy that will permit me to act in a consistent and responsible fashion.

Three general kinds of possibilities present themselves:

(A) The empirical circumstance can be removed. Of course, in the present case as described this option no longer exists, but in general we can imagine strategies designed to eliminate those empirical circumstances in which particularly difficult and troubling moral dilemmas arise. Still, such an alternative is often not very attractive, as the moral dilemmas that most concern us are typically related to common and difficult-to-avoid situations. For example, if the practice of borrowing things were eliminated altogether, then the dilemma described above could never arise; few of us, though, would be willing to take such a drastic step.

(B) The general moral principles can be altered so as to avoid the contradiction in imperatives. Thus, we could rewrite our first principle to read, "things borrowed should usually, though not always, be returned to their rightful owners," and we would hope to add to the principle a description of those kinds of instances in which things should not be returned. In doing this, we would eliminate our moral dilemma. Of course, in the process, we would have significantly adjusted and compromised at least one of the original principles in the interest of the other, something we might seriously regret. Nonetheless, I take it that this strategy is the most common one for dealing with such dilemmas.

(C) We can choose to hold our moral principles as originally stated, but avoid the contradiction in imperatives by reinterpreting one or more of the concepts upon which our principles are based. For example, in the present case we might discover that "borrowing" does not quite mean what we thought it meant, in that one cannot really borrow something from an insane person. Of course, we would have to have sound conceptual reasons for deciding this, reasons which I cannot now fathom. Nonetheless, if the concept of borrowing were so changed, then we would have to say that we did not "borrow" the weapon at all; hence, our first general moral principle simply would not apply to the present case and there would be no conflict of imperatives.

I believe that this kind of analysis applies equally to the problem of individual and society. The principle of the individual suggests that we should secure and expand the opportunity of the person to be different. The principle of society requires that we support and defend the rules and patterns of society. Given the usual empirical circumstances in which people find themselves, we frequently face contradictory imperatives: actions need not conform to the rule-governed patterns of society and actions must conform to them. Strategy (A) would suggest that the empirical circumstances be somehow altered so as to avoid the dilemma, e.g., we could demand that everyone become a hermit. Such an approach may seem to be of little use to political theorists, although some important variations of this strategy will be touched on in a later chapter. Strategy (B) would suggest that we accommodate the basic principles to one another, i.e., we should adjust and compromise one or both of the principles in the interest of the other. Strategy (C) would suggest that the concepts upon which the two principles are based—concepts of spiritual difference, person, rule coordination, and the like—can be suitably reinterpreted so that the apparent moral dilemma does not in fact arise.

I would argue that most political theorists of the modern period adopt some version of Strategy (B). Some of these proceed by emphasizing the principle of society at the expense of the principle of the individual; opportunities for being different would thus be compromised in the interest of a smoothly functioning social order. Others emphasize instead the value of the individual and would narrow the reach of those rules aimed at establishing patterns of coordination. Of course, most writers seek a kind of middle ground in which the value of distinctiveness and of coordination are sensibly and realistically balanced. But in all of these cases, the problem of individual and society is not dissolved but only circumvented on the basis of considerations external to the concepts themselves.[3]

But there is also an important tradition of modern political thought that relies essentially on one or another version of Strategy (C). Theorists in this tradition, and I include here Hegel, seek to

3. There is yet a more problematic version according to which the rules of society in fact serve the interests of individuality. Typical here would be Locke's view that law actually increases individual freedom. Such a position is considered briefly in section 4 of this chapter.

resolve the problem of the individual and society through a kind of conceptual analysis. To foreshadow the general argument, writers who employ Strategy (B) typically extend or flesh out the bare-bones concepts of individual and society in such a way as to leave the underlying moral dilemma between them untouched; hence, such theories are largely attempts to find a basis for accommodating the individual to society, and vice versa, without changing the essential character of either. The Hegelian approach, on the other hand, seeks to enrich the bare-bones concepts of individual and society in such a way as to show the dilemma to be a problem only for a shallow and unenlightened understanding; it claims to do so by offering a deeper account of individual distinctiveness and of rule-governed interaction, an account that demonstrates their mutual compatibility and, indeed, mutual dependence.

But for both approaches, it is clear that the issue of individual and society is a fundamental and unavoidable problem. On the one hand, this appears to be a straightforward consequence of the fact that political philosophy is necessarily concerned with the rules of society and with the welfare of those individuals who comprise it. It is hard to imagine a political philosophy which did not somehow manifest these interests, and I can certainly think of no counterexamples. To be concerned both with society and with the individuals who comprise it is almost necessarily to encounter the kind of problem I have been describing. But further, and more generally, I would suggest that virtually all of the other major preoccupations of political philosophy—e.g., the problem of who should rule, the question of church and state, the problem of justice, the issue of political obligation—themselves raise the question of individual and society. For example, the problem of who should rule presupposes the validity of rulership itself, hence of laws which establish patterns of interaction and regulate the eccentricities of individuals. Similarly, the question of justice necessarily involves the possibility of rules and patterns designed to ensure outcomes that are just or fair. In all such cases, the attempt to solve some difficult problem in political philosophy appears to presuppose a satisfactory answer to the problem of individual and society, a problem which therefore cannot be plausibly ignored.

The problem also appears to have emerged with particular force in the modern period. This is undoubtedly related to the distinctive emphasis which writers since (roughly) the Reformation have placed on the value of the individual apart from the social or transcendent contexts in which he lives. It may be thought, then, that the ancients, lacking any clear notion of the individual qua free agent, were largely insensitive to, and unconcerned with, the problem of individual and society. From this perspective, a work such as *Antigone* deals not at all with that problem but, rather, with a conflict between two social codes, one political, the other religious. The point is debatable. Antigone herself is without a doubt representative of a particular kind of institution having to do, roughly, with something like family piety; her actions do indeed emerge out of a particular set of social injunctions. And yet, those same actions also seem to emerge from a kind of individual distinctiveness, or even moral freedom. In this regard, the contrast between her and the timid Ismene is particularly instructive. Antigone cannot be simply a product of her family, for she alone of the sisters is willing to act. She must be understood as, in effect, a strong-willed individual, an agent who bears a deep personal responsibility for her deeds. Ismene makes this clear, both in her admonitions to Antigone and in her own inability to "will" that which is morally right.

In any case, it appears that the ancients may in some sense be eligible for a kind of retrospective interpretation or reconstruction in terms of the problem of individual and society; and it is absolutely certain that Hegel felt this way, as evidenced in his account of Plato in the *Philosophy of Right* and of Sophocles in the *Phenomenology*.

2

My premises, then, are threefold. First, the concepts of individual and society are such that to value those things described by the one is often to compromise those things described by the other. Second, the problem that this raises is a characteristic and perhaps necessary preoccupation of modern political philosophy. And third, in the face of this problem, we can either (A) change the empirical circumstances, (B) revise one or both of the principles so as to make their imperatives mutually consistent, or (C) avoid the contradiction by reinterpreting one or more of the concepts upon which our principles are based. In the account to be presented here, Hegel's political philosophy may be thought of as a particular and quite powerful version of Strategy (C). But in order to understand this more clearly, it will be useful to work through with some care the kinds of political philosophy against which Hegel is reacting, in particular, the standard versions of Strategy (B) as well as a version of Strategy (C), which prefigures, though only in a most incomplete and unsatisfactory way, the mature Hegelian formulation.

Again, the dominant tendency in modern political thought has been to adopt some version of (B). That is, the characteristic theorists of the modern period, dating roughly from the Reformation, have sought to reconcile the principle of the individual and that of society by reformulating—qualifying, softening, limiting, compromising—either one or the other, or both. By "characteristic theorists" I refer essentially to Hobbes and to authors working generally within the parameters of the Hobbesian revolution: Locke, Hume, the English utilitarians and their French Enlightenment counterparts, the American founders, J. S. Mill, certain democratic socialists, T. H. Green, English pluralists such as Figgis, Barker, and the early Laski and their heirs in American political science, and contemporary philosophers of liberalism such as Rawls, Gewirth, and Nozick. There may well be errors in this list, and some may complain about the notion that these are the characteristic theorists of the modern era. However, my purpose is not historical but theoretical. And my claim is that philosophers such as these at least implicitly share the view that the problem of individual and society can only be addressed by revising or qualifying the principle of the individual and that of society so as to accommodate the one to the other. For lack of a better word, I shall call these theorists *accommodationists*. Without minimizing the enormous differences among them, I believe that they represent one distinctive way of thinking about the crucial problems of political life. And indeed, I believe further that the clearest formulation of the approach is to be found in the work of Hobbes himself.

The particulars of Hobbes's political thought are too well known to merit a detailed rehearsal here; on the other hand, its perplexities raise questions that would take us far beyond the parameters of this work and beyond my expertise as well. Still, certain features of Hobbes's formulation are worth considering once again, for they well illustrate the strategies associated with what I am calling accommodationism.

The first book of *Leviathan* is, in large measure, a discussion of those things which distinguish individuals from one another. Now individuals evidently share a great deal. They are all creatures of sense, of memory and imagination, and of reason. As such, they are oriented toward the things of the world in roughly the same way: they acquire knowledge of the world by experiencing it sensually, their thoughts are rooted entirely in sense impressions, and they act in the world in terms of passions or appetites. Moreover, if we were to take men as we know them and, through a thought experiment, consider what they would be like and how they would act if there were no common power above them, we would find them all participating more or less equally in a war of every man against every man.

But it is in terms of these selfsame factors that Hobbes also chooses to distinguish individuals from one another. Humans differ largely insofar as their passions differ. This can involve any number of things. You may desire X whereas I desire Y; or, your desire for X may simply be more intense than mine; or again, you may desire that *you* receive X whereas I desire that *I* receive it. In all such cases, as individuals we differ from one another in terms of the nature and intensity of our appetites and our aversions.

Now Hobbes tells us that such differences themselves are rooted both in physical and in environmental factors:

> [T]he difference of Passions, proceedeth partly from the different Constitution of the body, and partly from different Education. For if the difference proceeded from the temper of the brain, and the organs of Sense, either exterior or interior, there would be no lesse difference of men in their Sight, Hearing, or other Senses than in their Fancies and Discretions. It proceeds, therefore, from the Passions; which are different not only from the difference of men's complexions; but also from their difference of customes, and education. [*Leviathan*, Macpherson edition, pp. 138–39]

Thus, the distinctiveness of the individual, though in part a reflection of natural or biological factors, is also a manifestation of the uniqueness of individual human experience. But further, as the above passage implies and as is elsewhere made explicit, such differences are in turn related to other, more complex differences of an intellectual, moral, or spiritual nature. For example, notions of good and bad, which for Hobbes lie at the root of ethical theory, are based entirely on the passions and vary accordingly from individual to individual: "But whatsoever is the object of any man's Appetite or Desire; that is it which he for his part calleth *Good*: And the object of his Hate, and Aversion, *Evill*; And of his Contempt, *Vile*, and *Inconsiderable*. For these words of Good, Evill, and Contemptible, are ever used with relation to the person that useth them: There being nothing simply and absolutely so; nor any common Rule of Good and Evill, to be taken from the nature of the objects themselves . . . " (p. 120). Similarly, the difference in passion leads to differences with respect to the "intellectual virtues." For example, those with a particularly intense desire for power, riches, knowledge, and honor are likely to have a great deal of what Hobbes calls "judgment," i.e., the capacity to make reasonable and sensible discriminations among things; as a result, such persons are more likely to be successful and influential actors in the world. Or again, differences of opinion, belief, and political doctrine arise in the same way, from the difference in men's complexions, customs, and education via the resultant difference of desire: "men give different names, to one and the same thing, from the difference of their own passions: As they that approve a private opinion, call it Opinion; but they that mislike it, Haeresie: and yet haeresie signifies no more than private opinion; but has onely a greater tincture of choler" (p. 165).

Thus, for Hobbes the individual is distinguished largely in terms of his passions and in terms of those things derived therefrom. It follows, then, that in Hobbes's system the principle of the individual reads something like this: to value the individual is to value the opportunity of the person to think and act in ways that reflect the distinctive configuration of his desires. This does not commit Hobbes to the view that the desires of individuals should be satisfied. Such satisfaction, of course, would not guarantee the happiness of individuals, for one's desires may turn out to be irrational and counterproductive in the long run. But even if this were not the case, the satisfaction of desires would still be beside the point; for a person's individuality and his happiness are two entirely different things. There appears to be no logical or conceptual connection between them, and it is by no means clear that there is an empirical connection either. Thus, the principle of the individual says nothing about the value or satisfaction of the individual's desires. Rather, it commits Hobbes only to the view that we should seek to secure and expand the individual's opportunity or ability to pursue the satisfaction of his desires. As such, it commits him to valuing something that will produce a situation in which particular demands for satisfaction are numerous, quite insistent, and often in deep conflict with one another.

There is, however, no reason to believe that Hobbes must prefer individuality, so defined, to all competing values. If anything, readers would surely be predisposed to believe the opposite. For it is abundantly clear that Hobbes is explicitly committed to supporting and defending the rules and patterns of society. Among Hobbes scholars, there is much disagreement as to the bases and precise nature of these rules and patterns. For some, they are rooted in the historical context of an emerging capitalism; as such, they express the political requirements of a market-oriented society and its spirit of possessive individualism. For others, they are based rather on objective ethical judgments, comprising a "strict deontology" ultimately sanctioned by the tenets of divine law.

But there is also a more general kind of reading, consistent with either of these but perhaps more useful for our particular purpose. Specifically, Hobbes's project may be viewed as an attempt to discover or deduce the *concept* of political society. This deduction is based on certain premises about mankind, such as those described above, along with a hypothetical account of human relations in a state of nature. The statement of these premises amounts to what Hobbes calls the apt imposing of names and the settling of plausible definitions—e.g., definitions of human distinctiveness, human motivation, and the natural condition of mankind (p. 105). Such definitions are, in turn, analyzed through the faculty of reason, understood as the "reckoning (that is, Adding and Subtracting) of the Consequences of general names agreed upon, for the marking and signifying of our thoughts" (p. 111). On Hobbes's account, this process of reasoning, when undertaken in a particularly systematic and perspicacious manner, comprises the activity of "science" and, as such, produces general "theorems of reason" which stand as the highest forms of human knowledge. Thus, to reckon the consequences of the premises regarding human nature and human distinctiveness is to engage in what we may call political science. Its theorems of reason are the "laws of nature" which, among other things, require that every man ought to endeavor peace, honor the covenants he has made, strive to accommodate himself to the rest, and the like. From these theorems is deduced, in turn, the basic feature of the concept of political society, viz., that individuals in the state of nature "conferre all their power and strength upon one Man, or upon one Assembly of men that may reduce all their Wills, by plurality of voices, unto one Will . . ." (p. 227). For Hobbes, therefore, political society is characterized above all by the presence of an entity that has a virtual monopoly of legitimate power, a sovereign entity. Again, it cannot be emphasized too strongly that this is a conceptual analysis. Hobbes is not engaged in the empirical description of political societies, nor is he asserting a mere preference or inclination for one kind of society over another. Rather, his concern is to stipulate a set of plausible names or definitions, to reckon the logical or conceptual consequences of those definitions—"to proceed from one consequence to another" (p. 112)—and to arrive ultimately at an account of political society that must be true if our definitions and reckonings are correct.

Of course, Hobbes seeks to deduce further characteristics of the concept of political society and of the sovereign entity in particular. But these are largely attendant to the fundamental claim regarding the centrality of sovereignty in the definition of political society. This claim, understood as a conceptual claim—i.e., a claim about the meaning of the concept of political society—establishes a kind of formal requirement. For there to be political society, there must above all else be a sovereign entity; to the degree that such an entity is lacking or is unrecognized, the requirements of political society are not fully met. As such, the claim seems to be largely indifferent to the particular form that sovereignty takes. While there is rather clear textual evidence to suggest that Hobbes preferred monarchical forms of government, it also seems clear that many other particular institutional arrangements can satisfy the Hobbesian criterion. For example, a democratic system based on majority rule would seem to qualify as a political society provided that the majority were, in each and every case, understood to be a sovereign entity possessing a virtual monopoly of legitimate power. I believe that even a Madisonian/Jeffersonian hybrid as embodied in the United States Constitution would qualify, insofar as the provisions of the Constitution explicitly depend upon the sufferance of a democratically constituted—albeit extraordinary and difficult-to-muster—majority. Which is to say that even the most basic and sacred principles of American government, for example, the individual rights described in the First Amendment, exist through the good graces of "the Legislatures of three fourths of the several States, or by Conventions in three fourths thereof . . . " (see also *Leviathan*, p. 238).

For Hobbes, then, to value political society is necessarily to value rules or patterns of behavior prescribed by an entity possessing a monopoly of legitimate power. In a sense, these rules and patterns do not conflict with the ultimate interests of individuals, for their interests can—on the whole—be better satisfied in political society than in the state of nature (e.g., p. 262). But in another and, for our purposes, more decisive sense, Hobbes recognizes as clearly as we do the inherent conflict between the rules of society and the desires of the individual. Hobbes writes that "the Lawes of Nature . . . are contrary to our naturall Passions, that carry us to Partiality, Pride, Revenge, and the like" (p. 233). He speaks of the "incommodities" suffered by men at the hands of government. He notes that "all men are by nature provided of notable multiplying glasses, (that is, their Passions and Self-love) through which every little payment [to government] appeareth a great grievance . . . " (p. 239). And the fact that these grievances are far less than the "miseries and horrible calamities" of anarchy in no way obviates the further fact that the power of the sovereign entity is precisely the general power to deny individuals the opportunity to act in ways that reflect the distinctive configuration of their desires. It may be true that if the government prevents me from seeking some object X, I'll be better able on that account to seek and even obtain both Y and Z; it may also be that seeking and obtaining Y and Z will ultimately make me happier than seeking X would have. Still, it might be the case that, in the absence of such a constraint, I would have chosen to pursue X. Hence, the government's rule specifically and pointedly undermines my opportunity to act according to my particular passions, i.e., those things that distinguish me as an individual. In Hobbes's thought, therefore, the principle that we should value the rules and patterns imposed by the sovereign appears to exist in considerable tension with the principle of the individual.

It might be objected that, insofar as the sovereign's rules actually make me happier, they must then be satisfying my desires and hence cannot be thought to undermine the principle of the individual. But, as indicated above, the satisfaction of my desires is not related to my happiness in any obvious or straightforward way; it may well be that I will be happier if I am prevented from doing those things which my passions would otherwise move me to do and which, therefore, distinguish me as an individual. The rules and patterns of political society threaten my distinctiveness and individuality by claiming—or indeed having—the legitimate right to prohibit certain acts. Such a right is based on society's putative capacity to make individuals happy; as such, it might well be fully justified. Nonetheless, even in cases where society has done its job well, the happiness of the individual may well have been purchased at the cost of his individuality, at least to the degree that his opportunity to act has been suppressed.

It may also be objected that the rules of society do not violate the principle of the individual since, in Hobbes's theory, that society is based on the consent of the governed. More specifically, the individuals who are ruled are, nonetheless, the "authors" of those rules (p. 218); and in several places Hobbes draws the conclusion that, for example, a person who has been punished for breaking the law has suffered no injustice since he is the author of his own punishment (pp. 229ff.). But again, this has to do rather with the justification of political society and its rules than with the tension between them and the principle of the individual. The point is well made with reference to Hobbes's famous distinction between author and actor. As author, the individual suffers no injustice, hence the rules of political society are fully legitimate. As actor, however, the individual may simply be prevented from acting: hence, it follows from Hobbes's own premises regarding human distinctiveness that the principle of the individual is thereby compromised.

Thus, given the usual empirical circumstances in which we find ourselves and which Hobbes himself fully recognized, there is a serious tension in his thought between the principle of the individual and the principle of society. Implicitly, Hobbes's approach to this problem is to accommodate the two principles to one another by altering them so as to make them mutually consistent. Most obviously, the principle of the individual is altered with a proviso or qualification having to do with the satisfaction of interests: we should indeed value the individual's opportunity to act in ways that reflect the distinctive configuration of his desires, but only insofar as this does not compromise the maximization of the happiness of all individuals. In principle if not in practice, this proviso is a very exacting one, for it places the individual's opportunity to act under a perpetual threat. Any time the sovereign deems an act suppressible, it becomes suppressed. It is for this reason that most readers will be disposed to say that in Hobbes's thought the principle of the individual does rather more accommodating than does the principle of society.

Nevertheless, individuality does seem to get its due. Specifically, the rules and patterns of society must serve the interests embodied in the social contract. To do otherwise is to dissolve the contract, hence to render the sovereign's rules nugatory. Of course, the sovereign entity itself cannot violate the social contract since, qua sovereign, it is not party to the contract. Nonetheless, when the sovereign acts in a way that threatens the welfare of the citizens, the agreements between them—in virtue of which they establish a sovereign whose pronouncements have the status of legitimate rules or laws—are abrogated. Now as regards the individual, one implication of this is that persons have a right to resist the sovereign when their life is endangered. That is, the rules and patterns of society lose their normative force when they threaten one particular desire which comprises, in part, the individuality of the individual—viz., the desire for *self*-preservation. The purpose of the contract is, in large measure, to secure peace and safety for the parties, hence to forestall or minimize the possibility of violent death. When the sovereign proposes to kill an individual, that individual's duty to obey is thereby nullified. This does not mean that the sovereign has no right to execute people, only that those condemned people have an equal right to resist (pp. 268ff.). We may say, therefore, that at least one of the distinguishing desires of the individual—the desire to avoid violent death—has a privileged position in Hobbes's theory. And to that extent, the interests of society must accommodate to those of individuality.

In Hobbes's thought, then, the principle of society reads something as follows: we ought to value those systems of rules and patterns of coordination imposed by the sovereign entity, but only insofar as they serve the individual's desire for peace and self-preservation. When juxtaposed to the reformulated principle of the individual, we now encounter no contradiction. There may indeed be severe disagreements as to the application of these principles to particular cases, e.g., what actually constitutes the maximization of happiness or how do we know if the desire for peace is being best served? But these are matters of practical judgment or of empirical fact and do not pose any moral dilemma for us. In Hobbes, the deep tension between the two principles is resolved by building into each an escape clause which describes the kinds of considerations that should guide us in selecting one principle for the other. We should value individuality except insofar as doing so compromises the maximization of self-interest; we should value the rules and patterns of society, except insofar as doing so undermines the individual's desire for self-preservation. When the maximization of self-interest and an individual's desire for life come into hopeless conflict, the individual's contractual obligations simply dissolve and he falls into a state of war. While this may not be very pleasant, as a moral agent he faces no ethical dilemma.

This sketch provides us with materials for characterizing the accommodationist position in general. When faced with two competing principles—one requiring that we value individuality, the other the rules of society—the accommodationist strategy is to accept their incompatibility as a given and seek to deal with it by amending either or both of them. The principle of individuality is amended so that it specifies those conditions under which individuality can and should be overridden; the principle of society is amended in a like manner. As a result, each value must, in certain circumstances, give way to some other, higher value. When amended in this way, the two principles present us with no contradictory imperatives: we may ignore the rules and patterns of society unless certain overriding considerations pertain; and we may ignore the value of individuality unless certain other considerations pertain. In Hobbes's thought, the maximization of self-interest requires that the rules and patterns of society be given priority, and that the value of individuality be therefore subsumed; there are, however, other situations involving self-protection in which the rules and patterns of society should take a back seat. In view of the empirical circumstances we normally expect to encounter, it seems that in Hobbes the balance is rather tilted in favor of the rules and patterns of society, but in other accommodationist theories, Nozick's for example, the balance is rather the other way. In all such cases, though, the tension between the two principles is seen to involve not a conceptual or philosophical error of some kind; the tension is, rather, an accurate and straightforward consequence of the principles themselves when encountered in typical circumstances.

Hobbes's theory also demonstrates another, evidently essential feature of the accommodationist strategy, viz., the need to justify the accommodation itself. There must be some account as to how we can compromise the value of individuality and that of society in a manner that is ethically persuasive. In Hobbes's thought, this is accomplished largely through a kind of utilitarianism. It is on the basis of a cost/benefit analysis relative to the real interests of persons that we can justify actions which compromise individuality in favor of society's rules or vice versa. Of course, there are many other kinds of arguments, some to be found also in Hobbes's thought, which may be used in this way: notions of consent and contract, the natural and inalienable rights of men, the harm principle, procedural circumstances that ensure ethically defensible decisions, and the like. Such notions function, at least in part, to justify actions that threaten things the value of which is not denied. For example, the theorist of inalienable rights does not deny the value of society's rules and patterns, but he does propose to undermine those rules and patterns when they violate authentic rights claims; similarly, the theorist of absolute popular sovereignty does not ignore the value of individuality, but he does propose to undermine it insofar as it disrupts the pursuit of the public will.

As a result of these kinds of concerns, accommodationist theories typically focus on two basic philosophical issues: the issue of authority—i.e., under what grounds is it legitimate to coerce persons who refuse to obey? and the issue of the scope of government—i.e., to what extent should persons be free to deviate from or ignore the rules and patterns of society? But again, such questions assume the prima facie difficulty of the problem of individual and society as we have defined it. It appears that any solution to this problem will necessarily involve a compromise; one of the things we value will have to make room for the other. The question for accommodationists is not how this can be avoided but, rather, how it can be explained and legitimized.

3

There is one variant of the accommodationist position that requires some further scrutiny. This is a view which claims that imposing limits on distinctiveness in the interest of society is in fact the surest way of maximizing the opportunity to be different. Typical here would be the Lockeian notion that law is essential to freedom. For Locke, law restricts certain individual freedoms so as to establish an orderly civil society; such a society, though clearly based on a degree of unfreedom, in fact conduces to more freedom than would be the case if society did not exist.[4] Thus, the rules and patterns of society tend to serve, rather than undermine, our interest in distinctiveness. This position differs from Hobbes's in that individuality is limited not in order to maximize some other value (e.g., security, prosperity, happiness) but, rather, to serve the cause of individuality itself. Thus, it may seem that the Lockeian account is able to do full justice to both the principle of the individual and that of society without compromising either one.

In fact, though, I think it is clear that Locke does employ a variety of Strategy (B) and is thus as much an accommodationist as Hobbes. To begin with, the view that freedom is greater in civil society than in the state of nature is merely an empirical judgment and in no way alters the fact that rules and patterns tend by definition and by design to impinge on freedom. In this sense, the ultimate consequences or even the intentions of an action cannot

4. John Locke, *The Second Treatise of Government*, chap. 6, para. 57.

constitute an exhaustive description of the action itself. If we say that "we will fight fire with fire," our intention to put out the fire does not change the fact that we are lighting a match; similarly, if we execute a murderer in order to prevent further killing, either by the murderer himself or by others whose actions we are seeking to deter, our interest in doing so does not permit us to say that we have not killed, though it may well justify our deed.[5] Thus, restrictions on freedom in the interest of freedom remain, nevertheless, restrictions on freedom.

Further, Locke's view compromises the principle of the individual in that at least some of the freedoms of at least some of the people are to be abridged at least some of the time. This is done for practical reasons and, again, may well be fully justified. Nonetheless, we may say that in Locke's thought the maximum *conceivable* liberty is limited so as to secure the greatest *average* liberty in the light of typical empirical circumstances. This may turn out to be the most practical way of serving the interest of individuality, but it falls short of the full flowering of individuality that the principle contemplates.

It may be argued that in Locke's thought the only real accommodation occurs between the freedom of one person and that of another. That is, my freedom is balanced not against the interests of society but, rather, against the freedom of other individuals. Nonetheless, the freedom of those "others" is protected precisely by society's rules. It is perhaps for this reason, rather than some intrinsic reason, that Locke values those rules. But he does value them and, for present purposes, the reason is unimportant. Some freedoms are to be limited by the rules of civil society; that this is done in the name of freedom does not change the fact that Locke's political thought is based on an accommodation between individual and society necessitated by the particular exigencies of the world in which we find ourselves.

Locke thus adopts a version of Strategy (B). As a result, his basic task, like that of Hobbes, is to show not how accommodation can be avoided but, rather, how it can be justified.

---

5. It should go without saying that the fact that we have killed does not mean that we have murdered.

4

This last sentence may remind us superficially of that most famous passage of political philosophy: "Man is born free, and everywhere he is in chains. One thinks himself the master of others, and still remains a greater slave than they. How did this change come about? I do not know. What can make it legitimate? That question I think I can answer." But of course, the differences here can hardly be overestimated. Indeed, it seems that Rousseau's political thought in fact offered the first systematic and influential statement of Strategy (C), a perspective which I shall term, for lack of a better word, *perfectionism*.[6] Rousseau did not merely emend or depart from the tradition of accommodation but, rather, embarked on an approach that is, in terms of the discussion of the present chapter, its polar opposite. It is true that Rousseau shares much with Hobbes. Both seem to utilize what Michael Oakeshott has called the "idiom of individuality." They share certain individualist starting points, most notably thought-experiments involving a pre-political state of nature, and each employs the language of the social contract.

But whereas accommodationists like Hobbes seek to deal with the problem of individual and society through a process of mutual adjustment and compromise, Rousseau in particular, and perfectionists in general, attempt the rather bolder and more radical task of showing that in fact individuality and the social order can be—and can only be—jointly perfected. The difference is absolutely decisive. For accommodationism, the problem of individual and society is never really solved and is certainly never denied; it is merely managed, its more pernicious tendencies contained. But for perfectionism, the "problem" is shown rather to be the product only of a failure to understand either the individual or society, or both. When these concepts are seen in a clear light, the problem simply vanishes. There is no need to manage the tension between individual and society because, when each is properly conceived, there is no tension between them at all.

Of course, to pin down Rousseau on virtually any theoretical

6. My use of the term "perfectionism" is not intended to coincide with its use in certain contemporary ethical writings. See, for example, Rawls, *A Theory of Justice*, pp. 25 and 325.

question, much less a fundamental one such as we are pursuing here, is no easy task. As we know, he is seen variously as a great apostle of radical individualism, a holist and an organicist, a forerunner of democratic totalitarianism, a conservative, a romantic reactionary, a Jacobin, and the like. My purpose is certainly not to adjudicate among these views. Nonetheless, it may be that at least some of the various strands of Rousseau's thought can be shown to converge if we pursue in his work the theme of perfectionism as a response to, and a rejection of, the tradition of accommodation.

That the problem of individual and society is crucial for Rousseau is apparent very early on in the *Emile*, where we encounter the distinction between man and citizen. Rousseau identifies three kinds of education, those which come to us from nature, from things, and from men. It is important that the lessons we learn from these be mutually consistent; but there is a particular problem with respect to the first and third of them, the education from nature and that from men:

> It is then to these primitive dispositions that everything must be related; and this could be done if our three educations were only different. But what is to be done when they are opposed, when instead of raising a man for himself, one wants to raise him for others? Then the harmony is impossible. Forced to combat nature or social institutions, it is necessary to choose between making a man or a citizen; for one cannot make both at the same time. [*OC*, vol. 2, p. 6][7]

To make someone a citizen is to mold him in the image of the community, to inculcate habits of obedience and conformity, and to teach him to value above all the social order of which he is a part. But it seems that this can only be accomplished by extirpating certain traits that we normally and quite plausibly associate with the individuality of the individual, in particular, certain natural and essentially personal impulses. Indeed, for Rousseau, in order to create a good citizen it is necessary to "denature" the individual: "Good social institutions are those which know best how to denature man, to take away from him his absolute existence for

7. All references are to *Oeuvres complètes de J.-J. Rousseau* (Paris: Librairie Hachette, 1913).

himself while giving him a relative one, and to transport the *I* into
the common unity, with the result that each particular no longer
believes himself to be a 'one' but [rather] a part of a unity, and
to no longer have feeling except within the whole" (*OC*, vol. 2,
p. 6). As with Hobbes, then, we seem to confront here a kind of
zero-sum game in which the achievement of citizenship involves
the denial of those natural traits crucial to the development and
enjoyment of individuality, and vice versa. If we were to demand
the full development of individuality, understood as a set of personal and private capabilities, then this would appear to undermine
our interest in defending the rules and patterns of a just and well-
ordered society; if, on the other hand, it is the good community
that we are after, then we must educate for citizenship, and this
seems to require eradicating at least some of those natural, personal capabilities. As Rousseau says: "He who in the civil order
wants to preserve the primacy of the sentiments of nature does
not know what he wants. Always in contradiction with himself,
always floating between his inclinations and his duties, he will never
be either man or citizen . . . " (*OC*, vol. 2, p. 7). The seeming
"impossibility" of harmonizing these contrary tendencies suggests
not simply that Rousseau is well aware of the problem of individual
and society but that, like the accommodationists, he despairs of
discovering a solution that would be anything other than a compromise; but, further, his language also suggests that a compromise
would not be especially appealing to him, and that he would perhaps prefer either a well-formed man or a well-formed community
to a watered-down version of both.

At this point, we may wonder where Rousseau's ultimate preference lies, whether he would have us educate for manhood and
individuality or for citizenship and the community. And what is
immediately clear is that his work, considered as a whole, seems
to provide ample evidence in both directions. On the side of individuality, there is, of course, the undeniably central Rousseauian
theme of liberty—i.e., the liberty of the individual, a theme he
pursues or alludes to in virtually all of his important works. Certainly such a notion lies at the heart of the Second Discourse,
especially in the image of natural man as perfectly free, unfettered,
characterized by a kind of pure, ingenuous feeling of self-love,
and, so it seems, an individual unto himself. This theme is elab-

orated further in the Second Discourse, where society itself emerges as a kind of malignant force in which *amour de soi* is replaced by *amour-propre*, undermining thereby the natural origins of individuality. In society a person ceases to be an individual in any meaningful sense and becomes, instead, a kind of culturally generated stereotype, one of a discrete number of stock figures largely indistinguishable from all those others who perform similar roles in the social comedy. The subversive force of society, and the tension between its imperatives and the will of the true individual, is, of course, an important topic in virtually all of the autobiographical writings; but indeed, it is central also to the *Emile* itself where, after all, the education of the boy must occur in a realm isolated and protected from the corrupting influences of the social world.

It is perhaps not easy to identify what Rousseau means by individuality in these various works, whether it involves the simple independence of presocial man, the private sentiments and attachments characteristic of family life, or a certain developed capacity for principled, "disinterested" choice and action.[8] On this score, the case of Hobbes is rather more straightforward. Nonetheless, there can be no doubt that we find in Rousseau an insistence on the importance of individuality, however understood, over against the unsavory tendencies of social fashion.

Yet, it is surely not hard to find a Rousseau at least equally committed to defending the rules and patterns of society. In a not uncharacteristic work such as *The Government of Poland*, for example, we encounter a defense of Polish customs and traditional forms of government, as well as a list of recommendations designed, or so it seems, to limit individuality and encourage an intense and even unreflective kind of patriotic conformity. Rousseau envisions a community in which, "all citizens feel themselves continually under the eyes of the public . . . and everyone . . . shall be so completely dependent upon public esteem as to be unable to do anything, acquire anything, or achieve anything without it"

8. See Judith Shklar, *Men and Citizens: A Study of Rousseau's Political Thought* (Cambridge: Cambridge University Press, 1969); and Stephen Ellenburg, *Rousseau's Political Philosophy: An Interpretation from Within* (Ithaca, N.Y.: Cornell University Press, 1976), pp. 201ff.

(*OC*, vol. 5, p. 286). In the *Letter to d'Alembert*, it seems certain that what we now call the liberty of expression should be sacrificed in the interest of the community, that the value of individual creativity is overridden by the value of society's established patterns wherein "individuals, always in the public eye, are born censors of one another and where the police can easily watch everyone . . ." (*OC*, vol. 1, p. 217). Indeed, in the "Dedication to the Republic of Geneva" of the Second Discourse itself, the simple yet sublime glory of that city seems to rest on an obedient citizenry: "It is on your constant union, your obedience to the laws, and your respect for their ministers, that your preservation depends. . . . Where the laws lose their force and those who defend them their authority, security and liberty are universally impossible" (*OC*, vol. 1, p. 75).

We may say, then, that Rousseau sometimes writes for individuality, sometimes for the community, and that at times he seems more interested in educating men than citizens, at times the other way round. Surely this need not betoken any kind of serious inconsistency or logical flaw; it may simply be that Rousseau's focus is appropriately influenced by the nature of whatever he happens to be writing at the time. The purpose of an essay such as the *Poland* is plainly different from that of, say, the *Emile*, and this difference will manifest itself in ways that should not surprise or disturb us.

Still, we are understandably at pains to discover some underlying animating spirit, perhaps even a common theoretical orientation, which is authoritative for all of these various writings and which can lend some substance to Rousseau's claim that his philosophy is internally consistent. I believe one useful approach in this regard would be to pursue the theme of perfectionism, particularly as embodied in the concept of the general will.

At the outset, we may suggest that the very purpose of the *Social Contract* is to justify certain principles which properly resolve the problem of individual and society. But what must be emphasized is that, for Rousseau, a proper resolution would compromise neither the individuality of the individual nor the legitimate ends of the body politic. As we have seen, Rousseau is well prepared to accept the validity of both sets of claims, the personal and the political. Thus, the task of his major political treatise seems to be to demonstrate how it is possible to conceptualize a mode of living together wherein, so to speak, men are citizens truly and citizens truly men. Such a project would involve, in effect, a reconciliation of the classical political ideal, in which the claims of the community are the only valid claims, with the modern ideal, in which individuality alone is natural and valuable. In this sense, the classical vision would have to be emended insofar as it ignores the full requirements of individuality; but the modern view is equally inadequate, at least in part because it rests on a contrived, insubstantial notion of citizenship and solidarity.

The concept of the general will is at least one of the forms that Rousseau's solution takes. Above all, this concept contemplates the absolute exclusion of particularity from the realm of politics. The general will considers only general questions, and it promulgates principles in a strictly "disinterested" fashion, laws that apply to all equally, without reference to particular, personal considerations. It is comprised of, and is concerned with, persons in the abstract. Thus, its criteria for judgment are universalistic. Only principles of justice and right are considered, and these principles are in turn attendant on a vision of the community's good.

With such a conception, then, Rousseau seeks to reestablish the grounds for something analogous to classical civic virtue. Selfishness and egoism are bracketed out or neutralized; the concerns of the particular individual are overridden by those of the community as a whole.

But equally important, the general will also involves the full development of the individual as an autonomous rational being; coincident with, and basic to, the general will is the moral elevation of the person. Rousseau's citizen acts in terms of justice, right, and duty; his orientation is public-spirited and his devotion to the community is quite complete. And yet, he retains—in altered and improved form—his personal liberty and his independence, i.e., those traits which, for Rousseau, are indispensible to individuality properly understood. For the citizen of the well-ordered community, by virtue of his participation in the general will, obeys only himself. He conquers his selfish inclinations, overcomes the tyranny of others, and thereby becomes his own master.

With this account, of course, I follow the now controversial though, in my view, still enlightening tactic of reading certain elements of Kantian morality back into the general will. For Rousseau, as for Kant, the full realization of individuality involves the capacity to act in terms of human reason. This means, on the one hand, resisting the influences of social fads, of insubstantial and petty demands which lack any rational justification and which, we may say, foster a pathological psychology of "other-directedness." But, on the other hand, it means also resisting the demands of one's own body, with its irrational desires and impulses. In each case, the individuality of the individual is conceptualized in terms of its opposition to some external force which cannot be plausibly identified with the person's own rational will.

Rousseau thus sought to elucidate principles that involve the complete *interpenetration* of the social and the individual without subsuming either one to the other. The individual's freedom, his self-mastery, and his autonomy are not merely incidental to the establishment of civic order; they are, in fact, necessary conditions of that order. Citizenship, properly conceived, must be based on free and voluntary choice. An imposed or manufactured sense of loyalty would ignore the autonomy of the individual while providing, at best, an uncertain, unreliable foundation for society. Thus, a healthy community requires citizens whose allegiance is not only complete but also freely, rationally, and self-consciously given.

With respect to the individual, then, we see that in civil society he does indeed give up his natural liberty but gains something which, from the standpoint of individuality, seems even better:

> The passage from the state of nature to the civil state produces in man a very remarkable change, by substituting in his conduct justice for instinct and giving his actions the morality they had formerly lacked. . . . [D]uty takes the place of physical impulses and right of appetites . . . [and] he is forced to act on different principles, and to consult his reason before listening to his inclinations. Although, in this state, he deprives himself of many advantages which he got from nature, he gains in return others so great, his faculties are so stimulated and developed, his ideas so extended, his feeling so ennobled, and his whole soul so uplifted, that, did not the abuses of this new condition often degrade him below that which he left, he would be found to bless continually the happy moment which took him from

it for ever, and instead of a stupid and limited animal, made him an intelligent being and a man. [*OC*, vol. 3, pp. 315–16; *Social Contract* I, 8]

One becomes a human being, an individual in the full sense, by participating in a general will according to which choice and action are the product of rational and collaborative deliberation. In the well-ordered community, the individual acquires what Rousseau, preceding Kant, calls moral liberty, a liberty "which alone makes him truly master of himself."

In this way, it seems that the very concept of individuality undergoes a crucial change. By strong implication, the individuality of the individual is now said to be a matter, not of natural inclination or independence, not of certain presocial dispositions, but rather of the capacity to engage in rational, principled choice, a capacity which itself can flourish in a well-ordered community. Whereas Hobbes sees individuality to lie in the particular and distinctive configuration of a person's passions, Rousseau seems to find it in the capacity of the individual to act in spite of and even against those passions, i.e., the capacity to obey principles of a rational nature that one has thoughtfully and reflectively legislated for oneself.

From the standpoint of the community, then, it seems that the rules and patterns of society must be understood in terms of citizens so conceived. That is, the solidarity of a well-ordered state must be based on the virtue—the moral liberty—of those who comprise it. In the "Discourse on Political Economy" Rousseau writes that "The community [*La patrie*] cannot exist without liberty, nor liberty without virtue, nor virtue without citizens. You will have everything if you create citizens; without them, you will have only miserable slaves, beginning with the heads of State themselves" (*OC*, vol. 3, p. 291). We may, of course, continue to be puzzled when Rousseau tells us elsewhere that it might be necessary to force citizens to be free. But we can at least see how this may be intended to communicate, in part, Rousseau's conviction that political society thrives not over against but precisely on the basis of the true individuality of the individual.

And thus, when we reconsider the *Emile*, we see that the "impossibility" of having both men and citizens turns out to be historical rather than conceptual; it is a result simply of the fact that there are, unfortunately for Emile, no true states any more. Rousseau tells us that Plato's *Republic* is the "most beautiful educational treatise ever written," but that it has lost its practical value. For "[p]ublic instruction no longer exists and can no longer exist, because where there is no longer fatherland [*patrie*], there can no longer be citizens. These two words, *fatherland* and *citizen*, should be effaced from modern languages" (*OC*, vol. 2, p. 7). We may say that in the modern world, with its culture of Hobbesian individualism and its resultant conceptions of political legitimacy, it is nearly impossible to find a well-ordered community in which to practice the true art of citizenship. It is for this reason, and this reason only, that Emile must be educated in private. But even so, there remains in Emile's intimate world an element which might be called civic. For Rousseau insists that "there is only one science to teach children; it is that of man's duties" (*OC*, vol., 2, p. 19). And as one recent commentator remarks: "Educated in a miniature republic, the mature Emile becomes both man and citizen: his inclinations are his civic duties. . . . Society and absolute liberty are perfectly reconciled in *Emile*, for Emile's transformation is the 'common' education of a single citizen."[9]

Ellenburg argues that Rousseau is, in the broad sense, an "anarchist." Regrettably, that term remains somewhat unclear in his account but, on the whole, it seems to comport with the interpretation of anarchism provided by Alan Ritter. According to Ritter, anarchism is most certainly a variety of what I am calling perfectionism insofar as it contemplates simultaneously fulfilling the values of individuality and community: "For all of [the anarchists] communal awareness springs from developed individuality, and developed individuality depends in turn on a close-knit common life. For all of them, community and individuality, as they develop, intensify each other and coalesce."[10] Whether Rousseau should be counted as "anarchist" is a historical question that need not detain us. But he appears to share with Ritter's anarchists this particular view of the mutual dependence of individuality and community.

9. Ellenburg, *Rousseau's Political Philosophy*, pp. 273–74.
10. Alan Ritter, *Anarchism: A Theoretical Analysis* (Cambridge: Cambridge University Press, 1980), p. 29.

And as we have seen, such a view is, in turn, based on an effort to reinterpret the constituent concepts themselves. Specifically, according to the perspective I have called perfectionism, individuality is regarded not in terms of particular and idiosyncratic passions or desires but, rather, in terms of a certain capacity for rational thought and decision. Similarly, the rules and patterns of society are understood not as a force external and opposed to the individual but, rather, as emerging out of a reciprocal, collaborative process of rational deliberation. The very mark of individuality, i.e., the ability to act in terms of principles sanctioned by human reason, is—when undertaken vis-à-vis other, similarly endowed persons—the proper source of social rules and patterns; hence, to conform to those rules and patterns is, at least potentially, to affirm rather than deny one's own individuality. On such an account, then, when individuality and society are correctly understood, the problem that we have been concerned with—that of individual and society qua logical contradiction—simply vanishes.

We may say that perfectionism constitutes an important, alternative tradition of modern political thought. It may include such diverse figures as Rousseau and Bakunin, Proudhon and Marx, John C. Calhoun and George Sorel.[11] That the differences among such theorists are quite decisive does not undermine the claim that their disputes all occur on one side of the theoretical terrain, quite apart from and alien to the perhaps more familiar terrain of accommodationism. Perfectionists all agree that the problem of individual and society is amenable to a complete conceptual solution; they disagree only as to the form that solution takes and the sense in which it can guide actual political practice.

One clear implication, then, is that this perspective in fact includes an otherwise quite diverse range of views. In particular, it seems unlikely that perfectionism needs to be anarchist in the sense of rejecting the very notion of legal government. But exactly how far it can go in the other direction is not immediately clear. It is in this light that we may turn now to the question of Hegel and

11. The inclusion of Calhoun here may seem particularly eccentric. But for a discussion along these lines, see Peter J. Steinberger, "Calhoun's Concept of the Public Interest," *Polity* 13 (Spring 1981).

consider the degree to which the dichotomy of accommodationism and perfectionism pertains to the fundamental doctrines of the philosophy of Right.

5

The revival of interest in Hegelian philosophy, beginning about two decades ago, has been accompanied by a new regard for his political thought. This renewal has not, as far as I can tell, directly confronted the issue of accommodationism and perfectionism. Nonetheless, we may say that the emergent picture of Hegel's political philosophy, at least in the English-speaking world, tends to suggest—by default, as it were—an interpretation which can be loosely termed accommodationist.[12]

In part, this has been due no doubt to the effort to reestablish the respectability of Hegel's political views. Against the excesses of traditional Hegel criticism, embodied above all in the work of Karl Popper, apologists such as Knox and Kaufmann and, in a later period, Pelczynski and Avineri, have demonstrated quite convincingly that the philosophy of Right contains much that orthodox Western liberals would find plausible and attractive.[13] In so doing, they have revived a line of thought which dates back at least as far as the work of Karl Rosenkranz in the nineteenth century.[14] For Rosenkranz, Hegel's political thought indeed represents an effort to find a middle ground—the so-called *Hegelsche Mitte*—between the extremes of conservative reaction and radical revolution; and this middle ground can, in some general sense, be called liberal. Against Haym and others, Rosenkranz emphasized the continuity of Hegel's political ideas from the Jena period to the

12. For an excellent source, see Henning Ottman, *Individuum und Gemeinschaft bei Hegel: Band 1* (Berlin: Walter de Gruyter, 1977).

13. Karl Popper, *The Open Society and Its Enemies: Volume Two* (Princeton, N.J.: Princeton University Press, 1950); Walter Kaufman, ed., *Hegel's Political Philosophy* (New York: Atherton, 1970); Shlomo Avineri, *Hegel's Theory of the Modern State* (Cambridge: Cambridge University Press, 1972); Z. A. Pelczynski, "Introductory Essay," in G. W. F. Hegel, *Hegel's Political Writings* (Oxford: Oxford University Press, 1964); and Z. A. Pelczynski, "The Hegelian Conception of the State," in Z. A. Pelczynski, ed., *Hegel's Political Philosophy* (Cambridge: Cambridge University Press, 1971).

14. Karl Rosenkranz, *Apologie Hegels gegen Rudolph Haym* (Hildesheim: Gerstenberg Verlag, 1977).

Berlin period in order to refute the claim that the mature Hegelian philosophy was merely an apology for the established Prussian state. He emphasized further the palpable differences between Hegel's rational constitution and the actual practice of politics in Prussia: "Hegel can not have copied the Prussian state of that time; for he taught the necessity of constitutional monarchy, representative government, the equality of all citizens before the law, the public administration of justice, the jury system, and the freedom of public expression. Did these institutions exist in Prussia? No."[15] Certainly Rosenkranz recognized that the rational state of the philosophy of Right was not a democratic state; rather, it was best seen as an organically structured system of groups or estates, a kind of pluralist society characterized by a certain diffusion of political authority and governed ultimately by the rule of law. As such, it was thought to be quite consistent with a great deal of modern political theory and practice.

The accounts of Pelczynski and Avineri (and, in French, of Weil and Fleischmann) seem to follow this general line of interpretation. These writers surely agree that Hegel was far from being a classical liberal in the sense of, say, John Locke. But in their effort to rescue Hegel from established philosophical prejudices, they tend to regard him as a moderate and something of a reformer, for whom many of the advances of the modern age—including especially the very concept of individual freedom and subjectivity—were to be valued and preserved. There is, in the philosophy of Right, nothing especially radical or outrageous.

It would be simply wrong to claim that these authors view Hegel as an accommodationist. As far as I can tell, they provide no clear judgments regarding the concepts used in this chapter. Nonetheless, the very terms of the debate tend in this direction. We may say that the critics of Hegel, preeminently Popper, see him as confronting head-on the problem of individual and society and dealing with that problem by coming down firmly on the side of the social order. For such critics, Hegel tramples on individuality and personal freedom by expanding greatly the authority of the state. It is this that makes him an enemy of the open society and a forerunner of twentieth-century totalitarianism. Hegel's defend-

15. Ibid., p. 38.

ers refute this account by finding in his work a much more equitable balance between individual and social values. Far from eradicating the claims of individuality, the philosophy of Right in fact recognizes the legitimacy of those claims and seeks to preserve them over against the incursions of the state. The issue, then, is not whether Hegel is an accommodationist but, rather, exactly what the particular terms of the accommodation are.

The result is a kind of domesticated Hegel whose political thought "is not radically different in approach, method of argument, and level of theorizing from the political theory of Hobbes, Locke, Montesquieu or Rousseau."[16] That this picture is the ascendant view may be discerned in some contemporary writing, the primary focus of which is not on Hegel. For example, in his fine treatment of freedom and equality, Charvet provides a brief but well-informed and quite sophisticated account of certain themes in the philosophy of Right.[17] It is an account which suggests, by implication, that Hegel's political thought was of a quite different order from that of accommodationism. Nevertheless, Charvet ultimately treats Hegel precisely in terms of the balance between individuality and the state and ends up offering a conclusion that seems to be a more moderate and philosophically more challenging version of Popper's view: "The devaluation of the particular individual is thus a central requirement of Hegel's philosophical scheme. The individual, as this person, has no value as an end, but only as a means. In this sense individuality is absorbed into and destroyed by the life of the universal."[18]

A rather different view is to be found in Michael Oakeshott's magisterial book *On Human Conduct*, in which Hegel appears as one of the model philosophers of *societas*, hence as someone quite unlikely to deny so freely and so completely the value of individuality.[19] But with Oakeshott, as with Charvet, the treatment of Hegel occurs as internal to the orthodox tradition of accommodation; any dispute between them regarding Hegel would be, so

16. Pelczynski, "Introductory Essay," p. 135.
17. John Charvet, *A Critique of Freedom and Equality* (Cambridge: Cambridge University Press, 1981).
18. Ibid., pp. 134—35.
19. Michael Oakeshott, *On Human Conduct* (Oxford: Oxford University Press, 1975), pp. 257–63.

to speak, a family argument. Hence, in both cases, as for Pelczynski, Avineri, and the others, the notion that Hegel is doing something quite radically different, that his political thought is in fact a profound challenge to modern orthodoxy, is rejected, either explicitly or by default.

There is, to be sure, substantial textual support for such a view. The fact is that Hegel's political doctrines do appear, at least superficially, to be well within the limits of established modern practice. We find in his political writings rather few specific proposals that would be called outrageous, radical, or even odd. There is no effort to deny the very possibility of legal government, as by the anarchists; no rejection of private property, as by Marx; no "infallible" general will, as by Rousseau; no attack on the family, as by Plato; no notion of a complete transvaluation of values, as by Nietzsche.[20] Indeed, we find Hegel making a variety of quite ordinary recommendations—constitutional monarchy, the rule of law, a legislative system based on the representation of established groups and estates, freedom of the press, religious toleration, and the like.

Moreover, it is clear that he held these views, or similar ones, throughout his professional career. This is evident, for example, in three well-known occasional essays on political subjects which Hegel wrote at intervals over a span of some thirty years.[21] In "The German Constitution"—written in the early part of the Jena period, hence prior to the development of anything approaching the full philosophical system—Hegel prescribes a rather conventional politics of balance and accommodation involving, in particular, a system of limited government that "demands from the individual only what is necessary for itself" and "restricts accordingly the arrangements for ensuring the performance of this minimum."[22] Similarly, in his essay on "The Württemberg Estates," roughly contemporaneous with the publication of the *Encyclopedia*, he supports a structure of shared power rooted in bicameralism and

20. There are, of course, exceptions, as in Hegel's pronouncements regarding the "march of God in history" and the like.
21. These essays are translated in Pelczynski, ed., *Hegel's Political Writings*. This discussion borrows from Peter J. Steinberger, "Hegel's Occasional Writings: State and Individual," *Review of Politics* 45 (April 1983).
22. "The German Constitution," in *Hegel's Political Writings*, p. 154.

in a system of voter qualification designed to ensure that all established corporate entities are fully represented while simultaneously limiting the excesses of atomistic democracy. Finally, in "The English Reform Bill," written just prior to his death, Hegel leaves the basic and traditional features of English political practice largely untouched and defends, by strong implication, the Whig-liberalism of the English constitution.

Again, all of this suggests that, at the least, the tone and temper of Hegel's political thought is rather similar to that of the standard, accommodationist tradition. Yet, there are at least three even stronger prima facie reasons for considering seriously the thesis that the philosophy of Right is, in fact, radically different from this, that it is representative of the perspective we have called perfectionism, and that, as a result, it contemplates the complete conceptual dissolution of the problem of individual and society.

First, historical factors argue for such a thesis. In brief, the generation of intellectuals in Germany who came of age at the end of the eighteenth century was caught up precisely by the thought of dissolving once and for all the seeming contradiction between personal freedom and communal integration. At first this manifested itself as a call for anarchist revolution, understood as an "instrument for the creation of a community of self-legislating moral subjects who would not require the coercive control of political government."[23] Later, as political revolution began to lose some of its appeal, the fundamental aim remained the same: "It was precisely through the development of his individuality that man affirmed his essence as a communal and universal being. In social interaction and communication men gave concrete existence to their unique individual capacities and at the same time came to a mutual recognition of their common participation in the fellowship of divine life."[24] Such a notion was not simply peripheral or of marginal influence, but in fact was at the center of the ascendant movement of German intellectual life as represented by Schelling, Schleiermacher, Novalis, and Schlegel.[25] While Hegel appeared

---

23. John Edward Toews, *Hegelianism: The Path toward Dialectical Humanism, 1805–1841* (Cambridge: Cambridge University Press, 1980), p. 33.

24. Ibid., p. 44.

25. Ibid., p. 45.

always to have resisted its more anarchist implications, it seems certain that he too embraced this general project of solving, finally and definitively, the oppositions of political life:

> In the sphere of sociopolitical or communal relationsips... Hegel [like Schleiermacher] constructed a model of integration in which the subjective autonomy of the individual was conceived as fully actualized through the process of identification with the historical "substance" of the communal totality of which he was a part.... The emancipated egos of civil society were to be integrated into an ethical community that transcended the merely mechanical harmonization of individual interests through a process of moral and theoretical cultivation in which identification with the ethical substance of communal relationships would emerge as the culminating fulfillment and actualization of the subjective will of the individual.[26]

It is thus hard to imagine that Hegel would have been immune to, and uninfluenced by, the political concerns of this emergent movement when, in other respects, his career and his philosophy were so obviously shaped by it.

Second, these same concerns are quite clearly identified in the preface to the *Philosophy of Right* itself as providing the basic subject matter of social and political theory. For Hegel, political philosophy, like all philosophy, is not concerned with "external" things, with appearances or empirical manifestations; nor is it a matter of simply recording and ratifying the "play of fancy" or the hegemony of feeling and instinct; nor, again, is it a matter of creating fantastic utopias or fleeting ideals to be realized in some misty future. Rather, it is a matter of conceptual analysis wherein one discovers and explores the necessary structure of rationality itself: "To comprehend what is, this is the task of philosophy, because what is, is reason" (*PdR*, p. 16). Moreover, with respect to matters of a social or political nature, the question of what is, turns on precisely those issues we have been discussing. In a famous but, I think, still underappreciated passage, Hegel writes as follows:

> To recognize reason as the rose in the cross of the present and thereby to enjoy the present, this is the rational insight which reconciles us

26. Ibid., p. 64.

to the actual, the reconciliation which philosophy affords to those in
whom there has once arisen an inner voice bidding them to comprehend, not only to dwell in what is substantive while still retaining
subjective freedom, but also to possess subjective freedom while
standing not in anything particular and accidental but in what exists
absolutely. [*PdR*, p. 17]

The goal of philosophy is to understand the nature of the world
as it is, or as it must be comprehended by human reason, hence
to separate out the inessential appearances of things from their
"actuality," their essence. With respect to social and political life,
this means seeing how it is possible to conceive of "subjective
freedom" in its truth, not simply as a matter of particularity and
accident but, rather, as the genuine feature of individuality which
is part of, and utterly coherent with, the "substantive" actuality
of human society. The goal of the philosophy of Right is to show
that the subjectivity of the individual and the substantiality of the
community are equally a part of that rational core which is the
"rose"—the joy and consolation, the essence—of our real world.
It seems certain, then, that a perfectionist strategy lies at the heart
of Hegel's stated intentions.

In this connection, it may be thought that Hegel's quite principled distrust of utopia-building is itself inconsistent with the bold
and sublime claims of perfectionism. To contemplate the complete
dissolution of the problem of individual and society seems rather
a utopian business. But such a view would badly misconstrue the
nature of Hegel's project as he himself understood it. For Hegel,
the dissolution of the problem of individual and society is based
on conceptual truths that are already immanent in the experience
of modern politics. Again, the goal of philosophy is simply to
describe with particular clarity those various truths and to show
how they emerge logically from the conceptual apparatus of a
rational being. Such a project cannot generate purely hypothetical
blueprints for some as yet unheard-of world. To the contrary, it
can only generate standards, inherent in reason itself, against which
to judge particular social and political arrangements. Those standards will likely be most exacting and even, in some sense, un-
attainable. But they will still be rationally connected with real
human experience in a way that utopias are not.

Finally, and relatedly, I believe that a perfectionist strategy is implicit in Hegel's philosophical method itself. This method is, in large part, an attempt to confront the apparent contradictions of the world as it presents itself to us and as we appropriate it, and to demonstrate that those contradictions can somehow be absorbed by a system of reason which is coherent and whole. If the philosophy of Right is a part of such a system, then it seems that the contradiction between individual and society must turn out to be not a contradiction at all or, at best, one whose contradictory force somehow dissolves in the light of human rationality. I think this latter claim is decisive in forcing us to consider a perfectionist approach to Hegel's political thought; it suggests, further, that any attempt to deal with the fundamentals of the philosophy of Right must, at some point, pay attention to the philosophical method itself as embodied, above all, in Hegel's Logic.

2

Varieties of Conceptual Analysis

In recent years it has become rather common to hold that the philosophy of Right can be understood and evaluated without reference to the more mysterious regions of Hegelian philosophy. That this has been so, and continues to be the case today, must be regarded as something of a curiosity. For the fact is that, among the great political authors, Hegel alone seems to have been accorded this kind of treatment. No one would propose to deal with the political ideas of Plato or Saint Augustine or Hobbes, for example, without due consideration of their larger philosophical views. Even those writers for whom there is no apparent wider system, such as Machiavelli or Rousseau, are frequently interpreted in the light of their implicit and unstated philosophical prejudices.

But the curiosity goes well beyond this. For perhaps no writer has insisted on the systematic character of his philosophy as strenuously as did Hegel. For him, the various regions of thought—metaphysics, the philosophy of history, aesthetics, politics, and the like—are bound together in a dual sense: they proceed in terms of a single methodological protocol, only partly grasped in the concept of the dialectic; and they describe aspects of a single historical process, the self-unfolding of what Hegel calls World Spirit. Moreover, Hegel's philosophy of Right is itself explicitly and pointedly embedded in the larger system. Its first published version takes up fifty-three paragraphs of the original edition of the *Encyclopedia of the Philosophical Sciences*, where it plays a specific role in the overall structure of the work. In subsequent versions, the posthumously published lectures on the philosophy of Right and the presumably definitive version, the so-called *Philosophy of*

Right itself, Hegel is quite explicit: "it will be obvious from the work itself that the whole, like the formation of its parts, rests on the logical spirit. It is also from this point of view above all that I should like my book to be taken and judged. What we have to do with here is philosophical *science*, and in such science content is essentially bound up with form" (*PdR*, preface). Thus, while it may in fact be the case that his political philosophy can be fully comprehended without reference to the larger system, it is absolutely clear that Hegel himself thought otherwise.

I begin, then, with the presumption that the philosophy of Right should be treated as Hegel intended, viz., as one of the several "sciences" animated by the methods and categories of the Logic (*EL* 24). But this suggests that we need an account of Hegel's philosophical method itself, and it is to such an account that we now turn our attention. The discussion that follows will be quite limited in scope. It will ignore most of the particular claims that Hegel makes pertaining to being and becoming, appearance and actuality, the Absolute, and the like; in short, it will largely ignore the substantive metaphysical arguments that comprise the greater part of the Logic. The focus instead will be on the kind of argumentation that Hegel employs in arriving at philosophical conclusions. What does it mean to do philosophy? What are the criteria by which we determine whether or not a particular conclusion is warranted? How do we distinguish a good argument from a bad one? Hegel's answers to such questions provide the methodological basis of the Logic which, in turn, controls and authorizes the particular sectors of his system, including the philosophy of Right.

Of course, even such a narrow focus presents extraordinary problems, for the question of method is perhaps the most difficult and controversial question for students of Hegel. I would certainly not claim that the following discussion is in some way uniquely correct. In general, my goal is to present one plausible account of Hegel's philosophical method, without denying that alternative accounts are possible. More ambitiously, I would hope that my account comports with the "real" Hegelian system—whatever that might be—in such a way that whatever I say could be assented to as at least a part of what Hegel had in mind. That is, if I am presenting merely one chunk of that system, but am doing so in a way that is faithful to the original, I will be satisfied. For to have traced out accurately a part of Hegel's method, and then to have examined its application in a particular substantive area such as the philosophy of Right, is presumably to have said something important about Hegel's work on Right which could not have been said otherwise.

I must admit, nonetheless, that this chapter is motivated in part by a certain dissatisfaction with a standard kind of approach to Hegel's system. That approach is essentially a matter of paraphrase. Its strategy is to restate Hegel's arguments in terms perhaps more familiar to contemporary readers, to trace out the sources of those arguments, and to suggest certain of their putative implications. Such a strategy can provide alternative images of the Hegelian system, and these can often be extremely illuminating. Still, one can read a great deal of excellent and suggestive literature on Hegel without fully emerging from a kind of metaphorical language nearly as obscure as Hegel's own. While it is often easy enough to see what it is that Hegel rejects, e.g., Hume's empiricism or Kant's critical system, it is not always easy to specify the precise nature of Hegel's alternative, and much of the secondary literature is—beyond a certain point—not all that helpful. (Notable exceptions would be the works of Mure and Findlay and, more recently, three remarkable books by Taylor, Burbidge, and Inwood.)[1]

My specific goal, then, is to describe some of the distinctive features of philosophical analysis as Hegel understood it, relying as little as possible on unclear words and unexamined claims. In pursuing such a goal, a number of tasks will unavoidably arise.

---

1. G. R. G. Mure, *An Introduction to Hegel* (Oxford: Oxford University Press, 1940); G. R. G. Mure, *A Study of Hegel's Logic* (Oxford: Oxford University Press, 1950); J. N. Findlay, *Hegel: A Re-examination* (New York: Oxford University Press, 1976); Charles Taylor, *Hegel* (Cambridge: Cambridge University Press, 1975); John Burbidge, *On Hegel's Logic* (Atlantic Highlands, N.J.: Humanities Press, 1981); M. J. Inwood, *Hegel* (London: Routledge and Kegan Paul, 1984). The "analytic" approach has come to influence certain Hegel scholars in Germany as well. For example, see Dieter Henrich, "Was Heist Analytische Philosophie?" in *Ist Systematische Philosophie Möglich: Hegel-Studien* 17. Still, perhaps the most influential recent account of Hegel's Logic in Germany is Michael Theunissen, *Sein und Schein* (Frankfurt: Suhrkamp, 1978). Theunissen's approach is quite different from the one presented here. For a discussion, see Hans Friedrich Fulda, Rolf-Peter Horstmann, and Michael Theunissen, *Kritische Darstellung der Metaphysik* (Frankfurt: Suhrkamp, 1980).

First, it will be necessary to consider in general terms how the dialectic operates and to characterize the role played therein by the Hegelian idea of sublation. It will be important to determine just what dialectical reasoning purports to achieve, what kinds of problems it seeks to resolve, and what general principles it invokes in arriving at philosophical conclusions.

It will also be necessary to distinguish, as well as possible, the goals of the Hegelian system from those of other philosophical traditions. It seems quite clear that Hegel's philosophy is a kind of conceptual analysis, but this claim may be a mere tautology. Philosophy itself may well be nothing other than conceptual analysis and, thus, it becomes important to differentiate the particular nature of Hegelian concepts and modes of analysis from those of, say, Plato or Kant or Wittgenstein.

Further, and perhaps most crucially, it will be important to determine the sense in which Hegel understood philosophical proof or demonstration. There is no doubt that he felt he had demonstrated a great deal, but there are serious questions as to what he meant by this. If we can discover the criteria by which he sought to determine the warrantability of conclusions, we shall have gone a long way toward understanding the dialectic in general.

Overarching all of this is a perhaps more basic question: How does Hegel's dialectical logic differ from conventional logic? More particularly, what is the relevance for Hegel of the standard rules of reasoning and rational inference, what Frege called the laws of truth?[2] These laws—the canons of logic—appear to be utterly indispensable to correct thinking in general and to philosophical analysis in particular. Yet there is a good deal of textual evidence to suggest that Hegel either sought to go beyond the standard principles of logic or else rejected them altogether, and that he understood dialectical logic to be somehow different and superior. If, then, the laws of truth are indispensible, how could Hegel have dispensed with them while still producing a rationally defensible philosophy?

A particularly crucial aspect of this general problem concerns the issue of contradiction. Of all the laws of reason, the principle

2. Gottlob Frege, "The Thought: A Logical Inquiry," in P. F. Strawson, ed., *Philosophical Logic* (Oxford: Oxford University Press, 1967).

of contradiction is perhaps the most fundamental; at least Hegel thought this to be the case. Yet he appears explicitly to reject the principle (*WL*, II, pp. 58–62) and systematically to violate it with such notorious formulations as "the identity of identity and non-identity." Indeed, he emphasizes time and again his judgment that contradiction is fundamental to everything. We must, therefore, try to determine exactly what this means and how it relates to our usual assumptions regarding rational thought.

Finally, there are a few general metaphysical issues that are crucial as regards the philosophy of Right and will thus require some brief attention. We shall have to touch on the Hegelian concept of "infinity"; and we shall have to consider the relationship between the logical, phenomenological, and historical self-unfoldings of Absolute Spirit as Hegel saw it. Further, we shall have to consider Hegel's claim to have established a presuppositionless philosophy and his further claim to have offered an apodictic proof of the necessary structure of the world. Naturally, these issues will take us rather far from the central topic of this book; as a result, they will be treated only insofar as an acquaintance with them is helpful in understanding the arguments of the philosophy of Right. My hope, then, is to offer an introductory discussion that will establish for the reader at least one possible account of Hegel's larger project, a project which I then proceed to trace in some of its peculiarly political or ethical aspects.

1

Let us begin with a simple, one might almost say simplistic, example of thinking which may be understood from the perspective of the Hegelian dialectic. Imagine that we have before us an object we are seeking to understand in such a way that we can answer satisfactorily the question "What is it?" Exactly how to do this in general is, of course, an old problem. Do we rely on the images the object imposes on our consciousness via the senses, then formulate some useful and plausible theory about it? Or do we bring a preestablished set of criteria in virtue of which the object is categorized and conceptualized? Do we attend merely to certain properties of the thing, or do we in fact think about the thing in itself? Setting questions aside, we might nonetheless agree that the effort to say what the object "is" leads us to suggest a more or less adequate description of what is commonly called the "nature" of the thing.

Let us suppose further that in the present case we articulate our claim in the following way: "The object before us is a body of water." Now we can hardly imagine a more staightforward assertion. Yet, exactly what it expresses is not entirely clear. Presumably in claiming to answer satisfactorily the question "What is it?" by saying that it is a body of water, we are attending to one or more of a wide variety of features. The object is a depression in the ground filled with water. It is fed by a source of water which itself is composed of two parts hydrogen and one part oxygen. The object is not the same as other objects that we call meadows, forests, deserts, and fields. At this particular moment, two ducks are floating on its surface. Its water is green; sometimes people take boats out on it; homes built on the edge of it are more expensive than homes built elsewhere. Clearly, there is an enormous variety of observations that might help us to describe the object. But in simply saying "The object is a body of water," the precise nature of these observations and, more especially, the particular kind of contribution that each one makes, if any, to our claim about what the object really is, is at this point unclear. Among the specific questions left unanswered are:

—Is the assertion saying something important about the object or something trivial?

—Upon what kind of evidence is the assertion based?

—Which features of the object are important to the claim that it is a body of water?

—Does the assertion imply that the object is different from certain other objects? If so, what are those other objects and what is the nature of the difference?

—Does the assertion imply that the object is similar to certain other objects? Again, which objects and why?

—In what ways could the object be changed and still be a body of water?

—What kinds of changes would turn the object into something other than a body of water?

In short, the assertion as it stands, without qualification or elaboration, is rather primitive. We would surely say that it is an account of what the object is, but as such it operates at a relatively low level. By this I mean that it fails—in and of itself, i.e., in virtue of its literal meaning alone—to suggest specific answers to those questions which seem to be crucial in arriving at an understanding of what the speaker is really trying to say. We can imagine the speaker of this assertion appending to it a variety of similar assertions: "the object is green," "it is a good place for boating," and the like. Still, the sum total of these assertions would not on its own account provide answers to those questions which are necessary if we are trying to determine what the speaker thinks the object really is, why he thinks that, and whether or not he's correct.[3]

Nonetheless, such assertions are undoubtedly based on something. Indeed, when a person says, "The object before us is a body of water," his claim is, in normal conversational contexts, necessarily reflective of certain answers to at least some of the questions outlined above, and to other questions as well, whether he knows it or not. That is, the very fact of his assertion strongly suggests (though perhaps does not prove) that he indeed has—in some sense of "has"—answers to those questions, despite the fact that he had not explicitly formulated or reflected upon them. To borrow H. P. Grice's terminology, the assertion ideally should implicate not merely the claim itself, but also those answers to judgments upon which the claim is based.

According to Grice, the meaning of a conversational utterance generally includes not simply the literal meaning of the words themselves but also the gamut of further meanings deducible from the contexts in which the utterance occurs.[4] While standing by my immobilized car, I remark to a passerby that "I'm out of gas." The passerby replies as follows: "There's a gas station around the next corner." Literally, his words convey a simple and perhaps unhelpful empirical claim. But in fact, the utterance may generally be thought to express a great deal else, including, for example, the idea that the gas station is or may well be open, has gas to

3. Of course, I assume here that the speaker is in fact trying to tell us what the object is. There are many other kinds of claims one could make about the object— e.g., "It is pretty"—which are not intended to answer the question "What is it?" and which therefore do not rest on the kinds of questions listed above.

4. H. P. Grice, "Logic and Conversation," in *The Philosophy of Language*, ed. A. P. Martinich (New York: Oxford University Press, 1985).

sell, is staffed by people who understand my language, and the like. Grice would call this the "implicature" of the utterance, and he claims that much human conversation depends on the ability of hearers to deduce from the context that which an utterance is intended to "implicate" beyond the words themselves. Thus, when someone says "The object before us is a body of water," this ought to implicate at least some of those further judgments on the basis of which we can truly understand his answer to the question "What is it?"

But as Grice notes, there are many circumstances in which such judgments are not clearly implicated: the words might plausibly be thought to implicate any number of contradictory judgments, are uttered in inappropriate contexts, provide insufficient clues for the listener, and the like. In the present case, to the extent that the underlying judgments remain for whatever reason opaque, we cannot say that the assertion truly expresses anything but the brute claim—the literal meaning—itself. In such a circumstance: (1) the listener can have no certain idea as to what particular judgments the assertion reflects but fails to express, and (2) the speaker also does not know—or at least has failed to articulate—which judgments comprise the basis of his own claim.

When we make those judgments explicit by, for example, asking the speaker some of the crucial questions, then the assertion might well come to be seen as a quite adequate description of the object. But it would now be, in a sense, a rather different assertion. For when fully explicated, it does indeed express not simply the claim that the object is a body of water but a great deal else having to do with the meaning and justification of that claim. That is, the assertion, when spoken and heard in the context of the judgments upon which it is explicitly based, in effect expresses those judgments as well; to utter it is necessarily to "implicate" them.

Thus, we really have two assertions, one which simply says that the object is a body of water, the other which says the same thing but also expresses or implicates some of the more particular judgments upon which that claim rests. We may call these the "brute assertion" and the "fully explicated assertion," respectively, and our conclusion is that they express quite different things despite the fact that the words are the same. Still, they are intimately related to each other in the sense that the second, by virtue of its known implications, merely makes manifest the unexpressed foundations of the first. Indeed, the fully explicated assertion is nothing but the brute assertion fleshed out; it simply indicates which of the many possible judgments the brute assertion would in fact express if it could.

I think it plausible to say that there is a hierarchical relationship between these two kinds of assertions. Fully explicated assertions are higher in the sense that they express not only everything expressed by their corresponding brute assertions but also much of the justificatory material upon which the latter are based. As such, they provide a far richer description of the object in question. But we should also note that the fully explicated and brute assertions do not exhaust the possibilities; they are, rather, simply two poles of a continuum. Along the continuum we find many degrees of "partially explicated assertions," and just how these would be classified in terms of descriptive adequacy is not immediately clear. Still, it seems evident that the more fully explicated the assertion, the "higher" it is in the sense just described.

In Hegel's Logic we encounter a similar hierarchy of claims. Hegel calls such claims determinations or, for reasons that are presently unimportant, definitions of the Absolute. Roughly speaking, what we have here referred to as brute assertions would be exemplified by what Hegel calls *qualitative determinations*—i.e., determinations that help to express the *quality* of the object in question (at least as understood by the speaker: *EL* 86ff.; Cf., *WL* I, pp. 111). A qualitative determination thus operates at a rather low level of discourse. It tells us something about the object in question—e.g., "it is a body of water"—but it fails to tell us why we believe this conclusion to be true, which features of the object are important in helping us determine that it is a body of water, what it is that distinguishes the object from other objects, and the like. As Mure puts it: "The categories of Being [of which quality is one] are in fact thought at the level where it is almost bare intuition below discursion."[5] A qualitative determination presents a claim about what a thing is, but it expresses virtually none of the arguments—none of the "discursion"—which claims should

---

5. G. R. G. Mure, *A Study of Hegel's Logic*, p. 28.

express or implicate if we are interested in a complete understanding of the object in question.

But when the assertion is fully explicated, we then have what Hegel calls an *essential determination*—a claim, correct or incorrect, about the essence of a thing.[6] Of course, the term *essence* is an extraordinarily difficult one, both in Hegel's system and in the philosophical literature generally. Moreover, it is by no means clear that Hegel's account comports with prevailing ones. Nonetheless, it seems generally true that to describe the essence of something is to say what it *really* is, not what it appears to be, and to claim both that this "what" is necessary and is exclusively so. If I say that F is the essence of *a*, then I in effect claim that F is necessary in the sense that without it *a* would not be *a*; and that, further, F is the only thing which has this property with respect to *a*.[7]

Now, for Hegel, we can make a claim regarding the essence of the object only when our assertion clearly implicates specific answers to at least some of the important questions that any simple description raises. Only by trying to answer such questions can we begin to distinguish assertions that pertain to the necessary/exclusive aspect of the object from those which pertain only to accidental or inessential features. For example, on Hegel's account one way of describing the essence of a thing is explicitly to differentiate it from other things. In Hegel's terminology, the category of difference is one part of the Doctrine of Essence. Thus, we might differentiate object *a* from object *b* in terms of some property F, the presence of which is essential to *a* for some specifiable reasons and the absence of which is again specifiably essential to *b*. In such a case, Hegel would say that our determination truly invokes the category of difference insofar as it clearly expresses specific judgments regarding difference. On the other hand, in describing object *a* we might say simply that it is different from object *b* without elaborating the nature of the difference and

6. On essential determination, see Robert Pippin, "Hegel's Metaphysics and the Problem of Contradiction," *Journal of the History of Philosophy* 16 (July 1978): 301–12.

7. Of course, this essence of the thing—F—may be in fact an extremely complex congeries of various elements.

without specifying the reasons why we consider that difference to be somehow "essential." For Hegel, such a description—involving something like a partially explicated assertion—would be closer to a mere qualitative determination.[8] It does indeed differentiate one object from the other. But again, it does not clearly tell us anything about the difference or, indeed, about what it means to differentiate in general. In Hegel's terms, then, the category of difference is only "implicit" in the qualitative determination. This means that the latter, while differentiating, nonetheless fails to express answers to important questions regarding differentiation, answers which in fact form the tacit basis of the determination itself and which are finally made explicit in the essential determination.

Thus, for Hegel, there is a complex, hierarchical relationship between qualitative and essential determinations. Presumably, for every essential determination there is a corresponding qualitative determination. The essential determination is higher in that it expresses both the rudimentary claim of the qualitative determination and the particular judgments upon which that claim rests. This means that the qualitative determination is "present" in the essential determination in the sense that the latter expresses the basic claim of the former. But in another sense, the essential determination or, more specifically, the particular judgments which comprise it, are "present" in the qualitative determination in that, upon inspection, it turns out to have been reflective of them.

We may summarize by saying that Hegel wants to distinguish assertions about *what a thing is* (qualitative determination) from assertions about *what a thing is in essence* (essential determination). We might say further that the former kinds of assertions express *pre-essential determinations*. Again, when we encounter the object, we assert that it is a body of water and we might add to that a variety of other qualitative determinations. The complete set of such determinations comprises what Hegel calls the "qualitative limits" of the object. Now it seems that these qualitative limits stand as a first answer to the question "What is the essence of the object?" For in setting out the qualitative limits, we rely on a series

8. Hegel does not explicitly operate in terms of a continuum between these various kinds of determinations; exactly where, or how, he would draw the line is not entirely clear.

of brute assertions; and those assertions reflect, although they do not express, the kinds of judgments characteristic of essential determination. Thus, to present the qualitative limits of a thing is strongly to suggest that those limits reflect that which is exclusively necessary—i.e., essential—though, again, they certainly fail to identify exactly what it is that is essential and why.

2

If we reflect a bit more about brute assertions, it seems that they can be of more than one variety. In particular, some assertions describe features of an object in quantitative terms while others do not. Indeed, it appears to be the case that many kinds of features would be quite difficult to express quantitatively, while others are best expressed that way. We say that George is "Catholic," and it is hard to see how we could express this judgment using numbers or other quantitative language; for the trait of being Catholic seems to bear no relationship of "more-or-less-than" to any other trait. On the other hand, we also say of George that "he wears a 42-Long," and it is hard to see how we could avoid using numbers and still get a suit to fit him properly.

Now it may seem odd to suggest that brute assertions of a quantitative nature could be pre-essential in the sense described above. It is not likely that the assertion "George wears a 42-Long"—when fully explicated—could possibly be construed to mean that wearing a 42-Long is the essence of George, i.e., that feature which is exclusively necessary to his being what he is. If George gained fifteen pounds, he'd surely still be George. On the other hand, a little reflection will show that some fully explicated assertions of a quantitative nature can indeed be essential determinations (though not necessarily good ones), and that their corresponding brute assertions must therefore be pre-essential.

To begin with, consider those cases in which specific theories reduce seemingly nonquantitative features to quantitative terms. For example, many psychologists seem to believe that the human mind is purely material, and that its functions should be conceived of as empirically identifiable sequences of electronic impulses. Such a view suggests that ideas, emotions, personality traits, and the like, can be best understood as a series of quantitatively defined relationships between basic entities such as protons and electrons.

Of course, such entities are common to all objects and, thus, a brain differs from a frying pan only in the number of such basic entities it has and in their quantitatively defined relationships. On such an account, to describe these quantitative facts is thus to describe the essence of the brain, i.e., that which is exclusively necessary to its being what it is. In general, the tendency of scientists to reduce phenomena—colors, odors, sounds—to bits of matter distinguished from one another by molecular structure shows that quantitative assertions can be quite attractive as essential determinations.

But we can also think of more homely examples. I recall the case of the assembly-line worker in the bread factory whose sole job it was to place the finished, wrapped loaves in large cardboard boxes. After a time, or at least for long moments, the loaves of bread ceased to have for him any identity other than as homogeneous units of the same size and weight. The features that we normally associate with bread—its taste and smell, its nutritional value, its role in making sandwiches—were lost to him. From his perspective, the objects before him were otherwise characterless entities of a certain volume to be placed in boxes and shipped in trucks. Similarly, we can imagine the college admissions officer who thinks of candidates exclusively in terms of SAT scores; the investor for whom a corporation is the value of a share of its common stock; the cartographer who distinguishes one mountain from another solely in terms of altitude in feet.

Now it does seem that a *purely* quantitative determination would be extremely difficult to imagine. Even the brain and the frying pan are understood as "things" or "objects" or "material entities," concepts which are not intrinsically quantitative; and at some point, the protons and electrons that comprise matter—or whatever the basic entities happen to be—must probably be conceived of as having an essence not expressible in purely quantitative terms. Similarly, the fact that the admissions officer compares candidates solely in terms of SAT scores is certainly compatible with the fact that the set of candidates qua candidates may be nonquantitatively different from, say, the set of lawn mowers.

Nonetheless, what distinguishes essential determinations of a quantitative nature is that—within nonquantitatively determined groups—they identify essential differences as being differences in degree rather than in kind. The brain and the frying pan share certain features that are common to their essences, e.g., each is a "thing" or each has a molecular structure. But beyond this, that which is exclusively necessary to the brain, without which it would not be a brain, is different only in degree—i.e., in terms of quantities and/or spatiotemporal configurations of atomic entities— from that which is essential to the frying pan. Similarly, a particular candidate for admissions, though perhaps sharing many nonquantitatively defined essential features with the other candidates, is also described as "a 625"; and for the admissions officer, this might well be an essential feature—the candidate would not be what he is without it—which still is different from the essential features of the other candidates only in degree.

Thus, fully explicated assertions of a quantitative nature can be essential determinations and, therefore, their corresponding brute assertions can be pre-essential. But further, it seems that such assertions not only differ from but in fact specifically contradict nonquantitative assertions. The intuition that objects are essentially different only in degree contradicts the perhaps more conventional intuition that objects are essentially different in kind. To the ordinary consciousness, the brain and the frying pan are to be distinguished from one another not in terms of some quantitative scale; rather, they are different *kinds* of things. Hence, their essences are, in a certain sense, incommensurable. We would say that to compare them is "like comparing apples and oranges." This does not really mean that they cannot be compared at all but, rather, that their essential natures cannot be compared in terms of, say, a common, quantitatively defined dimension. The brain and the frying pan are different because of features that would be very difficult to place on a single scale. Similarly, it would be hard to compare in purely quantitative terms the admissions candidate who is a 625 with the candidate who is, say, a piano virtuoso. Thus, assertions which express the view that essential differences can be differences only in degree directly contradict the intuition that such differences are differences in kind.

Again, Hegel's Logic focuses on this contradiction. He distinguishes *quantitative determinations* from qualitative ones and, indeed, defines them as unique opposites (*EL* 99ff.). Both are roughly equivalent to what we have called brute assertions and are, therefore, pre-essential. But the judgments relative to essence that are reflected tacitly in quantitative determinations directly contradict those that are reflected in qualitative determinations. According to the former, essential differences are differences in degree; according to the latter, they are differences in kind. Thus, to assert the one is, by implication, to deny or "negate" the other.

For Hegel, quantitative determinations in fact reflect two related kinds of judgments. First, they reflect the view that the object is simply a single unit—it is one thing—amidst a range of other single things (or, if we are talking about a number of objects, that there are so many of them.) The object, that is to say, can be counted; and to count it is, in effect, to draw a conceptual circle around it which differentiates it as one unit among many other units. Findlay puts it well: "The notion of Quantity therefore involves an essential *discreteness* or apartness of units."[9] But, second, quantitative determination also involves the view of the object as itself composed of many constituent units having definite quantitative relationships. These might be electrons and protons; or they might be square feet or tonnage or points on an SAT examination. In each case, the object is seen to be a particular agglomeration and/or quantitatively defined configuration of such entities. The category of quantity is thus applied both to the object's relationship to other objects and also to its own internal make-up. Hence, from the standpoint of quantity, the object is both a discrete unit and a composite of discrete units; in each sense, the judgment can be rendered in terms of one or more numerical scales. But again, such judgments pertain to essence, i.e., they purport to describe that which is exclusively necessary to the object being what it is. Thus, assertions reflective of them will, when fully explicated, contradict assertions reflective of the view that objects are essentially different not in degree but in kind.

For Hegel, then, there appears to be a logical contradiction between qualitative and quantitative determination. We may return now to our original example. We characterized the object before us as "a body of water," and in so doing we set out (at least some of) its "qualititative limits." These limits tell us what the object *is*. But we can imagine that someone else comes by—

9. Findlay, *Hegel: A Re-examination*, p. 167–68.

perhaps an urban planner or a tax assessor—and says, rather, that
the object *is* "a thing having a surface of 10,000 square feet and
a volume of 150,00 cubic feet." Insofar as the "is" in these assertions merely predicates certain properties of the object, there is
of course no contradiction. But insofar as the "is" is the is of pre-
essential determination—i.e., insofar as the assertions, when fully
explicated, would express judgments regarding that which is exclusively necessary to the object being what it is—then we do
indeed have a straightforward logical contradiction.

It may be worthwhile at this point informally to schematize this
contradiction. We may call the object before us a and the qualitative limits of that object F. Thus, our first assertion is a^*F, where
* denotes "is" in the sense of what we have called pre-essential
determination. Our particular determination provides us with what
Hegel calls the quality of the thing, and we can call the category
of quality F. So, we may say that, for us, F is the F of a. Similarly,
the quantitative limits of a we will call G, so that a^*G. We can
call the category of quantity G so that for us G is the G of a.
(Retrospectively, we may say that F and G are applications of F
and G, respectively, to the object a). Assuming that F and G are
different from one another—indeed, for Hegel they are not simply
different but are unique opposites—and that, as a result, F and G
are similarly different, we face a logical contradiction since a cannot
be pre-essentially F and G (i.e., non-F) at the same time.

Hegel's task in the Logic is to resolve such contradictions by
showing that they are products of a comparatively undeveloped
mode of thinking. In the present case, while we cannot logically
say both that a^*F and that a^*G, our intuitions nonetheless tell us
that a is in fact both F and G. Our task, therefore, is to overcome
the logical contradiction; and this is achieved simply by concluding
that while F and G are each a part of the essence of a, neither is
by itself the whole of that essence. Each is necessary but not
sufficient for a being what it is. In order to express this intuition,
we need a new assertion which, when fully explicated, would express the essence of a as being something other than simply F or
G but, rather, F together with G (though the precise sense of
"together with" is not entirely clear). We can call this something
other H. And thus, our new assertion is a^*H, where H = F + G
and "+" denotes some sense of "together with." In making this

assertion, we are invoking a new category—F together with G—which we can call H and, thus, H is the H of a.

In Hegelian terminology, the concept of quality together with the concept of quantity is called *measure*. According to Hegel, measure is the "unity" of quality and quantity or, more briefly, the qualitative quantum "where quality and quantity are in one" (*EL* 107; cf. *WL*, I, pp. 332ff.). In asserting the measure of an object, the apparent contradiction between our qualitative and quantitative determinations is "overcome."

Now the question of how we derive this new category, and how we can give an adequate account of it, will be considered below. Indeed, it is my judgment that the bulk of Hegel's substantive philosophy, including most of the philosophy of Right, is devoted precisely to such questions as "how should we understand and articulate this or that 'third' category which we have initially defined as the conjunction of two seemingly opposed categories?" Chapters 3 through 6 of this book treat several such concepts—punishment, marriage, and the organic state—in precisely these terms.

But putting such questions aside, Hegel's resolution of the apparent contradiction has certain implications that demand our immediate attention. To begin with, the original contradiction—as originally stated—remains a contradiction. That is, since F is different from—or, perhaps, is the unique opposite of—G, it cannot be that both a^*F and a^*G. The introduction of H does nothing to change that. Nor does it change the fact that at least some of the judgments which were reflected in the original assertions remain true, viz., the judgments that F and G are both essential to a. Moreover, if we were, for some circumstantial reason, to lose sight of or forget about H, then we might well encounter once again the original contradiction. Indeed, it seems that such circumstantial factors arise quite frequently: the worker in the bread factory reverts to his benumbed state, the admissions officer feels pressure to increase median SAT scores, and the like. There is a sense, then, in which the *appearance* of contradiction is preserved, even while it is in fact being overcome.

Further, in our new assertion F and G continue to be crucial in determining a, hence the concepts F and G are also crucial. Indeed, H is *nothing other* than $F + G$. Of course, this in no way changes that fact that F is different from or even the opposite of G. Thus, in H the distinction between them is preserved; in Hegel's phrase, they continue to be "at war" with one another. But in another sense, our understanding of F and G does change somewhat. For when we employ them in determining the object before us, we no longer think of F apart from G, but, rather, together with G. That is, the discovery of H leads to the conclusion that (at least with respect to the object a) we must use F in conjunction with G, and vice versa; the one must be situated, so to speak, with the other. It is, of course, possible to avoid doing this, negligently or perversely to ignore this conjunction-in-use; but to do so is, in Hegelian terms, to think "abstractly" rather than "concretely," to risk lapsing back into contradiction, hence to forfeit the opportunity adequately to understand the object a. Thus, for a mind employing the category H, F ceases to be simply F and becomes, instead, the F-that-goes-along-with-G; and, of course, G becomes the G-that-goes-along-with-F. In this way, the original concepts are in one sense retained, in another sense altered. At many points in the Logic (and elsewhere) Hegel emphasizes that the progress of philosophy does not leave concepts untouched, and we have here an example of this. Both the original contradiction and the concepts it reflects are expressed yet altered in the later assertion; they retain their identity, their distinctiveness, yet we now understand them in a very new light.

I believe that many examples of the Hegelian dialectic follow a pattern roughly like this one. A contradiction between two kinds of intuitions leads to the discovery of a contradiction between two categories of thought. The contradiction appears to be very troubling since, owing to the strength of our intuitions, we would want to give up neither category. We somehow discover a third category which is, in fact, nothing but the two original categories taken together. This third category simply reflects the discovery that the first two were each necessary but insufficient; and recognition of this prompts us to see the two categories in a new light. Each is seen to be most useful only in the context of the other, hence as part of a more complex, composite category. In Hegel's words, each is now to be understood concretely rather than abstractly.[10]

---

10. For a nice introduction to this notion of the concrete, see J. Glenn Gray, "Hegel's Logic: The Philosophy of the Concrete," *Virginia Quarterly Review* (Spring 1971), pp. 175–89.

Each is to be employed in its crucial connection with the other, rather than in isolation. For Hegel, the result is that the abstractness of our earlier judgments is annulled, while their rational core is preserved and elevated. Our original judgments, $a*F$ and $a*G$, are cancelled by the new judgment, $a*H$, which preserves that in them which was valuable and correct.

As regards our original object of inquiry, then, we come to see that both its qualitative and quantitative limits are crucial in arriving at an adequate pre-essential determination. That is, we must make note of the fact that the object is a body of water, but this fact must be considered in the context of the object's size; and/or we must note its size, but only together with the fact that it is a body of water. In this way, we come to see that it is not simply a body of water, and that it is not simply an object of 150,000 cubic feet, but in fact that it is a "pond" rather than a puddle or a lake or an ocean. Clearly, the difference between a pond and an ocean is one that we would want to take into account; and it is Hegel's view that recognizing such a difference requires the concept of measure qua the mutual conditioning of quality and quantity.

3

The discussion thus far has focused solely for illustrative purposes on the dialectic of quality, quantity, and measure. There is, of course, a quite broad range of concepts that receive explicit treatment in the Logic. These include such categories as being and becoming, identity and difference, substantiality and causality, among very many others. The sum of these categories may be said to comprise the foundation of Hegel's general metaphysics. They are, at one and the same time, the fundamental ways in which Mind—as manifested in particular human minds—appropriates and understands the world and, also, the necessary forms of the world itself. The meaning of the word *necessary* here and in related contexts will be considered in section 4 below. For now it may suffice to say that the categories are thought to be the logically deduced tools of all intellection and that the world "out there," whatever it may be, can only be understood—intellected—in terms of those tools.

But for our purposes, there is a more important point to make about these concepts, and that is that they are, strictly speaking, categories appropriate only to a discussion of general metaphysics. They pertain to ontology in the abstract, not to particular ontologies having to do, say, with the nature of art, religion, social life, and the like. Thus, in the particular case, the philosophy of Right does not proceed in terms of such categories as quality, quantity, and measure; rather, it operates on the basis of concepts peculiar and appropriate to its own particular nature. This is true of all the individual regions of Hegelian philosophy. While each one is part of the larger system and emerges out of the teaching of the Logic, its connection to the Logic cannot be understood straightforwardly in terms of the categories of Hegelian metaphysics.

The connection of these various regions with the Logic is, in fact, twofold. To begin with, each operates according to the inferential method established in the Logic and introduced above with reference to quality, quantity, and measure. That is, in each case something of interest is encountered and described in terms of different, ultimately contradictory determinations of a pre-essential nature; and in each case, the contradiction is dispelled by introducing some third determination which somehow subsumes the other two. But second, this inferential method itself can be described in terms of a certain common set of Hegelian categories that are, in some sense, supplemental or attendant to the categories of metaphysics strictly understood. These supplemental or, perhaps, metatheoretical concepts are, in effect, the tools not of metaphysics—nor of any other substantive region of philosophy—but of thinking itself considered as a process; they describe, so to speak, the activity rather than the content of thought. Since all realms of philosophical science operate methodologically in the same way, their various connections can be best understood with reference to this supplemental set of concepts. In the particular case, then, the philosophy of Right will reflect the Logic not in terms of the categories of metaphysics but, rather, in terms of these broader metatheoretical concepts.

Included among such concepts would be certain of the better-known terms of Hegelian philosophy. We have already touched on these in passing, but it will now be useful to treat them in some detail:

1. *Mediation.* For Hegel, the process of logical inference is one of progressive mediation in which particular formulations are qual-

ified or refined in the light of other, alternative formulations (see *EL* 65–70). Specifically, any chain of reasoning begins with what Hegel calls an immediate claim. Our original qualitative description of the body of water would be an example. Such a description is immediate (*unmittelbar*) in the sense that it presents itself initially as a brute, intuitively evident account of the object at hand. The truth of it is, so to speak, immediately apparent to us, and we may at first be inclined to accept it without qualification. It is a claim that we hold to without deep reflection, without having asked all of those questions which, once answered, would change it from a pre-essential to an essential determination. In a similar way, of course, our quantitative determination of the object would also be an immediate claim. In the first instance, Hegel would say that the object exists for us immediately as a body of water; in the second, that it exists for us immediately as an object of a certain size. But the very awareness that we are making two competing, seemingly incompatible claims provides an impetus for our comparing, contrasting, and evaluating each in the light of the other. Again, the qualitative limits of the object come to be seen in terms of its quantitative limits, and vice versa. In this way, each claim ceases to be merely immediate and, instead, comes to be mediated—that is, qualified, recast, conditioned, situated—by the other. An object, when fully mediated, exists for us as the set of all its relevant determinations understood explicitly in terms of their various mutual relations. In every example of the Hegelian dialectic, an immediate claim is confronted by an alternative immediate claim, and the resolution of this conflict leads to our understanding of the object in question as fully mediated.

2. *The negation of the negation.* While the concepts positive and negative do have a particular role in Hegel's general metaphysics (*EL* 119), they also function more broadly with respect to the dialectical process itself. As we have just seen, any chain of reasoning necessarily begins with an immediate claim. But we may also understand this claim to present, not simply a first determination of the object, but also an initial account of its integrity or unity as an object—i.e., the object as a single, whole thing, an identity. In Hegel's terminology, the object stands for us as something positive, something that has been affirmed and appears as an "identical self-relation." In a certain sense, our second, alter-

native determination operates in precisely the same way, present-ing a different "positive" account of the object. But since this second account is apparently incompatible with the first, our aware-ness of this leads us to say that it is, in fact, the negation of the first. Returning to our example, to claim that the object is (pre-essentially) an object of a certain size is to deny that it is (pre-essentially) a body of water. Of course, the reverse is also true. Hence, when viewed in a certain light, any positive claim may be seen as a negative claim, a fact which simply reflects the manifest instability of claims that are as yet unmediated. With the resolution of our contradiction, we come to see that in fact neither claim successfully negates the other. Our final determination of the ob-ject, therefore, stands as the negation of the negation. As such, it is surely a positive claim, since two negatives do make a positive; but it is now a positive claim understood precisely in terms of the particular negatives that it has negated, and it cannot be adequately comprehended without making explicit reference to those earlier determinations. Thus, to have before us a fully mediated object requires that our account of it stand as the negation of the negation.

3. *The concrete.* As we have seen briefly above, Hegel's use of the terms *concrete* and *abstract* is distinctive, and has nothing di-rectly to do with, say, the difference between the empirical and intellectual realms (*EL* 164). For Hegel, an object is known to us concretely—its determination is concrete—when it is understood not simply in itself but in terms of its basic connections with other things. These connections, in turn, are provided by all of those determinations which, though initially immediate and isolated, are shown to be each a necessary and unavoidable part of our descrip-tion of the thing. To define the object as simply a body of water without referring to its quantitative limits is to understand it ab-stractly, i.e., as a fleshless, disembodied, unconnected, and ulti-mately insupportable phantasm. For any object can be really comprehended only in terms of its place in the entire structure of our determinations of the world. We understand not simply that the object before us is a body of water, but also that it is of a certain size, that it is specifiably different from a meadow and different, in a specifiably different way, from an automobile or from a cow or from a book, and that, in a sometimes important, sometimes trivial sense, all of these facts—the fact that it is dif-

ferent from things like books, in addition to the fact that it is filled with H_2O—are a part of what makes it what it is. Only when we are able consciously to appropriate the objects of the world in this way, in the light of their various connections of various kinds, can our understanding of them be truly concrete.

4. *Sublation*. The most well-known of the concepts we are now treating is the Hegelian *Aufhebung*. The following is the key passage:

> We should recall here the double meaning of our German expression *aufheben*. By *aufheben* we mean, first of all, to clear away or annul, and thus we say, for example, that a law or a regulation is annulled or cancelled, i.e., *aufgehoben*. But further, we use *aufheben* also to mean "to preserve" or to keep, and we say in this sense that something has been well preserved or well maintained, again, *aufgehoben*. This double meaning in linguistic usage, whereby the same word has both a negative and a positive meaning, should not be seen as accidental, nor as something for which to criticize language as giving cause for confusion. Rather, we should recognize in it the speculative spirit of our language overcoming the mere either-or of the understanding. [*EL* 96 *Zusatz*; Cf. *WL*, I, pp. 93–95]

In the Hegelian system, every dialectical process involves the sublation—the simultaneous annulling and preserving—of the constituent elements. As we have seen with our body of water, each of the initial determinations is annulled; neither the qualitative nor the quantitative descriptions can stand as pre-essential, since both are necessary to the object being what it is. But our resolution of the contradiction involves the introduction of some third concept that is nothing but the first two taken together. Hence, in this third concept the first two are very much preserved, though now understood in a rather different way. Indeed, the contradiction itself is in a sense preserved, since we continue to be aware of the difference and potential opposition between our original qualitative and quantitative determinations. All of Hegelian philosophy involves this notion of particular moments sublated or *aufgehoben*. Moreover, the general position seems to rest, not on some kind of arbitrary assertion or mystical claim but, rather, on the quite plausible presupposition that everything we say about a particular object is—in one way or another—a part of any truly complete and total description of it.

These metatheoretical concepts have a certain relative status in Hegel's system. Specifically, what is in one context mediated and concrete may, in another, higher context, appear to be only immediate and quite abstract. For example, to understand something in terms of measure is, according to Hegelian metaphysics, to be more concrete than simply relying on unmediated qualitative and quantitative determinations. But measure is merely the culmination of the first part of Hegel's Logic, the doctrine of being, and is, as such, a quite abstract and unfulfilling formulation when compared with those categories outlined in (say) the doctrine of essence. Hegel's method, then, is based on an ongoing and systematic process whereby seemingly concrete and deeply situated claims are brought up against one another, are shown to be incompatible, to be mutually negating, hence to be as yet unmediated and relatively abstract—claims that are then annulled yet preserved, sublated, on the basis of some new, third formulation which is the negation of the negation and which, therefore, provides the basis for a more fully mediated, more concrete understanding of the object in question.

This kind of account suggests that any effort to deal with specific dialectical arguments in Hegelian philosophy must principally involve two tasks. First, one must specify the apparent contradiction upon which an argument rests, i.e., identify the precise claims and concepts that are in seeming conflict, as well as the nature of the conflict itself. Second, one must also describe that third formulation—the new concept—on the basis of which the contradiction is resolved or *aufgehoben*. Again, this new concept is often or typically the first two concepts "taken together"; as such, it stands as the negation of the negation. But the negation of the negation must also be something positive, and, as will be shown, much of Hegel's philosophy is concerned primarily with understanding such concepts in the sense of demonstrating and specifying exactly how the purely negative formulation can be translated—analytically, conceptually—into positive terms.

It is on the basis of this kind of account that I propose to deal with certain arguments from the philosophy of Right. But we are far from being ready to leave the Logic for, in a certain sense, the most fundamental questions still remain.

4

As should be clear from the argument thus far, Hegel is engaged in the analysis of concepts. But it is not yet clear just what kind of analysis this is. Philosophers since the pre-Socratics have analyzed concepts, have done so in many different ways and for many different reasons, and have as a result made many different kinds of claims. Thus, we would do well to specify the nature of what might be called "Hegelian conceptual analysis" insofar as it is distinct from, or indeed similar to, other varieties of philosophical analysis.

Perhaps a good way to begin would be to think in general terms about the process of using concepts to refer to and/or describe things in the world. We have already made a few remarks about assertions and some of the ways in which they reflect and express judgments. But it may be useful to examine a bit further some of the things philosophers have said about this process whereby concepts or categories are utilized in order to understand and talk about objects. Of course, the literature on this subject itself would comprise a fairly substantial library, but there may nonetheless be certain rudimentary areas of agreement that can be stipulated as such, if only provisionally. Thus, we may think of the use of concepts as typically involving a set of discrete elements which are bound to one another in some specifiable manner so as to constitute what might be called a "structure of conceptualization."

Among these elements, there is, of course, the *concept* itself. It may be, as some have argued, impossible to give an account of "the concept of a concept." But, if anything seems clear, it is that we cannot use concepts without having a thought of some kind, which, moreover, can be manifested in a word or group of words having, partly as a result of its manifesting the thought, a "meaning."

Beyond this, I believe most would also agree that the use of concepts is typically undertaken vis-à-vis specific instances which are understood as having identifiable attributes. More specifically, using a concept implies that the speaker has attended to, and made judgments regarding, the *recognized features of cases.*[11] This attending to and judging will, at least in part, be a matter of differentiating the features of one case from those of another; Austin was surely correct when he said that if there were no similarities and dissimilarities "there would be nothing to say."[12] Of course, these cases will not necessarily be empirical cases, though they often are. Also, there may well be disagreements regarding the features of particular cases, and to that extent there may be disagreements about the use of concepts. Nevertheless, it seems that to use concepts is generally to refer to something other than the concepts themselves—cases—and that this further presupposes some general sense as to what those cases are about.

Relatedly, using concepts also seems to involve an *interpretation of the features of cases.* Our judgments do not simply enumerate features but, rather, presuppose an account of them.[13] Thus, we often say that this feature is essential while that one is somehow secondary; or we claim that one attribute is the cause of another; or again, we argue that the same characteristic plays a very different role in two different objects. Of course, we may again disagree strenuously about such judgments, but it seems that our use of concepts typically involves some judgment (though perhaps only tacit) about the nature of, and relationship between, at least some of the facts of specific cases.

In the light of concepts, cases, and judgments, then, we strive to use our concepts in a manner that is consistent and reliable. Our use, that is, constitutes what might be called a *practice of usage*, i.e., the actual practice according to which some cases are subsumed under a concept/word. But further, the very fact of such a practice seems to imply an *account of usage*, i.e., a description of the kinds of cases that are subsumed under a concept and the kinds that are excluded. Our use of concepts and words is, perhaps, typically unreflective. But, when pressed, it seems that we usually would be able to offer at least some kind of explanation as to why

11. P. F. Strawson, "Introduction," in Strawson, ed., *Philosophical Logic*, p. 3.

12. J. L. Austin, "Truth," in George Pitcher, ed., *Truth* (Englewood Cliffs, N.J.: Prentice-Hall, 1964), p. 22.

13. It is not clear that this element is really different from the former one. The question, though, is not central to my argument.

these cases are to be distinguished from those, and why this particular concept is a good way of distinguishing them.

We may say, then, that to use concepts to refer to and/or describe things in the world typically involves, at a minimum, these five elements: a concept, a judgment regarding the recognized features of various cases, an interpretation of those features, a practice of concept/word usage, and an account of that practice. But it also seems reasonable to think of these elements as comprising a structure in the true sense; that is, they are typically connected to one another in important and specifiable ways. To be sure, there is a great deal of dispute regarding the precise nature of those connections. On some accounts, for example, concepts and usage are connected in the sense that a change in usage leads to a change in the concept, whereas others would argue that concepts can in fact resist this kind of change. Such issues need not concern us here. What is important is the fact that the various elements may well have certain implications for one another such that, if one changes, some of the others may have to change as well.

We may suppose that much of the time the use of concept occurs unproblematically. In normal discourse, we think and communicate in terms of cases whose features are not generally disputed, concepts whose meanings are widely shared, patterns of usage that are venerable and well-established, and the like. Most of our efforts to use concepts do not raise difficult questions about the concepts themselves or about the ways in which they are used; as a result, we are able to achieve many of the goals that depend upon communicative interaction.

There are, however, important circumstances in which an attempt to use a concept seems somehow not to work, and it is in such circumstances that we come to investigate—sometimes philosophically—our conceptual practices. Specifically, we often encounter in the world some reason for believing that a particular "structure of conceptualization" is not quite right. In the light of such an encounter, we may thus be led to revise the structure somehow—to revise one or more of the five elements—so that this sense of inadequacy can be dispelled.

Indeed, I believe that we can think of situations in which a problem appears with respect to each of the five elements. For example:

—Problems sometimes arise with respect to judgments regarding the recognized features of cases. Typical here would be situations involving empirical discovery. When we discover that a female impersonator is, in fact, a male, we are naturally led to subsume this individual under a different concept; when we find that water is composed of two parts hydrogen and one part oxygen, our concept of water might change, at least to the extent that the concept now includes this new bit of information.

—There may also be situations in which the facts of a case do not change but our interpretation of them does. For example, it may be possible to think of alternative scientific theories that claim to offer different explanations of the very same facts. To be sure, there is some dispute as to whether this can actually occur—i.e., whether *all* of the facts can possibly remain the same and still yield two complete yet incompatible theories. Nonetheless, some situations may at least appear to be of this type, and they will surely prompt us to inquire about the adequacy of our interpretation of the facts. This in turn may lead to some further adjustments in the conceptual structure; that is, if we revise our interpretation of the facts, we may be motivated to accommodate this revision by looking for new facts, changing our practice of usage, and the like.

—Similarly, we face difficulties when our patterns of usage themselves are thrown into question. It is certainly common to encounter individuals who use a particular word differently from the way we do. For example, I might say that Warren Harding was a statesman; you might respond by saying that he was no such thing. It may turn out that I simply do not understand the word *statesman*. Or it may be that we disagree about the nature of the concept "statesman," about the particular features of the case called Warren Harding, about the interpretation of those features, and the like. In any event, conflicting patterns of usage may raise difficulties which prompt us to examine concepts, cases, and the rest.

—Related but perhaps more difficult problems occur when we meet someone whose account of usage differs from ours. We may agree, for example, that Warren Harding was a statesman, but disagree as to why that was so and, perhaps, disagree as to the general types of cases that can be subsumed under the concept "statesman." In other words, we may have difficulty explaining an otherwise unchallenged pattern of usage, and the resultant inquiry might prompt us to decide, for example, to use certain words differently in the future.

—Finally, we may run into trouble regarding the concept itself. Most typically, we may be asked about the meaning of a particular concept and discover, upon reflection, that we are unable to provide a very good account of it. Consider the example of Socrates asking Cephalus and then Polemarchus about the meaning of justice. It seems clear that the practice of using this concept in Attica of the fifth century B.C. was fairly well established, or at least about as well established as it is for us today. It also seems clear that Cephalus and Polemarchus were experienced speakers whose usage was in no way exceptional or eccentric. Yet, when forced to give an account of the concept, and when forced to apply it to certain difficult cases, they were unable to do so. This circumstance appears to put the entire conceptual structure in jeopardy and prompts the discussants to look not just at the concept but also at the features of cases and their interpretation, accounts of usage, and the like.

I believe that all of these situations describe circumstances in which the activity of conceptualizing—normally unproblematic and taken for granted—runs into difficulties which demand further analysis. Consider once again the body of water lying before us. Assume that in the light of its qualitative/quantitative attributes we assert that "it is a pond." This seems to require that we have a concept of pond, that we have made some judgments regarding the recognized features both of the object before us and of other objects from which it has been differentiated, that we have some sense as to the interrelationships between those various features, and that we use the concept/word "pond" to refer to objects like the one lying before us but not to other kinds of objects. It is clear that many things could happen which would cause us to reexamine this structure of conceptualization. We might, for example, move closer to the object and discover that it is not filled with water but, rather, with a hard plastic substance ingeniously painted to look like water from a distance. Or, we might run into another observer who denies that the object is a pond and claims that it is, instead, a tarn. Or again, someone else might come by and agree that it is a pond but wonder why we call it that rather than a tarn or a pool or a lake. In each circumstance, questions are raised that might motivate us to think about the various elements in our structure of conceptualization, perhaps to revise one or more of them, and possibly to adjust the others so as to accommodate this revision.

One might say, then, that conceptual analysis—in the broadest sense—is a matter of considering such revisions. Clearly, there are numerous strategies for doing this, and choosing among them will likely depend upon the particular kind of difficulty encountered. But I would hypothesize that, in most circumstances, revisions tend to emerge from a common kind of analytical protocol. Simply stated, when an element in a structure of conceptualization is thought to be deficient, we seek somehow to test it vis-à-vis an established standard taken from outside of that structure:

—To pick the simplest case, when we have doubts about our usage, we can test our practice by comparing it with that of other, more experienced speakers. Since language is a rule-governed practice, we can test our usage by searching for and specifying the appropriate rule. In this way, some of the difficulties with a particular structure of conceptualization can perhaps be solved simply by *learning the language* or, more typically, by learning it better.

—At other times, of course, the problem involves our account of usage, and we often turn again to experienced speakers, not for the purpose of learning a rule, but rather in order to understand the putative logic behind the rule. We may feel that we usually use a word correctly, yet still not be sure as to what that usage implies. By systematically examining general patterns of usage, we try to discover not the rule itself—for we already know that quite well insofar as we use the word correctly—but the rule's rationale. I take it that this search for an account of usage is what is generally done under the name of *ordinary language philosophy*.

—When questions arise regarding the recognized features of cases, we can test our judgments through *empirical analysis*. That is, we seek to employ some more rigorous process of data collection designed to improve our knowledge of those features. Again, this involves relying on some element from outside of our particular structure of conceptualization against which we can evaluate our judgments.

—There appear to be other circumstances, less well known, in which the facts of a case remain largely unchanged but we still come to reinterpret those facts, to see them in a new light. In Plato's *Laches*, for example, an issue is raised with respect to the use of the concept "courage."[14] The crucial fact in the case is that Crommyon's sow does not flee in the face of danger. On the basis of this fact, we are led to conclude that the sow is courageous. Nicias points out to Laches and Socrates, however, that there is a difference between fearlessness, which might be rash, blind, foolish, or instinctive, and courage, which involves a kind of knowledge about how to deal with fearful things. Nicias imports a distinction from outside of the structure of conceptualization—a distinction perhaps rooted in psychology—which suggests that certain facts of the case ought to be reinterpreted.

In all of these circumstances, then, a challenge to a particular structure of conceptualization is met by testing one or more of the structure's elements against some external standard. Of course, it is possible, indeed highly likely, that no such conceptual analysis will be final or definitive. In part, this is because analysis is difficult and analysts sometimes make mistakes; in larger part, it is because the external standards we rely on—ordinary language, empirical data, and the like—frequently change, sometimes as a result of further conceptual analysis. Nonetheless, it seems clear that the effort to free our structures of conceptualization from the kinds of difficulties described above is necessary if we are to achieve a reasonable measure of coherence.

But there is one kind of conceptual problem deriving from our scheme, the solution of which has not yet been discussed. This occurs when we have difficulty specifying the concept itself, as in the case of Socrates, Cephalus, and Polemarchus mentioned above. Again, the discussants in the *Republic* appear to be in the habit of using a particular concept/word—justice—without undue controversy. When asked to give a convincing account of this concept, however, they are unable to do so. Or, rather, the accounts that they do offer—e.g., doing good to friends and harm to enemies—seem somehow inadequate; they are descriptions of concepts, to be sure, but they fail to satisfy us as descriptions of the particular concept we are looking for. As a result, the discussion of the *Republic* is aimed at developing just such a concept. Its

14. For this example, I am indebted to Neil Thomason.

purpose, I would suggest, is not to uncover or reinterpret the facts of cases since, in the *Republic*, such facts are pretty well stipulated. Nor is its purpose simply to discover a rule of language, since the interlocutors seem quite prepared to subvert the most widely accepted uses of the word *justice*. Whereas those engaged in, say, empirical analysis or ordinary language philosophy seem to be concerned primarily to clarify, enrich, and otherwise improve concepts that we already have, the Socratic search for justice appears to be one in which existing concepts are actually undermined and replaced with concepts that are in some sense new.

Whether this is in fact what occurs in the *Republic* is not entirely clear. But presumably, concepts—like empirical judgments, patterns of usage, and accounts of usage—must be tested somehow vis-à-vis a standard external to the particular structure of conceptualization in question. Is there, then, some such standard particularly appropriate for the judging of concepts themselves, in the way that usage is tested against the practices of experienced speakers or empirical judgments are tested against rigorous scientific observations? It is impossible here to answer this question with any certainty. But clearly one way to judge a concept would be to examine it in relation to other concepts. Specifically, when we encounter a concept that seems to us somehow inadequate, a plausible strategy would be to look at other concepts of ours that are not currently under suspicion in order to determine whether the concept in question is consistent with them. In the case of the *Republic*, for example, concepts of justice are tested by attempting to determine whether or not they are consistent with certain uncontested concepts pertaining to the nature of man, the human psyche, prudence, fairness, and the like. When we consider these various concepts, we find that Polemarchus's account of justice presents logical problems such that we cannot hold them and it at the same time. That is, the notion that we should do good to friends and harm to enemies is, on balance, inconsistent with the collective import of our uncontested concepts; since the latter are accepted as given, the former must be either wrong or, at least, for us untenable.

To be sure, there seems to be no good reason why some concepts or set of concepts should remain permanently uncontested. Still, it appears to be the case that a certain degree of consensus regarding concepts is necessary if we are to consider and discuss philosophical questions at all. If there were no such consensus—no communicative contexts based on a relatively stable set of shared meanings and judgments—then it is hard to see how we could enjoy anything but the most rudimentary kind of communication. The range of concepts included in this consensus is likely to be variable; concepts will move in and out of the "uncontested" category as particular questions arise or are, in some sense, resolved. Nonetheless, it seems that the kinds of problems that we are here considering presuppose the existence, at any particular time, of a broad array of uncontested concepts to which our troublesome concepts must be reconciled. This process of reconciliation is, I suggest, one important way of dealing with difficult conceptual problems.

Thus, for example, the Socratic concept of justice is said to satisfy us insofar as it is the only such formulation consistent with our other concepts. An analysis along these lines appears to prescribe rather than merely enrich or clarify concepts by, in effect, fashioning a particular formulation so that it comports with the set of concepts we have. Such an approach assumes—it seems to me correctly—that to accept and act upon an inconsistent set of concepts is to fail a most plausible test of what it means to make sense.

In my judgment, much of Hegelian philosophy involves roughly this kind of analysis. There are, to be sure, certain special features of Hegel's method that would distinguish it from the general account I have given here. Moreover, it seems clear that Hegelian philosophy is not of a piece, that Hegel's analyses are often more eclectic, more methodologically diverse, than he himself would perhaps have admitted. Despite this, I would suggest the following three hypotheses:

First, for Hegel, conceptual problems of the type here discussed generally arise with respect to those concepts on the basis of which an apparent contradiction is overcome (see page 60 above). We discovered that the apparent contradiction between concepts F and G is resolved with the discovery of concept H. We also defined H as being nothing other than "F together with G." But presumably we would also wish to have a characterization of H that tells us something more than this, that is not simply a restatement of H's role in resolving the apparent contradiction. That is, we wish to know "how to understand and articulate this or that 'third' category which we have initially defined as the conjunction of two seemingly opposed categories." I believe that, in Hegel's system, such "third categories" occur primarily as the kind of troublesome concepts we have just now been discussing, and I believe further than much of his philosophy is concerned precisely with the particular difficulties that they raise.

Second, the mode of reasoning prescribed by the Logic involves, among other things, the analysis of troublesome concepts precisely in the light of other, uncontested concepts. In Hegel, this general method has an added twist. The troublesome concept is reconciled with—shown to be logically consistent with—the set of existing concepts; but in doing this, it must also help to demonstrate thereby the internal consistency of that existing set. For example, H is initially defined in terms of F and G, which are, by this time, included in our set of uncontested concepts. In elaborating H more fully, we must provide an account according to which H continues to be fully consistent with those uncontested concepts. Yet H is also the means by which we come to understand that F and G are themselves mutually consistent. Thus, troublesome concepts must be tested in terms of the degree to which they cohere with, but also help to make coherent, our established range of concepts.

Finally, this general mode of analysis is embodied in, and is authoritative for, the particular "substantive" regions of Hegelian philosophy, including the philosophy of Right. Just as the aim of the *Republic* is to arrive at a concept of justice that comports with the range of uncontested concepts, so is the philosophy of Right concerned to discover the concept of Right in the light of our other, previously specified concepts. Of course, in the process, in moving from certain basic concepts to the full development of the concept of Right, Hegel seeks to derive a series of intermediary concepts, including, among many others, notions of punishment, moral intentionality, marriage, and the structure of the rational state. In each case, concepts are said to be derived from, or discovered on the basis of, the existing set of concepts, and to be ratified insofar as they comport with, and help to make internally consistent, that existing set. Hegel's concept of punishment, for example, is said to be the only such concept that is consistent with previously stipulated notions of freedom, personhood, property, and the like. Hence, if we are to retain those notions—and we appear to have no overriding reason for not doing so—then we must accept Hegel's account of punishment. In this way, Hegel seeks to show that our disagreements regarding punishment can be resolved by attending carefully to the logical implications of our broader conceptual scheme.

I believe that this general account may help to clarify somewhat the nature of Hegel's philosophical project and the sense in which it can be called a kind of conceptual analysis. A serious question remains, however. I have talked rather casually in terms of the "discovery" of concepts and also in terms of one concept being "consistent" with or "comporting" with another. But it is surely not self-evident how such terms are to be taken or how they might manifest themselves in Hegel's system. Indeed, the two problems of conceptual innovation and conceptual consistency are among the oldest and most difficult of philosophy. It is not clear to me that Hegel solved these problems, and it is abundantly clear to me that his attempted solutions are extremely difficult to understand. Nonetheless, my account of Hegel's method demands at least some brief attention to these issues, and it is to a discussion of them that we now turn.

5

The unfolding of Hegel's philosophy is the unfolding of concepts, the process by which a set of concepts—or, more precisely, an apparent contradiction within that set—leads to another concept that is discursively more advanced. It seems certain, further, that Hegel intends us to understand this process as a necessary one, that for him the unfolding of concepts occurs not haphazardly but according to an indisputable logic of some kind. Thus, the contradiction between *F* and *G* necessarily gives rise to *H*; and, similarly, each major concept of the philosophy of Right is thought to follow of necessity from those preceding it. We settle on concepts not because they seem to us merely interesting, plausible, or useful but, rather, because they can be shown to be discursively necessary.

But exactly what kind of necessity is involved here? This has been an issue of serious concern to Hegel scholars. Indeed, it may be that the effort to deal with this issue is ultimately what distinguishes one kind of Hegel interpretation from another. That is, in attempting to confront the question of conceptual necessity, Hegel's readers are forced to make certain basic judgments regarding the very nature of the Hegelian project itself.

At the risk of much oversimplification, we may identify three general approaches. According to one—pioneered by Schelling himself, adopted by many philosophers of the late nineteenth and early twentieth centuries, and argued somewhat more recently by J. N. Findlay in his important reexamination of Hegel—the claims of conceptual necessity simply fail. This is to say that Hegel's efforts to show how one concept necessarily "follows from" another are unpersuasive, that the "new" concept is no more necessary than any number of potential surrogates, and that, as a result, the nature of the connection between concepts is something other than a logical and necessary one. To be sure, Findlay is far from denying that Hegel's work contains many interesting and profound insights and that it repays the closest possible attention. Indeed, Findlay's book is, in part, an appreciation; as such, it has played a crucial role in reviving interest in Hegel among English-speaking philosophers. Nonetheless, his conclusion is that the Hegelian project as Hegel himself conceived it, a project in which philosophical conclusions are to be apodictically proven, is ultimately a failure, and that Hegel's claims regarding necessity are simply and demonstrably false.[15]

A second kind of approach substantially agrees with this conclusion but goes on to argue that Hegel's work cannot be adequately judged in this way. That is, the attempt to evaluate Hegel's philosophy in terms of standard notions of truth and rationality ignores the fact that the Logic is entirely different from logic as we generally understand it and, thus, resists the kinds of evaluations Findlay and others have made. So, while it is true that Hegel's various conclusions are not necessary in the *usual* sense of logical

---

15. Findlay, *Hegel: A Re-examination*, e.g., pp. 74ff. A similar argument, of course, is made with reference to the philosophy of Right. See, for example, Henning Ottmann, "Hegelsche Logik und Rechtsphilosophie: Unzulängliche Bemerkungen zu einem ungelösten Problem," in Dieter Henrich and Rolf-Peter Horstmann, eds., *Hegels Philosophie des Rechts: Die Theorie der Rechtsformen und ihre Logik* (Stuttgart: Klett-Cotta, 1982); also, Z. A. Pelczynski, "Political Community and Individual Freedom in Hegel's Philosophy of State," in Z. A. Pelczynski, ed., *The State and Civil Society: Studies in Hegel's Political Philosophy* (Cambridge: Cambridge University Press, 1984), p. 63.

entailment, this fact has no real force because Hegelian philosophy is of a wholly different order.

This approach has been formulated most recently by Michael Rosen in his book on Hegel's dialectic. With reference to the unfolding of consciousness in the *Phenomenology of Mind*, Rosen poses the basic question with uncommon clarity:

> The forms of consciousness which lead to Absolute Knowledge are to be shown to be a rational, necessary sequence. Each form must show itself to be the result of the previous one until the final, completed form is reached. . . . Yet by what right is each form to be taken to be the *result* of the previous one? . . . [W]hat right has Hegel to adopt a perspective according to which the breakdowns of forms of consciousness do not constitute an adventitious sequence but go together to make a single, progressive movement?[16]

The problem is perfectly transportable to all of the regions of Hegel's philosophy, including and especially the Logic. Why should we not regard the unfolding of concepts presented by Hegel as merely adventitious and convenient rather than logically or conceptually necessary? Rosen's conclusion is that as long as we operate in terms of standard modes of inference and rationality, Hegelian philosophy does indeed fail, but that to do so is to misunderstand what Hegel is really up to.

According to Rosen, Hegel's philosophy is fundamentally "non-inferential."[17] It is entirely unlike thinking in the usual sense; it "differs from the common conception of rational argument, not just in making use of stronger than normal principles of connection," it "actually *undermines* their normal individuation into semantic atoms."[18] Indeed, Hegelian philosophy might be called a kind of "hyperintuitionism," i.e., "a non-inferential form of development whose specific character consists in being *beyond* the 'inner picturing' which intuition is normally taken to be. . . ."[19]

16. Michael Rosen, *Hegel's Dialectic and Its Criticism* (Cambridge: Cambridge University Press, 1982).

17. Ibid., p. 76.

18. Ibid., p. 49.

19. Ibid., p. 77.

Hegelian thought does not proceed inferentially; but this is a virtue, not a defect. In Hegel's view, standard modes of rationality, including those embodied in formal logic, are inadequate. They operate at the level of crude "understanding" rather than true reason. Hence, to be criticized for being inferentially unsound—by Findlay, among many others—is not to be criticized in a very important way.

Rosen's account seems unsatisfying in a number of respects. To begin with, his argument that Hegel's philosophical method differs from standard methods is based on a rather determinedly one-sided reading of the textual evidence. It is quite clear that Hegel seeks to distinguish his work from what he calls "formal reasoning" or "formal logic," but this in itself is inadequate to show that his philosophical method is utterly foreign to thinking and philosophy as we generally understand it. Indeed, there are numerous passages where Hegel emphasizes the value, indeed the indispensability and truthfulness, of what look very much like conventional modes of inference (e.g., *EL* 160 and 181). Further, it is not entirely clear what Hegel meant by "formal" reasoning or logic. Strictly formal logic was still rather crude in the early nineteenth century, and it has been plausibly suggested that more recent advances in formal and symbolic logic might have satisfied Hegel quite well.[20]

Beyond this, we must wonder what Hegel's alternative to ordinary reasoning could possibly be. In this regard, Rosen's account is particularly disappointing, for he admits that he cannot really explicate the Hegelian method:

> [W]hen we characterize an experience we try to answer the question "what is it like?" But the experience of Thought is an experience which is *sui generis*; the point is that it is not *like* finite experience at all. . . . Hegel's Science, animated by the "movement of the notion" is the *radically non-metaphorical discourse*. Its deep truth is imageless. . . . So the question "what is Thought like?" is unanswerable if we expect to be able to give an account in terms of a positive analogy. What *can* be done, however, is to explain the nature of

20. Clark Butler, "On the Reducibility of Dialectical to Standard Logic," *The Personalist* 56, p. 416; and Taylor, *Hegel*, p. 318.

Thought in terms of what it is *not* like—to express its distinctness from alternative conceptions of the nature of rational experience.[21]

It is understandable that Rosen cannot give a positive account of this noninferential kind of thought, since it is by no means clear that a truly alternative logic—a way of making sense without regard to the usual canons of correct reasoning—is even possible, much less communicable. Rosen's claim is that Hegel's logic must be "experienced" rather than discussed, analyzed, and rationally evaluated. In view of this, it is hard to know what to do with Rosen's presentation, at least in a context—such as the present one—devoted to discussion, analysis, and rational evaluation.

A third approach to the question of necessity in Hegel is to argue that his project does not fail, at least not in any obvious way, and that it does in fact provide a highly plausible account of the unfolding of concepts even when judged on the basis of standard rational criteria. This is, in many ways, the emergent approach. A number of scholars have recently been concerned to show that Hegelian philosophy is rationally defensible and that it comports, indeed explicitly rests upon, the canons of reason as we normally understand them.

As may now be apparent, this is a general viewpoint with which I am extremely sympathetic. Nevertheless, existing accounts along these lines fail to come to grips with the ultimate question: exactly how are Hegel's philosophical conclusions warranted? Thus, for example, in his magisterial book on Hegel, Taylor captures quite well the sense in which Hegelian philosophy involves the unfolding of concepts as governed by a kind of "conceptual necessity."[22] But I believe that Richard Bernstein is quite correct when he complains that Taylor neglects to tell us just what this involves: "he [Taylor] fails to clarify or analyze what is *meant* by 'necessity' when we speak of the necessity of inference or ontological necessity."[23] It is one thing to assert—albeit quite correctly—that Hegel's method invokes a kind of conceptual necessity and quite another to dem-

21. Rosen, *Hegel's Dialectic and Its Criticism*, pp. 92–93.

22. Taylor, *Hegel*, pp. 227–31.

23. R. J. Bernstein, "Why Hegel Now?" *Review of Metaphysics* 31 (September 1977): 29–60.

onstrate just how this necessity works; and ultimately, Taylor must conclude that perhaps it does not work.[24]

Similarly, Terry Pinkard purports to explicate the "Logic of Hegel's *Logic*" and, to a great extent, succeeds. However, in describing the sequence of categories or concepts, he merely says that "one infers to" a new concept or that an established concept "leads to" a more advanced formulation.[25] As in Taylor's notion of conceptual necessity, it is simply not clear how phrases such as "infers to" or "leads to" should be understood. Pinkard does try to specify what is *not* involved when he insists that the unfolding of concepts is not deductive.[26] But this does not suffice to tell us exactly how Hegel arrives at and justifies philosophical conclusions.

Even so perspicacious a reader as Hans-Georg Gadamer appears to fail the test of specificity. Like the others, Gadamer sees and appreciates the fact that Hegel's is a philosophy of categories in which "the advance from one thought to the next, from one form of knowing to the next, must derive from an immanent necessity." But Gadamer accounts for this by saying that "each concept calls for another" and that "[n]one stays by itself, but rather . . . ties itself in with another. . . . "[27] Again, it would be important to know just how this "calling for" occurs and how it is that concepts can "tie themselves" into each other. In this respect, Gadamer provides us with little concrete guidance.

We may simplify the problem somewhat by saying that in philosophy the issue of necessity is often bound up with the notion of deduction. Indeed, when we speak of philosophical or rational

24. Thus, it is perhaps more difficult to classify Taylor's approach than the above paragraphs suggest.

25. Terry Pinkard, "The Logic of Hegel's *Logic*," *Journal of the History of Philosophy* 17 (October 1979): 423–34.

26. Ibid., pp. 431 and 433.

27. Hans-Georg Gadamer, *Hegel's Dialectic* (New Haven, Conn.: Yale University Press, 1976), pp. 83 and 85. Elsewhere, however, Gadamer does refer to Hegel's "aprioristic deduction of all ideas from the self-unfolding of the absolute," thus hinting at a much stronger account not dissimilar to the one presented here. Hans-Georg Gadamer, *Wahrheit und Methode* (Tübingen: J. C. B. Mohr, 1972), p. 215.

necessity, or of necessary inference, we are typically talking about a matter of logical "entailment" or deducibility. Sound deductions display a kind of necessity that other forms of thinking appear to lack; as such, deduction is the model for all thinking that aspires to apodictic proof. The trouble with treating Hegelian necessity as deductive, however, is twofold.

First, Hegel himself denies that his system is deductive, at least in the ordinary sense of the term. He consigns the normal rules of rational inference to the realm of the "Understanding," a realm that is authoritative for most philosophers but is decidedly inferior to the critical thought of the "Dialectic" and the ultimate truth of "Reason." It seems that, for Hegel, deductive systems are unable to acknowledge and account for the complexity, dynamism, contradictoriness, and interrelatedness of the world; as such, they cannot penetrate to the truth.

Second, and as important, Hegel's system, as described thus far, appears to involve the development of new concepts. That is, the unfolding of concepts in any dialectical sequence seems to be a matter of conceptual innovation; on the basis of an established set of concepts, new concepts arise. But if this is in fact the case, then Hegel's system cannot be deductive, for it seems that deduction itself cannot generate new content. Deduction merely clarifies or brings to the surface that which is already present and, thus, one cannot deduce new concepts from old ones.[28] But again, if Hegel's system is not deductive because it generates new content, then how can we make sense of its claims to necessity?

In answering this question, it will be helpful briefly to reconsider our sketch of the dialectic. In the light of the apparent contradiction between two concepts F and G, we somehow discover concept H. Again, H is initially defined as "F together with G" and helps to show that those two concepts are only in apparent contradiction with one another; whereupon we seek to provide a fuller account of H according to which we understand, among other things, that it is indeed consistent with F and G (and with the rest of our uncontested concepts as well.) Thus, two questions arise: How did

28. Findlay, *Hegel: A Re-examination*, p. 81; Pinkard, "The Logic of Hegel's *Logic*," p. 431.

we arrive at *H* in the first place? And how do we provide a fuller account of it?

I believe that, in each case, the answer can only be that we relied on a kind of analytic judgment. According to Kant, of course, an analytic judgment is one in which "the predicate B belongs to the subject A as something contained (though covertly) in the concept A."[29] In other words, the conclusion of an analytic judgment is already at hand; the judgment itself merely serves to uncover that conclusion, to clarify or illuminate it. Kant says that "our knowledge is in no way extended by analytical judgments, but that all they effect is to put the concepts which we possess into better order and render them more intelligible."[30]

In the present case, *F* and *G* are utilized in the assertions a^*F and a^*G respectively, where, again, "*" denotes what we have called a pre-essential determination. The two assertions contradict one another, yet our intuitions tell us that both F and G are essential to *a*. Thus, any account of *a* must express at least three facts: (1) F is essential to *a*, (2) G is also essential to *a*, and (3), *a* cannot be pre-essentially F and G at the same time. I take it that the assertion a^*H—where H = F + G—is nothing but a shorthand way of expressing (1), (2), and (3). It is simply a restatement of, a synonym for, the conjunction of those three facts, hence it is discovered analytically. Moreover, we derive certain of its particular logical consequences—for example, the consequence that F and G can each be only a part of the essence of *a*—in a similar fashion; and we provide a fuller account of H and the concept it applies, *H*, as we would any assertion and concept, i.e., analytically.

Similarly, in the account of the pond lying before us, we concluded that (1) it is an essential feature of the object that it is a body of water, (2) it is also an essential feature that it consists of 150,000 cubic feet, and (3) neither of the assertions can be pre-essential in the sense of being exclusively necessary for the object to be what it is. Any adequate determination of the object would have to take into account all three facts. In this sense, the concept

29. Immanuel Kant, *Critique of Pure Reason*, Introduction IV.
30. Ibid.

of measure is nothing more than a synonym for this "taking into account." It has no meaning apart from but is, rather, a shorthand way of expressing the conjunction of (1), (2), and (3). As such, to "discover" the concept of measure is to make an analytic judgment in the way that the statement "all bachelors are unmarried" is analytic; and the discovery of its various conceptual implications—for example, that qualitative and quantitative determinations cannot be pre-essential—is simply a matter of further analysis.

There is, of course, a great controversy in philosophy, spurred in part by Quine's famous essay, regarding the degree to which we can truly gain purchase on the idea of analyticity at all.[31] Such questions aside, however, it seems that there is a very close relationship between analyticity and logical deduction. In this respect, I follow the work of Schlick as emended by Friedrich Waismann.[32] According to Waismann, "a statement is analytic if it can, by means of mere definitions, be *turned into a truth of logic*, i.e., if it is *transformable* into such a truth." In other words, if an analytic judgment is true, one should be able to reformulate it into a sound deduction from premises. For example, we concluded that the concept of measure, as the conjunction of (1), (2), and (3), implies analytically that neither qualitative nor quantitative determination can be pre-essential. If this is a true analytic judgment, then we should be able to see how it can be transformed into a truth of logic, a deductive truth.

That this demonstration is easy enough to make should already be quite clear; as such, it can be formalized without any difficulty. Consider the following simple argument:

1	(1) Fa	Premise
2	(2) (x) (Fx⊃ -Gx)	Assumption
2	(3) Fa⊃ -Ga	1, 2 UE
1, 2	(4) -Ga	1, 3 Modus Ponens
5	(5) Ga	Premise

31. W. V. O. Quine, "Two Dogmas of Empiricism," in *From a Logical Point of View* (New York: Harper, 1963).

32. Friedrich Waismann, "Analytic-Synthetic," *Analysis* 10 (December 1949).

| 1, 2, 5 | (6) -Ga·Ga | 4, 5 Conjunction |
| 1, 5 | (7) -(x) (Fx⊃ -Gx) | 1–6 Indirect Proof |

In this formulation, we shall say that F refers to qualitative determination and G to quantitative determination. Whereas step 1 establishes qualitative determination as a premise, step 2 assumes that such determination is exclusive, hence pre-essential. With the introduction of the second premise at step 5—quantitative determination—we face a contradiction which necessitates our rejection of the assumption at step 7; qualitative determination cannot be pre-essential, given our premises. With the assumption disproved, the conjunction Fa·Ga presents no logical problems and we can simply redefine it as Ha where H refers to measure.

While this kind of simplistic deduction can hardly serve as a model for all of Hegel's arguments, I would nonetheless contend that Hegelian philosophy does generally follow, or at least intends to follow, the rules and methods of standard logical inference. Thus, my claim is that—despite what Hegel appears to tell us—the necessity of his system is indeed a matter of deduction in the usual sense. Again, such a claim raises two difficult questions: How do we explain Hegel's express views regarding ordinary forms of reasoning and inference? And how can we account for the appearance of conceptual innovation in his system? I shall deal with each of these questions in turn.

6

It is, of course, quite well known to every beginning student of Hegel that he has many unkind things to say about the standard modes of rationality and logic. In the specific case, he contrasts his own Logic with what he calls "formal logic" as developed largely by Aristotle and adopted by most of the Western philosophers with whom we are familiar. More generally, he consigns conventional modes of reasoning, including those upon which formal logic is based, to the realm of Understanding, which is seen to be important as a constituent of, but is ultimately different from and inferior to, the faculty of Reason. To claim, then, that Hegel's dialectic proceeds in terms of standard forms of inference seems to violate what Hegel himself says. Indeed, it seems inappropriately to domesticate Hegel, to reduce him to our own primitive level of intellectual development, to make his system seem simpler than it really is.

In this sense, it will be useful to examine a bit more closely just what Hegel has to say about Understanding (for example, at *EL* 80). For him, Understanding does indeed describe the ordinary way of thinking about things as well as the kind of thinking that most philosophers are engaged in. As such, it can never penetrate to the truth and reality of the world. It is content to "analyze," to separate things out into their constituent elements without putting them back together, hence to ignore the important connections between those elements. Indeed, a central goal of Hegel's Logic is to go beyond Understanding, to transcend its "mere formalism" and to describe the objective and absolute nature of things.

We may say that this account contains three specific and central charges. First, Understanding is said to operate in terms of "finite" rather than "infinite" categories. Hegel's notions of the finite and the infinite are very difficult and can only be treated here in a most rudimentary fashion. We should say that concepts or categories of thought are treated as *finite* when their necessary interconnections are overlooked, when their individual separateness or distinctiveness is considered to be fundamental and definitive. Thus, for example, when writing of the "old metaphysicians"—essentially pre-Kantian rationalists such as the medieval Schoolmen—Hegel claims that their "terms of thought [i.e., the categories they employed] were cut off from their connection, their solidarity; each was believed valid by itself and capable of serving as a predicate of the truth" (*EL* 28). The faculty of Understanding rigidifies or, to use a more fashionable word, hypostatizes the distinctions among various concepts: "Thought, as *Understanding*, sticks to fixity of characters and their distinctness from one another: every such limited abstract character it treats as having a subsistence and being of its own" (*EL* 80). One rather indirect result of this is that Understanding is unable to capture the "totality" of things, i.e., the systemic or organic character of the world:

> The metaphysic of understanding is dogmatic because it maintains one sided thought determinations in their isolation; whereas the idealism of speculative philosophy has the principle of totality and shows

that it can reach beyond the one-sidedness of the determinations of the Understanding. Thus, idealism comes to say: The soul is neither *simply* finite nor *simply* infinite; rather, it is essentially the one *as much as* the other, and thus *neither* one *nor* the other exclusively. That is, determinations in their isolation are invalid and acquire validity only when sublated as elements of a larger concept. [*EL* 32 *Zusatz*]

For Hegel, then, Understanding simply fails to notice the unavoidable interconnectedness or mutual dependence of our categories of thought. He tells us that a fixed category such as "blue" is nonetheless dependent upon, because unintelligible without, such evidently distinct categories as "yellow" and "white" (*EL* 119). If blue were the only possible or imaginable color, then it would be hard to see how the category of color could come into play at all, since such a category would not help us to distinguish some particular objects from others. For us to predicate "blue" of some object requires that we have in our possession certain other possible predicates. In a crucial passage, Hegel declares this to be a general principle:

> Positive and negative are thus essentially postulated through one another and only in their mutual relation. The north pole of the magnet cannot be without the south pole, and vice versa. If one cuts a magnet in half, one does not have a north pole in one piece and south pole in the other.... In opposition, the "different" is confronted not only by *an* other but, rather, by *its* other. The ordinary consciousness considers different things as unaffected by one another. Thus, one says: I am a man, and around me are air, water, animals, and other things in general. All things thus fall outside of one another. The goal of philosophy, on the other hand, is to dispel indifference and to know the necessity of things so that the "other" is seen to stand over against *its* other. [*EL* 119 *Zusatz*; cf. *WL* II, pp. 54ff.]

It would seem, further, and despite what Hegel appears to say, that each particular category does not have just one opposite but, rather, has different definite opposites in different contexts. In certain contexts, blue is the opposite of yellow; but in other contexts, blue—a color—might be opposed to acrid—an odor; or again, blue—a "sensuous generalized image" *EL* 119—might be the opposite of right—a normative or categorical property. Thus, virtually *all* of our categories are bound up with one another, are linked in discursively important ways, and this is a fact that mere Understanding fails to consider. In Charles Taylor's words: "seeing things in the world as simply diverse, involving as it does seeing them as being merely contingently related to each other, is a superficial view. Understood at a more fundamental level, each thing is what it is only in a relation of contrastive and interactive opposition with another, which is thus 'its other'."[33] Taylor goes on to talk about "reality as necessary interconnection" and concludes that, for Hegel, "we are dealing with a system of related beings, a totality of external being which is systematically and necessarily related."[34] This notion of necessary interconnectedness is at least a part of what Hegel means by "infinity."

The second charge against Understanding and against ordinary forms of inference in general is that they depend upon presuppositions which are left unproven. Hegel simply has in mind here the notion that an argument can be logically valid yet its conclusion completely false because its premises are false. It is in this sense that the "truth" of Understanding is merely formal. Hegel found the controversy concerning the existence of God to be a typical case in point:

> The main point is this, that demonstration [*Beweisen*]—as the Understanding has it—is a matter of the dependence of one determination on another. In demonstration, one has a presupposition, something firm and fast, from which something else follows. Thus, one here exhibits the dependence of a determination upon a presupposition. Now, should the existence of God become demonstrated in this way, it can only mean that the being of God is dependent upon other determinations and that these constitute the ground of His being. One sees here, then, that this must involve a distortion; for God is simply and solely the ground of everything and, hence, is not dependent on anything else. [*EL* 36 *Zusatz*; cf. *EL* 50]

The faculty of Reason, on the other hand, is not content with mere formal adequacy. It demands, rather, that the content of its claims

33. Taylor, *Hegel*, p. 261.
34. Ibid., p. 263.

also be true. This requires, in turn, that all presuppositions be proved, and hence cease to be presuppositions at all: "The demonstration of Reason indeed also has something other than God for its starting point. However, in its progress it does not leave this other untouched in its immediate existence. Rather, while it shows the other to be something derivative and posited, it also shows that God is to be considered as self-mediating, self-subsisting, truly immediate, and primary" (*EL* 36 *Zusatz*). Hegel's philosophy, relying as it does on the faculty of Reason, must be fundamentally presuppositionless and, in this sense, is intended to go well beyond the limitations of Understanding.

The third charge against Understanding follows directly from the second. The "truths" of Understanding are not simply empty and formalistic; they also, as a result of this, say little or nothing about the reality of the world. This particular criticism has several aspects. On the one hand, to accept presuppositions uncritically, merely to assume certain features of the world as Understanding does, is by implication to give up the very possibility of determining whether or not those assumptions are true. Indeed, if all arguments depend upon unexamined and, in some sense, unexaminable presuppositions, then we can never know whether our arguments have anything to do with the real world, no matter how "valid" they may be. All of our conclusions might well be fundamentally false while nonetheless fulfilling the formal requirements of what we generally call logic. As a result of this, those who rely solely on Understanding either make arguments about ultimate reality which cannot be taken seriously or else take the position that such arguments are finally indefensible. Of course, for Hegel the culmination of this latter view is to be found in Kant's critical system; and it is against such a position that Hegelian philosophy asserts and insists upon the necessary relationship between thought and reality. For Hegel, philosophy is concerned with truth not simply in an abstract and formalistic sense but in the fullest and most concrete sense.

In sum, Hegel argues that Understanding typically ignores the interconnectedness of concepts, relies on unexamined presuppositions, and fails to make serious claims about ultimate reality. We may judge these charges in any number of ways according to our own philosophical convictions. But be that as it may, I would contend that Hegel's criticisms say virtually nothing about the *rules* of logic and inference themselves, about the laws of clear and correct thinking which Understanding invokes and prescribes. The failure of Understanding to consider and explicate the interconnectedness of concepts stems not from the basic principles of rational argument. Rather, it stems from a tendency to see those principles as the sum total of truth; and this tendency, in turn, derives not from the principles themselves but from a kind of extrarational, perhaps even ideological, short-sightedness rooted in the relatively primitive development of *Geist*. The fact that conventional argumentation rests upon unexamined premises is not itself a criticism of the discursive principles upon which such argumentation relies. The view that Understanding is content with "validity" rather than truth does not imply that its view of validity is somehow mistaken or even inessential. Hegel's criticisms deal not with the standard laws of thought but with the limited way in which those laws are typically employed.

Of course, it is true that Hegel sees great merit in Understanding insofar as it is a step in the hierarchy of the mind which prepares the way for Reason. He tells us that "the merit and rights of the mere Understanding should unhesitatingly be admitted," that it performs the crucial discursive function of fixing and specifying the distinctions between things in the world (*EL* 80 *Zusatz*). This in itself might look like rather faint praise; Understanding performs a crucial service but must, nevertheless, be regarded as something wholly inferior, something to be surpassed by Reason.

But the fact is that, for Hegel, the logical principles of Understanding, its rules of thought, far from being left behind are, indeed, a crucial part of Reason itself. Reason, every bit as much as conventional thought, is bound by those rules. Hegel is quite clear on this score. Whereas he criticizes the "mere formalism" of Understanding, he still insists on the absolute centrality of the informal element in thought and truth: "We usually say that Logic is concerned with *forms* only and that *content* comes from some other place. But logical forms are not an "only" in comparison with all other content; rather, all other content is an "only" in comparison with these forms. They are the absolute ground, existing in and for itself, of everything else" (*EL* 24 *Zusatz*). But are the forms of *Hegel's* Logic the same as those of standard logic? I think Hegel makes it clear that they are, at least up to a point. He tells us that truth is essentially a matter of "consistency" (*EL* 24 *Zusatz*) and that the differences between Reason and Understanding, though in one sense very large, are in another sense not so large after all. Indeed,

> as great as the difference between the concept of formal logic and the speculative concept may be, closer consideration nonetheless shows that the deeper meaning of concepts is not so foreign to the general way of speaking as might first seem to be the case. One speaks of the deduction of a content, e.g., deriving the specific provisions of the law regarding property from the concept of property itself; and similarly the reverse, of tracing back from such a content to the concept. [*EL* 160 *Zusatz*]

Time and again Hegel refers to his own formulations in the terms of ordinary logic. For example, the original development from Being to Nothing, with which Hegel's Logic begins, is said to be "the logical deduction and the movement of thought exhibited in sequel" (*EL* 87). Still, we might press again: does Hegel mean by "deduction" the same thing that we generally mean? And again, the answer seems to be plainly yes. Consider the following passage from Hegel's famous discussion of the syllogism:

> The name of reason is much and often heard, and appealed to: but no one thinks of explaining its specific character, or saying what it is, least of all that it has any connection with Syllogism. But formal Syllogism really presents what is reasonable in such a reasonless way that it has nothing to do with any reasonable matter. But as the matter in question can only be rational in virtue of the same quality by which thought is reason, it can be made so by the form only: and that form is Syllogism. And what is a Syllogism but an explicit putting, i.e. realizing of the concept, at first in form only, as stated above? Accordingly the Syllogism is the essential ground of whatever is true: and now the definition of the Absolute is that it is the Syllogism, or stating the principle in proposition: Everything is a Syllogism. [*EL* 182; cf. *WL* II, pp. 308ff.]

On the one hand, Hegel tells us that the syllogism is far indeed from Reason in the full sense. It is, again, the problem of an empty formalism that concerns him here. Syllogism does claim for itself the mantle of truth, but this claim cannot be taken too seriously. For the syllogism is in fact a mere logical protocol, hence cannot by itself be understood as an adequate account of truth. Reason has a specific content, i.e., the truth of the world. But the syllogism is merely formal, is indifferent to content, and thus is "reasonless." As such, it "has nothing to do with"—it does not in and of itself represent or even imply—"any reasonable matter." And yet, Hegel insists in effect that rationality is rationality and, more especially, that what is rational in the world must share something fundamental with what is rational in thought. This shared something is the *form* of reasoning, and that form is, of course, the syllogism. Further, the syllogism is not merely a matter of "triplicity"—i.e., a structured relationship containing three elements—but also a particular kind of relationship between those elements, namely, a relationship utilizing standard principles of logical inference. The implications are twofold: (1) to think rationally means to think in a manner governed at least in part by formal logic as exemplified by the syllogism; and (2) the truth of the world itself reveals this logical form. As a result, the syllogism is "the essential ground of whatever is true." The syllogism is not the truth itself; but it does describe the formal properties which necessarily govern all adequate truth claims.

Now we should note and emphasize the fact that Hegel distinguishes the "syllogism of Understanding" from the true syllogism. But the distinction seems to be precisely the one we have just been dealing with. The syllogism of Understanding presents itself, so to speak, as the sum total of the truth. As such, it locates truth in those formal rules which govern the activity of the knowing mind. In Hegel's terms, the syllogism of Understanding presents the truth as something subjective, something imposed on the world by human thought. The true syllogism, on the other hand, sees the formal properties of truth to inhere not simply in the mind of the knower but in reality itself. The laws of thought, the principles of rational inference, subsist not exclusively in the realm of human consciousness; rather, they are embodied in the world "out there." It is in this sense that the true syllogism is objective. But for our purposes, the important point is that those laws of thought which find their embodiment in objective truth remain the same laws of thought with which we are generally familiar.

For Hegel, then, Reason does have certain crucial formal properties, and those formal properties essentially reflect the standard rules of logic and inference. This is not to say that Reason is no different from conventional modes of thought. For again, Reason is much more than simply a set of formal properties; it has a necessary content which is objective and true. But the reverse also holds; the content of Reason is not fully explicit or adequately developed until it attains the *form* of rationality, and that form comports with the rules of thought as generally understood. Hence, when Hegel talks of deduction, of drawing inferences, of the necessary dependence of one idea on another, and the like, the relations that he sees are, at least in a formal sense, the same as those embodied in standard logic.

Now to deny this, to argue instead that Hegel is willing to suspend the laws of thought, including—to pick the most notorious example—the principle of contradiction, requires at least two things. First, it requires that one discover alternative laws or principles of thought in the body of Hegel's writing, laws which Hegel sets out as superior to those with which we are already familiar. Second, it requires that one is able to give an account of laws which will convince us, both that they are different, and that there is something about them that is plausible. As regards the first of these, to my knowledge Hegel provides no such alternatives. This is to say that nowhere does Hegel offer an account of how it is possible to "make sense" while violating conventional logical principles. When he talks of consistency, of rational inference, of the form of Reason, etc., he appears to have in mind principles of thought which are, as far as they go, quite unexceptional. This is not to say that Hegel's own arguments always obey these principles. It is to say, however, that when they fail in these terms they are properly criticized, and that there are no unusual or hitherto unknown principles to which they could appeal for special validation.[35]

35. Stanley Rosen, *G. W. F. Hegel: An Introduction to the Science of Wisdom* (New Haven, Conn.: Yale University Press, 1974), pp. xiv, xix, 15, 34.

As regards the second requirement, I think that none of Hegel's interpreters has succeeded in describing the kind of thinking that would somehow circumvent and violate conventional principles while still making sense. To pick just one typical example, consider Findlay's treatment of contradiction. On the one hand, he appears to claim that Hegel does indeed violate the principle of contradiction, and he explicitly has Hegel rejecting "any view which makes the contradictions of Dialectic *merely apparent*, something that will vanish once Systematic Science has been achieved."[36] Presumably, then, there is some logic in Hegel that will permit him to make sense while at the same time affirming contradictories. But virtually in the next breath, Findlay says of Reason that "it succeeds in *uniting* or *reconciling* opposed characteristics, so that the unalloyed contradiction marking the dialectical stage, which is responsible for its unease, passes over into a state which is also one of harmony and peace." Thus, it seems that the unease of contradiction will indeed "vanish" in some higher, presumably noncontradictory order. Findlay pursues this general problem with what strikes me as a most useful illustration:

> The stability of the reasonable result, as opposed to the unrest of the dialectical phase, lies further in the fact that one of its aspects overreaches the other, and demotes it to a mere condition of itself— the infinite, e.g., overreaches the finite, the subjective the objective, etc. We are reminded in these accounts of those photographs in which several successive ballet-positions are projected on the same film: Reason sees together what in Dialectic are separate and incompatible.[37]

Despite Findlay's intentions here, the example seems perfectly to illustrate the view that Hegel does indeed accept the principle of contradiction, that the goal of his philosophy is to show that apparent contradictions are in fact not real contradictions. For it should be perfectly clear to all of us that there is no contradiction in the photographs Findlay describes. There is indeed the appearance of contradiction, but this appearance would be troubling

36. Findlay, *Hegel: A Re-examination*, pp. 63ff.; cf., Lucio Colletti, *Marxism and Hegel* (London: NLB, 1973), pp. 20ff.

37. Findlay, *Hegel: A Re-examination*, p. 68.

only to a relatively primitive or undeveloped observer. It is easy enough to see how such photographs came about and how they can be explained in such a way that perfectly satisfies everyday notions of what it means to make sense. Once we penetrate to the truth of the photographs, the contradiction does indeed vanish.[38]

Thus, when we encounter those passages where Hegel seems to deny the standard rules of rational inference—for example, in section 1, chapter 2 of the Larger Logic's "Doctrine of Essence"— we appear to have two choices. Either we can accept his denial at face value, at which point, since there is no clear "alternative" logic, we are left wondering what Hegel can possibly mean by deduction, inference, rationality, and the like; or else, we can understand Hegel to be rejecting these rules as the *whole* of the truth while nonetheless retaining them as the formal foundations necessarily shared both by the thought of the truth and by the truth itself. Certainly, my view is that the second alternative comports fully with what Hegel actually says, but it is of course up to the reader to make this judgment for himself. We should be clear, though, that the stakes are high. For if I am wrong in this, then Hegel's philosophy would indeed have to be seen as a kind of arcane mysticism, deeply unattractive to those of us who are interested in the warrantability of philosophical conclusions, and largely irrelevant to a modern age impatient with mystery, obscurantism, and the occult.

7

We must still briefly consider the question of conceptual innovation. I have argued that Hegel's Logic necessarily comports with the conventional rules of rational inference. Insofar as the particular substantive regions of Hegel's system are themselves governed by the methodological/procedural exigencies of the Logic, these too will reflect those rules. But then we face the question of how Hegelian philosophy can generate new concepts. In all of his substantive work, including the philosophy of Right, we encounter a

38. For a somewhat similar account, see the essays by Richard Norman in Richard Norman and Sean Sayers, *Hegel, Marx, and Dialectic: A Debate* (Atlantic Highlands, N.J.: Humanities Press, 1980), especially pp. 47–66.

sequence of concepts which, while somehow dependent upon one another, do not seem to be simply deductively related. In the first section of the philosophy of Right, for example, we move from notions of freedom and will to concepts of property, contract, crime, and punishment. Each of these concepts, while "following from" or "coming out of" the previous ones, seems also to add something new, to introduce into the argument an element that was not previously there. But if Hegel's system prescribes an essentially deductive mode of reasoning, then it is hard to see how we could generate such new content.

It is at this point that one of the central, and also one of the more puzzling, features of the Hegelian system comes into play. I refer here to what Hegel calls the Idea. As is well known, Hegel tells us that the full development of the Idea is the goal of philosophy. Indeed, he says that the Idea is the truth itself, the absolute truth, and that it includes all previous notions of the truth (*EL* 213). This conception of philosophy as aiming at the Idea is presented early on in the Logic and is traced more or less systematically all the way through (e.g., *EL* 6, 45, and 87). But it is not until the last division of the Logic, the so-called Doctrine of the Notion, that Hegel makes at least somewhat clear what he has in mind. It is impossible to present here anything like a full account of Hegel's teaching in this regard, but one or two of its salient features do require our attention.

We may say that, for Hegel, the Idea is the full and completely satisfactory account of the truth of the world. As such, it is intimately related to the notion of infinity. Again, Hegel's notion of infinity refers, at least in part, to the necessary interconnectedness of concepts. Our various thoughts about the world are each partial accounts of the truth; in pursuing these partial accounts, we come to see that they are mutually dependent in the sense that the one necessarily implies the other. For example, from our qualitative and quantitative determinations of an object, we necessarily deduce its measure. Measure is thus implied by quality and quantity; and by highlighting the inadequacy of each when taken by itself, it also expresses their own mutual interdependence. Philosophy proceeds by painstakingly pursuing all such interconnections until the complete set of concepts and their various necessary relationships are made explicit. The upshot is that each particular concept or determination is now understood to be bound up—directly or indirectly—with each of the others, resulting in what Taylor calls the "seamless garment of rationality" that is the necessary truth of the world.[39] I believe that this seamless garment is at least part of what Hegel means by the Idea. That is, the Idea is the sum total of particular determinations together with their necessary interconnections. Just as measure is the mutual conditioning of the qualitative and quantitative determinations of a thing, which dissolves their opposition while preserving their distinctiveness, so is the Idea the dialectical overcoming/preservation of all previous, partial accounts.

Certain implications of this are made clear at the beginning of the Doctrine of the Notion. First, Hegel tells us that the various concepts or categories of thought—the various ways of determining or defining the truth or some part thereof—are themselves but "constituent stage[s] in the Idea" (*EL* 160). When these stages are complete, the Idea is fully developed. But further, it is at this point that we come to see the truth of the world—as expressed in the Idea—to be not really a collection of disparate things but, in fact, one single thing that can be analyzed into numerous distinct but utterly dependent constituents. The image is, perhaps, an organicist one. The Absolute is this seamless garment composed of countless threads, each of which has its full meaning and identity only in relation to all of the others. Thus, at this stage "[t]he onward movement of the notion is no longer either a transition into, or a reflection on, something else, but *Development*. For in the concept, the elements distinguished are directly and simultaneously posited as identical with one another and with the whole, and the specific character of each is a free being of the whole concept" (*EL* 161). Hegel tells us, in effect, that we finally come to see that there is literally no "other"—"the other which it sets up is in reality not an other" (*EL* 161 *Zusatz*). As a result, the unfolding of truth is not a movement from one thing to something else but is, rather, a self-development in which the truth—as a *single* thing, albeit a very complex one—unfolds and becomes explicit. This single truth

39. Taylor, *Hegel*, p. 96.

includes everything, every particular determination, and these latter are now understood to be only partial realities whose real truth is essentially a matter of their participation in the Absolute.

But if this reading is correct, then it indeed becomes possible to see philosophy as a deductive enterprise. This is to say that Reason is essentially a matter of logically analyzing the Idea, making explicit its various constituents, and tracing out their interrelationships. The Idea, as the expression of the truth of the world, is rational. As such, it embodies the form of Reason, and the purpose of philosophical speculation is to bring to the surface the way in which the Idea's various elements rationally cohere with one another. We do not, then, produce the Idea. Rather, we uncover it and its many constituents. Or, more accurately, we consider the Idea as it appears in the everyday consciousness of humans, in their *Vorstellungen*, and seek to deduce its internal structure so as to make explicit its rational nature. All particular formulations are deduced from this preexisting Idea. As a result, strictly speaking, philosophical analysis generates no new content. Rather, it makes explicit a content which is already present, and which is already possessed by the ordinary consciousness, albeit only in an implicit and inchoate manner. Clearly, this kind of analysis can be extremely illuminating. It can help us to see things we had not seen before; and thus, in a psychological sense, we know something "new," something of which we were previously unaware. Nevertheless, this something new is not new content in the true sense, but rather, and more simply, a new and improved way of looking at a content that is already at hand.

This consequence, that philosophy generates no new content, is in fact made quite explicit by Hegel.

[I]n the process of development the notion keeps to itself and only gives rise to alteration of form, without making any addition in point of content. It is this nature of the notion—this proof of itself in its process as a development of its own self—which is chiefly in view with those who speak of innate idea, or who, like Plato, describe all learning merely as reminiscence. Of course that again does not mean that everything which is embodied in a mind, after that mind has been formed by instruction, had been present in that mind beforehand in its definitely expanded shape. [*EL* 161 *Zusatz*]

For Hegel, then, the sequence of concepts that philosophical analysis presents is in fact the gradual unfolding of a single thing—the Idea—which is extraordinarily complex in that it includes all possible determinations of reality. This unfolding is essentially a deductive process. Just as we "analytically" unpack the meaning of a particular word or sentence without thereby adding anything to it, so do we unpack the Idea in all its fullness by looking for the logical implications of this or that particular aspect of it. Such a project shares with the classical notion of *anamnesis* at least the general principle that philosophy is a matter of uncovering—bringing to light—notions which are present but hidden, which are perhaps felt but not truly known, and which, when fully revealed, exist in the mind in their "definitely expanded shapes" and, as such, represent the necessary truth of the world.

8

It will be evident to students of Hegel that the foregoing account leaves out most of what is important in the Logic. Since the Logic is ultimately a treatise in metaphysics, a description of methodology can hardly be said to do more than scratch the surface. But further, Hegel's system contains a number of specific substantive claims which, at least at first glance, would seem difficult to reconcile with the account I have provided. Included here would be a variety of judgments pertaining to history. While the unfolding of the dialectic is sometimes approached in purely conceptual terms, Hegel also treats—indeed emphasizes—the historical unfolding of concepts. This latter parallels the process of logical development, but the nature of the connection between the two remains very obscure (see *WL* I, p. 7). It is clear that the concept of *Geist*, of a transpersonal faculty of thought or reasoning, plays some crucial role in making this connection; but that concept itself is difficult to fathom. Indeed, the issue is further obscured by the fact that Hegel recognizes his own work to be historically situated and that, as a result, the historical dialectic impinges on the logical dialectic in a substantial and unavoidable way. There is a sense, then, in which history is philosophically prior to Logic; and yet the unfolding of history itself must be grasped in terms of the concepts or categories provided by the Logic, thereby suggesting the latter's priority.

To this we must add the further complication that the dialectic also has a phenomenological manifestation. Specifically, Hegel treats the development of human consciousness, and the appearance of the categories of thought, in terms of a philosophical anthropology. Of course, this anthropology itself has a diachronic aspect such that its relationship to history proper is, again, not immediately clear. Indeed, the interplay among the logical, historical, and phenomenological unfoldings of *Geist* remains a serious problem for Hegel scholars.

Of course, implicit in both the historical and phenomenological dialectic is the characteristically Hegelian emphasis on struggle, on the importance of a dynamic tension in the world and its role in human progress. Further, it is only in this regard that we forcefully encounter Hegel's teachings regarding self-consciousness and, thus, can come to appreciate fully the importance of such formulations as "thought thinking itself." Our rather prosaic discussion of logical contradiction and its dissolution in no way captures the far more sublime accounts of dialectical confrontation and self-awakening that Hegel provides, as, for example, in the conflict between master and slave, the famous treatment of *Antigone*, or, indeed, the entire grand sweep of the philosophy of history. To be sure, these are the formulations for which Hegel has become most famous in this century, and they derive not merely from the *Phenomenology of Mind* but from Hegel's most mature work as well.

Exactly what role, then, would the discussion of this chapter play in a complete account of Hegel's philosophy, assuming such a thing to be possible? Consider a homely analogy. Imagine that I wish to get in my car this evening and drive to a restaurant for dinner. Now it seems clear that my doing this will be dependent upon a number of things which, in some sense, must be taken to be necessary. It will depend, for example, on the laws of the physical universe which, among other things, make it possible for me to keep my car on the road and negotiate the curves. It will depend, additionally, on the successful invention of the gasoline engine, and on the correct functioning of that invention as it appears in my particular car. Further, it will depend, let us say, on the highway system, in which I would include the roads themselves (and the fact that they're not all dead ends), the system of maps, street names, and addresses, and also the rules of the road—stop signs, lanes, speed limits—which presumably improve my chances of arriving at the restaurant in one piece. Without the roads, it would be difficult or impossible for me to drive to the other side of the river where the restaurant is located; without some system of addresses, I'd have great difficulty knowing how to get there; without the rules of the road, I might get killed on the way; and without knowing those rules, I might get arrested and thrown in jail for a traffic violation.

We may think of these factors, then, as minimally necessary—or at least very important—requirements or conditions of my driving to the restaurant. Yet it is clear that in discussing and analyzing my performing that action such factors will be among the least interesting. We prefer to know, rather, why I chose this particular restaurant over that one, why I am in the mood for Chinese food instead of steak, why I prefer this route to another, why I made a reservation for seven o'clock rather than eight, and the like. In short, we typically take the minimal requirements for granted and focus instead on the more obviously germane elements of our behavior. Or rather, to put it perhaps more clearly, we tend to focus on those elements of our particular action which are in some sense special. The laws of physics and the rules of the road generally remain the same wherever we happen to drive, but our selection of this restaurant over that one presumably reflects something not quite so regular. Still, the minimal requirements are no less important for being ignored, and a complete analysis of my driving to the restaurant would have to take them into account.

My hope is that the discussion in this chapter provides some of the minimal necessary requirements of the Hegelian philosophical system. In describing the nature of conceptual analysis as Hegel saw it, we have charted something equivalent to the highway system—i.e., those rules and practices that must be followed if one is successfully to pursue philosophy. To have done this is not to have fully accounted for Hegel's particular conclusions regarding the structure of the world or the nature of human knowledge. But it is, I think, to have described certain features which are quite necessary, though by no means sufficient, for Hegel to have arrived at those conclusions in the first place. Thus, in discussing the particular claims of the philosophy of Right, for example, we must make note of and take into account the fundamental rules of the Hegelian system.

There is, of course, one especially important point at which our homely analogy breaks down. Whereas we may discuss my decision to drive to the restaurant in the light of other possible decisions, all of which may be consistent with the highway system, Hegel's ultimate position is that the conclusions of his philosophical system are absolutely true, and that the minimal requirements of his system, when coupled with certain key premises, necessarily entail those conclusions alone. It is as though all roads lead to one restaurant, so that to wind up somewhere else is to violate the rules, hence to be somehow incoherent.

Along these lines, Hegel's most audacious claim is that his system indeed describes the true and necessary structure of the world. This description is in no way hypothetical or contingent; it is absolute, apodictic, hence irrefutable.

Since we all live in the shadow of David Hume, such a claim will surely make us uncomfortable. The premodern notion of the world as a rationally constructed text, replete with a meaning imparted to it by some superhuman intelligence, and capable of being appropriated and interpreted by creatures of reason, is no longer very easy to sustain. We are either skeptics or else are quite certain of the limitations of human knowledge. And thus, Hegel's claim to have irrefutably described the necessary underlying structure of the world will strike many or most of us as untenable in principle. Yet, the fact is that Hegel himself lived in the aftermath of Hume and, indeed, quite consciously rejected the knowledge-limiting principles as espoused both by Hume and of course, though in a very different fashion, by Kant. Is there any way, then, that we can accept the distinctively modern insights of the empirical revolution while still finding something plausible, or at least possible, in Hegel's most audacious claim?

As far as I can tell, the only reasonable option we have is to view Hegel's system as being based on a series of transcendental arguments. In saying this, I am endorsing what is clearly an emergent theme in the literature on Hegel.[40] On such an account, and despite what Hegel says at various times, we must view the essential metaphysical claims of the Logic as being "absolutely true" in a way that is different from the sense usually accorded that phrase.

Though it may be that transcendental argument can be traced as far back as Aristotle, the modern source of the notion is Kant. Roughly, transcendental arguments claim to show what must be true if some particular kind of discourse or experience, especially scientific or cognitive discourse, is to be possible. Thus, for example, Kant thought that the possibility of human experience and knowledge necessarily presupposes, among other things, the unity of apperception; hence, this unity was said to be "transcendentally proven." More recently, and relatedly, similar kinds of arguments have been used primarily against those who have doubted the very existence of the external or "real" world. Thus, according to Jonathan Bennett, a transcendental argument is one "which aims to rebut some form of scepticism by proving something about the necessary conditions for self-knowledge, self-consciousness, or the like."[41] Typically, such arguments take the form of showing that skepticism is somehow self-defeating. As such, they have been utilized by various contemporary philosophers, including Wittgenstein, Strawson, and Putnam.[42]

40. See Charles Taylor, "The Opening Arguments of the *Phenomenology*," in Alasdair MacIntyre, ed., *Hegel: A Collection of Essays* (Notre Dame, Ind.: University of Notre Dame Press, 1976); Alan White, *Absolute Knowledge: Hegel and the Problem of Metaphysics* (Athens, Ohio: Ohio University Press, 1983), pp. 29–30 and 82; Pinkard, "The Logic of Hegel's *Logic*," p. 417; Gadamer, *Hegel's Dialectic*, pp. 11; Rosen, *Hegel's Dialectic and Its Criticism*, p. 61; and Bernstein, "Why Hegel Now?" p. 53.

41. Jonathan Bennett, "Analytic Transcendental Arguments," in Peter Bieri, Rolf-P. Horstmann, and Lorenz Kruger, eds., *Transcendental Arguments and Science: Essays in Epistemology* (Boston: D. Reidel, 1979), p. 50.

42. Ludwig Wittgenstein, *Philosophical Investigations* (New York: Macmillan, 1968), sections 269 and 275; P. F. Strawson, *Individuals* (London: Methuen, 1979), p. 40; Hilary Putnam, *Reason, Truth, and History* (Cambridge: Cambridge University Press, 1981), p. 16.

There is a great deal of controversy about how transcendental arguments actually work and, indeed, whether they work at all. But if they do work, it would seem to involve something like the following account, which relies especially on the writings of Barry Stroud and Hilary Putnam.[43] Consider, to begin with, Carnap's famous distinction between "internal" questions and "external" ones.[44] For Carnap, some philosophical questions occur within, or internal to, a particular theoretical language or framework; they assume the concepts and categories of that language and derive their meaning—including, most importantly, their criteria of verifiability—from it. Such questions are in principle answerable and, hence, have scientific or cognitive value. There are other questions, though, which seem to arise from outside of the accepted linguistic or theoretical framework; they are, ultimately, questions about the framework itself. According to Carnap, included here would be questions such as whether there is a real world independent of human consciousness. Now for Carnap, meaning can only be conferred by a framework; one can make sense only if one employs such an established theoretical language. Hence, to move outside of one's framework is to forfeit the opportunity to talk meaningfully, at least to those who remain within it. Questions pertaining to the existence of an external world, for example, are—from the standpoint of the accepted framework—quite literally nonsense and thus are lacking in any cognitive or scientific character.

Carnap thus regards the question of the existence of the external world as, in some sense, out of order. But others have extended this kind of argument to show that all skeptical claims can be proven false because self-refuting. Putnam, for example, asks us to consider again the famous Cartesian hypothesis that we are

43. Barry Stroud, "Transcendental Arguments," *Journal of Philosophy* 65 (May 2, 1968): 241–56; Barry Stroud, "The Significance of Scepticism," in Bieri, Horstmann, and Kruger, eds., *Transcendental Arguments and Science*, pp. 277–97; and Putnam, *Reason, Truth, and History*.

44. For a discussion, see Stroud, "The Significance of Scepticism," p. 282 and footnote 17.

brains-in-a-vat controlled by an evil demon.[45] To endorse such a hypothesis is, of course, to claim that we really are brains-in-a-vat. Now to take such a claim seriously requires, first of all, that it be a cognitive claim. For Putnam, however, the cognitive nature of utterances requires that they make reference to something, and making reference to something requires, in turn, an intention to refer to something and a substantial, typically causal connection between the thing to which we refer and our utterance. But, at least in certain easily imagined circumstances, there can be no such connection between a brain-in-a-vat and the utterance of a brain-in-a-vat that it is merely a brain-in-a-vat, since, having no senses, a brain-in-a-vat could not see itself or observe itself in any way. In certain imaginable circumstances, that is, there can be no causal connection between the fact of being a brain-in-a-vat and the utterance by such a brain that it is a brain-in-a-vat. For this reason, a brain-in-a-vat could not truly refer to itself as a brain-in-a-vat; hence, its assertion cannot have cognitive value. But further, it would seem that, for this same reason, virtually all of its utterances, being nonreferential, would be noncognitive. Nonetheless, the mere fact that we can make *this* judgment, and find it acceptable, requires that we believe that we can indeed make some referential, cognitive utterances. That is, our very discussion of the brains-in-a-vat situation presupposes and requires the possibility of cognition and, therefore, presupposes and requires that we are *not* brains-in-a-vat. In this way, then, the claim that we are brains-in-a-vat is refuted.

What is the precise nature of this refutation? It seems clear that it in no way proves that in fact we are not brains-in-a-vat. Rather, it simply proves that we are incapable of claiming cognitively that that is what we are. The assertion "we are brains-in-a-vat" is impossible coherently to endorse; hence, it must be rejected as untenable, as wrong. Stated otherwise, internal to our system of thought and knowledge the utterance is false. External to that system, it may be true; but since, for us, true and false can only be used within our system of thought and knowledge, we must regard the utterance as false, and leave it at that. This seems to

45. Putnam, *Reason, Truth, and History*, chap. 1.

be at least a part of what Putnam means by "internal"—as opposed to "metaphysical"—realism.[46] Metaphysical realism invokes claims about the world from a "God's-eye" point of view; such a point of view is external to our own and, presumably, can generate knowledge about the real world. But it cannot generate knowledge *for us*. For we are, quite evidently, bound by our own system of thought and knowledge, the "human's-eye" point of view. Within that framework, we shall plausibly and quite correctly use words such as *true, false, proven, known*, and the like; and we shall, for example, say that something is "true" when it is demonstrated to be true in the light of our system of thought and knowledge. But we shall understand that all such truths are true only "internally." Thus, Putnam's arguments for realism seem to be of the type: we must accept the propositions of realism for, from a human's-eye point of view, they have been shown to be true.

Such an argument goes well beyond the claims of Carnap and certain of the other logical positivists. For Carnap, while all truth emerges out of particular theoretical frameworks, there may—at least in principle—be many such frameworks. His position is thus a conventionalist or relativistic one. On the other hand, transcendental arguments claim that there are certain propositions which must be true for there to be human cognition per se. In Barry Stroud's words, they seek to "establish the necessity or indispensability of certain concepts."[47] All frameworks, that is, will presuppose those concepts.

Thus, transcendental arguments refute the skeptic not by showing that the external world exists but, rather, by showing that it is impossible for us coherently to believe otherwise. There appears to be some evidence to suggest that Kant himself thought that he had made the stronger claim that the external world really does exist, as, for example, in the famous refutation of Berkeley's idealism that appeared in the second, but not the first, edition of the *Critique of Pure Reason* (B275). Nevertheless, I think the bulk of the evidence supports a different view, as articulated by Günther Patzig: "the transcendental deduction of the categories does not,

46. Ibid., pp. 49ff.
47. Stroud, "Transcendental Arguments," p. 243.

so I think, amount to an actual proof that there is, after all, an objective world out there. It rather concentrates on the idea that the system of categories based on the table of judgments is the only possible system which allows the unification of our subjective intuitions into one consistent and coherent body of knowledge."[48] Of course, some critics, notably T. E. Wilkerson, have claimed that Kant's views are seriously inconsistent, and that the First Critique suffers from a constant tension between realism and idealism.[49] Nonetheless, it seems possible even for the idealist Kant to write in terms of objective knowledge:

> Through concepts of understanding pure reason does, indeed, establish secure principles, not however directly from concepts alone, but always only indirectly through relation of these concepts to something altogether contingent, namely, *possible experience*. When such experience (that is, something as object of possible experiences) is presupposed, these principles are indeed apodeictically certain; but in themselves, directly, they can never be known *a priori*.[50]

In such passages, Kant seems to suggest that transcendentally proven principles, though "internal" in Putnam's sense, may nonetheless be known with utter certainty. What this seems to mean, simply and straightforwardly, is that such principles must be assented to on pain of incoherence. The "must" here implies that the principles are objectively true in the sense of being unavoidable, irrefutable, or cognitively necessary. For skeptics, claims about the world can always be denied; but for those who offer transcendental arguments, some claims simply cannot be denied. Such claims, then, must be asserted and endorsed. Thus, given the system of human thought and knowledge, objective truth is indeed possible. This truth will always be relative to the "human's-eye" point of view; but since that is, for us, the only point of view, necessary truth relative to it will be, for us, absolute.

48. Günther Patzig, "Comment on Bennett," in Bieri, Horstmann, and Kruger, eds., *Transcendental Arguments and Science*, p. 71. See also, Kant, *Critique of Pure Reason*, A371 and A737–B765.

49. T. E. Wilkerson, *Kant's Critique of Pure Reason* (Oxford: Oxford University Press, 1976), p. 197; see also A. C. Ewing, *A Short Commentary on Kant's Critique of Pure Reason* (Chicago: University of Chicago Press, 1970), p. 68.

50. Kant, *Critique of Pure Reason*, A737–B765.

Again, it is by no means certain that transcendental arguments of this kind can ever be successful.[51] Moreover, the task of showing that Hegel in fact employs such arguments would be a monumental one indeed. However, there does seem to be a prima facie case for holding that such an account is at least consistent with much of what Hegel says. For example, when Hegel claims that there is no gap between thought and being, we might simply interpret this to mean that our thoughts about the world are necessary and unavoidable (i.e., transcendentally proven), that they cannot stand as proofs that the world exists, but they can stand as proofs that we must believe in the existence of the world, that this belief is relative to the human's-eye point of view—which is, of course, the only possible point of view for humans—and, thus, that it is simply incoherent to say that there is a gap between thought and being. On such an account, to criticize Hegel for failing to prove the existence of the real world, as is frequently done,[52] is in no way to undermine many of his most ambitious claims.

Of course, if Hegel does employ transcendental arguments, they are far bolder than even those of Kant. For Kant, the transcendental method requires us to believe virtually nothing about the real world of things other than that it exists; the thing-in-itself remains permanently beyond our ken. Hegel, on the other hand, would deduce an enormous range of necessary beliefs pertaining to the essences of things and to the underlying structure of the world itself, all of them "absolutely" true. Given the controversial nature of transcendental arguments per se, and the at least equally controversial nature of Kant's more "modest" proofs, we can hardly say that a grand Hegelian system of transcendental arguments would initially strike the modern reader as very attractive. Nonetheless, it would seem that such a system might, at least in principle, be more attractive than one that actually did claim to prove—from a God's-eye point of view—the existence and essence of the real world. If in fact Hegel is claiming to take a God's-eye

51. See Richard Rorty, "Verificationism and Transcendental Arguments," *Nous* 5 (February 1971): 3–14.

52. For example, Raymond Plant, *Hegel: An Introduction* (Bloomington: Indiana University Press, 1973).

point of view, and if by "God" he means something more than just another transcendentally proven principle, then it seems to me that his metaphysics would indeed violate some of the more sensible discoveries of modern philosophy and would be best viewed in the usual manner, as an obscure and rather odd collection of assertions worth considering only for antiquarian reasons.

PART TWO

The Concept of Right

3

Crime, Punishment, and Abstract Right

The philosophy of Right presents itself as an extensive series of concepts having to do with matters of a social and political nature. These concepts are presumably related to one another in that each is said to follow from its predecessors. Thus, any account of the philosophy of Right must make note of this connectedness. But, in addition, each concept is attendant to, or emerges out of, a particular argument of a substantive or doctrinal nature. The sum of such arguments comprises, in effect, the substance of Hegel's political teaching; hence it is to them that we must turn our primary attention.

There are, of course, literally scores of interesting and difficult philosophical arguments to be found in the philosophy of Right. A truly comprehensive investigation of them would certainly require more than one volume and would tax the resources of even the most skilled and assiduous commentator. My intentions are by comparison quite modest. In this chapter and the three that follow, I propose to provide an initial account of Hegel's political system by focusing on four sets of arguments that pertain, respectively, to punishment, Kantian morality, marriage, and the internal structure of the rational state. Each of these is strategically important in the process by which the concept of Right unfolds. Though hardly comprehensive, taken together they can be especially useful in providing an understanding of the basic principles and methods of Hegel's system of political philosophy.

It should now be clear that this presentation will be informed, substantively, by the dialectic of individual and society. As suggested in chapter 1, Hegel's political thought is importantly shaped by the apparent tension between social rules and patterns, on the one hand, and the individuality of the individual, on the other. It is at least plausible to hypothesize that this characteristic problem of modern political philosophy is at the very center of Hegel's project. My general purpose, then, is to support this hypothesis by showing that our understanding of the philosophy of Right is enriched and deepened when viewed in such a light. More particularly, I believe that at least one of the keys to Hegel's political philosophy lies in specifying the exact sense in which he adopts what we have called a strategy or philosophy of perfectionism.

Methodologically, the presentation will be informed by the discussion in chapter 2 of conceptual analysis. That discussion can be summarized in terms of the following general formulations, which we may think of as some basic "principles of the dialectical method":

1. Philosophy is a matter of analyzing those concepts that we utilize in making sense of the world, especially in the kind of "making sense" that involves saying what a thing essentially is.

2. Often this involves an encounter with seemingly contradictory claims, wherein each claim—invoking some particular concept—appears to present what is exclusively necessary to the particular thing in question being what it is.

3. Such contradictions are resolved with the introduction of some third claim, involving a new concept or set of concepts, on the basis of which we come to see that our first two claims must in fact be taken together as mutually accounting for the essence of the thing. The new concept is to be thought of as, in some sense, the conjunction of the first two, or what may roughly be described as the one "together with" the other.

4. The resolution of contradictions is understood in terms of a particular set of metatheoretical concepts that are authoritative for all regions of Hegelian philosophy. These include: immediate and mediated, abstract and concrete, the negation of the negation, and the Hegelian *Aufhebung*. It is on the basis of such notions that we can come to link particular substantive formulations in Hegelian philosophy to the overarching discursive principles of the Logic.

5. Though all of Hegel's mature philosophy involves resolving contradictions in this way, the bulk of his philosophical writing is devoted to the analysis of those "third" concepts on the basis of

which oppositions are *aufgehoben*. By *analysis* I mean here a fundamentally nondialectical process in which a particular concept is evaluated in terms of its own necessary conceptual implications or entailments, and in light of the degree to which it is consistent with those other concepts to which we are, for a variety of reasons, committed.

6. The sum total of those concepts that emerge as dialectically sound, as fully mediated and concrete, may be thought of as the set of transcendentally necessary concepts on the basis of which we are ultimately able to make sense of the world, i.e., to understand the world without contradicting ourselves.

These rules or principles suggest that an adequate account of particular arguments in the philosophy of Right requires two basic tasks. First, it involves specifying the nature of the contradiction out of which an argument emerges, and also specifying the identity of that "third" concept on the basis of which the contradiction is thought to be resolved. Second, it involves the analysis of this third concept with a view toward discovering its conceptual implications and entailments, and evaluating it in the light of our other, presently uncontested concepts. This second task, the analysis of concepts, comprises the bulk of Hegel's philosophy, and the discussions that follow will reflect this emphasis. Our particular focus will be on a discrete set of concepts—punishment, the ethical community, marriage, and the rational state—each of which is understood as a third concept that is instrumental in resolving some fundamental contradiction but which, at the same time, demands analysis such that its specific conceptual content—its positive content—can be known and evaluated. Stated somewhat differently, each such concept is initially presented as the negation of a negation. Our goal is to follow Hegel in tracing out the conceptually necessary positive content of this originally negative formulation.

The concepts of crime and punishment play a central role in Hegel's philosophy of Right. As the first moment in which the concept of Right truly encounters an "other," crime is thus the first, crucial stage in the mediation and actualization of Right itself. As the annulment or negation of this "other," punishment is, in effect, the first point at which Right is reflected back into itself, hence begins to know itself qua Right. For these reasons, it is in the discussion of crime and punishment that Hegel begins to treat the kinds of issues most closely associated with what we have called accommodationism and perfectionism.

There is a sense in which the theory of crime and punishment can also stand as a particularly good test case of Hegel's method in general. As one of the many "set pieces" that characterize so much of Hegel's work, it provides an opportunity to trace out in some detail just how he arrives at philosophical conclusions. It is, indeed, one of the first moments of the *Philosophy of Right* that clearly embodies and reflects the rules of the dialectical method.

More specifically, we encounter here a rather straightforward contradiction of the kind described in the previous chapter. Hegel's theory of crime and punishment emerges out of an analysis of property. According to this analysis, the human individual is fundamentally characterized as a free being, possessed of a free will. He can come to exercise his freedom, however, only if he recognizes this trait in himself; and, for Hegel, this recognition depends upon his being able to seize and control some object external to himself, an object which can then serve as a manifestation of his freedom. In short, the individual must have possessions. Such an account justifies a kind of egoistic acquisitiveness; to be self-consciously free, the individual must seize, possess, and enjoy those objects which strike his fancy. This kind of activity is virtually the first one sanctioned by the concept of Right; hence it can be restated as the most primary moral imperative of Hegel's political thought: one should seek to acquire possessions.

On the other hand, it is also clear that this imperative needs to be seriously qualified; for an unlimited right to acquire possessions would, in effect, put at jeopardy the possessions of every individual, setting the stage for a war of each against all. In such a war, no one's possessions would be secure. As a result, no one could be truly confident in his self-consciousness of freedom; indeed, such freedom would remain largely unrecognized by other individuals and would appear to lack a clear moral basis. Thus, to the original imperative regarding acquisition must be added a second: one should not attempt to acquire just anything that happens to strike one's fancy.

The result appears to be a contradiction. We are told that we should be acquisitive, for that is how to express our freedom; and yet we should not be acquisitive, for that can undermine our freedom. In both cases, we are expressing a claim about possessions sufficiently persuasive that we would not want to give it up. As we saw in chapter 2, the question "What is the object before us?" allowed of at least two contradictory answers, one qualitative, the other quantitative. Similarly, to the question, "How should we behave toward external items of value?" we again encounter two different answers the practical implications of which seem to be mutually incompatible. For Hegel, then, the claims must be merely immediate and quite abstract. In its original form, each exists in isolation, so to speak, hence neither is appropriately informed by the other. Of course, the solution to the contradiction is quite simple and manifests itself in the notion of property. Property is that "third" concept on the basis of which we see that our two original claims are each an important part of, but not the whole of, the truth. Acquisitiveness must recognize the limitations inherent in property rights; those rights limit and yet, at the same time, help to insure the possibility of acquiring possessions. That is, property is a matter of acquisitiveness "together with" limits, or limits together with acquisitiveness. The contradiction is thus *aufgehoben*. In the assertion that we have property rights, the various claims regarding possession become mutually mediated and attain a relative degree of concreteness. The concept of property is, in effect, the negation of the negation.

Looked at somewhat differently, we come to see that the concept of possession must be enriched so as to distinguish mere physical possession from rightful or legitimate ownership; to this latter kind of possession, we attach the word *property*. Thus, the concept of Right now contemplates the freedom of the will as manifesting itself not in possession simpliciter, but, rather, in a particular kind of possession, viz., property ownership. As a result, we encounter a new maxim that is no longer contradictory: one should seek to acquire possessions, provided they are not the property of another person.

The concept of property thus solves the apparent contradiction between two moral imperatives. With this solution in hand, our task then becomes a matter of philosophically analyzing the concept of property, i.e., what further concepts does it necessarily imply? Or, given our concept of property, what additional understandings of possession and human action must we subscribe to in order to be intellectually coherent? Hegel's particular analysis of property leads to (among other things) the concept of crime and, thence, to the concept of punishment. In crime and punishment, that is, we begin to specify the implications of the negation of the negation—property—by establishing some of its positive content.

We shall examine this positive content by considering three problems which, in different ways, present challenges to Hegel's approach. They concern, respectively, the necessity of punishment, the relationship between particular crimes and particular punishments, and the issue of crime and insanity. These problems Hegel either never explicitly considers or never systematically resolves. I shall nonetheless argue that Hegel's theory does contain *implicit* responses to these objections, responses that are clear, sensible, and ultimately decisive. By demonstrating the power of the Hegelian system to generate convincing answers to such objections, I shall be suggesting both the logical or rational cogency of Hegel's ideas and the utility of those ideas for the real world.

1

We begin with an overview.[1] In the Hegelian system the word *Right* refers to the entire normative structure of social life; as such,

1. The literature on Hegel's theory of crime and punishment is comparatively sparse. Three recent articles, however, provide a good starting point. David Cooper, "Hegel's Theory of Punishment," in Z. A. Pelczynski, ed., *Hegel's Political Philosophy* (Cambridge: Cambridge University Press, 1971), is a fine explication and defense, and raises a number of important theoretical issues concerning crime and punishment. Peter Stillman, "Hegel's Idea of Punishment," *Journal of the History of Philosophy* 14 (April 1976): 169–83, though different in several respects, nicely complements Cooper's piece and suggests the importance of Hegel's theory for his political thought in general. Lewis P. Hinchman, "Hegel's Theory of Crime and Punishment," *Review of Politics* 44 (October 1982): 523–45, offers a useful account of the development of Hegel's views over time, but provides only a skeletal treatment of the philosophy of Right. Together these essays offer an accurate and otherwise excellent summary. However, they are essentially expository. They do not challenge the Hegelian theory in a systematic fashion, hence do not convincingly demonstrate the persuasiveness of that theory in the face of pointed criticism.

I am especially sympathetic with Cooper's general account (especially at pp. 160–66). He properly emphasizes (except where noted below) the logical, rather than empirical, nature of Hegel's arguments. And his notions of "performatees"—

it includes what we generally think of as the morality of interpersonal relations, civil rights and liberties, the law, the legitimate bases of political authority, and the like. The purpose of the philosophy of Right is to trace out the logical and immanent development of Right in the world and to uncover thereby the underlying interrelatedness of all social norms, from the simplest to the most sublime. This is a difficult task, for Right, as the complex gamut of normative social principles, must be approached gradually, in a piecemeal fashion. The simplest norms must first be isolated and identified before other, logically necessary principles are added. Each such addition, to be sure, complicates and enriches the concept of Right; the task of the political philosopher is to trace out these various cumulative additions and to show that each builds upon and is logically compatible with, yet at the same time subsumes and envelops, its predecessors. The nature of this process is, of course, dialectical, as described in chapter 2 above. That is, it is a matter of encountering and resolving contradictions that emerge from the various ways in which we think about the world.

The first stage in the development of Right is described in the

---

i.e., things which can exist only by virtue of some rule-governed procedure—is an interesting way of doing this. However, his view is seriously deficient, I believe, for the following reasons:

(*a*). Cooper's discussion of performatees fails to demonstrate that punishment is related to rights in the way that, say, the phrase, "I promise . . . " is related to the existence of a promise. That is, the criteria for distinguishing a performatee from something else are never specified.

(*b*). To the extent that such criteria are suggested, they seem to be wholly alien to Hegel's view. Relying on Austin, Cooper appears to relate the existent (e.g., "rights") to the rule-governed procedure (punishment) in terms of conventions or generally accepted understandings. This may be correct, but it is not Hegel's view. For Hegel sought to demonstrate the *absolute* and *ineluctable* relationship among crime, punishment, and Right, regardless of particular conventions or circumstances.

(*c*). Finally, while Cooper does at least try to show the logical necessity of punishment, he fails to distinguish punishment from deterrence and rehabilitation in *these* terms. Rather, his discussion of the latter is presented in other, less central terms (pp. 152–56). Thus, for example, he fails to show why deterrence might not constitute the "procedure" that makes possible the "existent."

In general, then, I believe that Hegel's logic is both bolder and more successful than the logic of performatees.

section on Abstract Right; it essentially involves the rights of persons to own property. That is, at this initial stage the sole normative principle of social life has to do with property rights; one has a right to own property, and it is wrong to violate the same right of someone else.

Now as we have seen, this right to own property is important—it is the most basic norm—because of its role in the development of freedom. In this sense, it offers a precise example of what Charles Taylor calls "the principle of necessary embodiment."[2] For Hegel, the will, which is a defining characteristic of persons, is itself by definition free (5). Hence, if there are persons, there must be freedom. But this freedom can be "actualized," it can make its appearance in the world, only when the will knows itself to be free. Property helps make this self-knowledge possible. For the actual possession of property—its seizure, its use, its alienation—permits the will to observe the effects of its freedom in something external, something "out there." The will, knowing the object of its activity to be its property, can thus reflect from the property back into itself, thereby confirming to itself its own power or freedom.

Property is thus the necessary *embodiment* of the will's freedom (41, 43). But again, having a free will in itself is said to be a defining characteristic of persons. Hence, it follows simply and directly that there can be no persons unless there is property. If there are to be persons, i.e., repositories of free will, then each such person must have a right to own at least some property.

A world of persons with property rights, all contracting peaceably with one another and thereby recognizing and acknowledging one another as persons, would be a pleasant and uncomplicated world were it not for the presence of crime. For the act of the criminal—prototypically theft—is, in effect, an attack on this peaceful world in general, an attack on property rights. The criminal, by stealing one's property, is denying one's right to have and own that property; indeed, by refusing to recognize one's right, the criminal is in fact denying the concept of property altogether (95). That is, the criminal act suggests that there is no such thing

2. Charles Taylor, *Hegel* (Cambridge: Cambridge University Press, 1975), p. 83.

as property; rather, there are only possessions. Clearly we *do* have things, we possess them, use them, and alienate them; but for the criminal we have these things only as a matter of might or of accident, not Right; hence our having them has no normative force (45; cf. *EG* 499).[3]

There is a sense in which the existence of crime merely repeats, in a somewhat different form, the original contradiction that led to the concept of property in the first place. Property has emerged as that "third" concept on the basis of which we can dissolve the apparent opposition between acquisitiveness and the need to limit acquisitiveness. Despite being well established, though, property rights may still become subject to new claims of unlimited acquisitiveness, i.e. the implicit claims of the criminal. By strong implication, the criminal way of seeing things is, like the original impulse to acquisition, quite natural and initially not implausible. It says, in effect, that you can take anything you want, despite the alleged right of the "owner," as long as you get away with it, a perspective not unknown to some utilitarians. Thus, property rights have to be reaffirmed—and thereby made more concrete, more fully mediated—by considering them explicitly in the context of criminal activity.

Crime is thus a very complex thing. It is, of course, an attack on a particular person, the victim, and a limitation of that person's ability to embody his freedom. Moreover, it is an attack on the person's property rights, a denial that he has such rights, and hence an attack on his very personhood. But further, the criminal's choice of a victim is presumably accidental and contingent; it is thus not *your* particular right to property that he is denying, but rather the right to property per se. This is largely what Hegel means when he identifies crime as the "infringement of right as right" and as a "negatively infinite judgment" (95, 97). It is negative in that it stands as the negation of the right to own property; it is infinite in that it does not in itself distinguish between this or that particular victim, or this or that particular piece of property, but is rather a rejection of the very idea of personal property rights. And thus,

3. Of course, the typical criminal neither intends nor is aware of all this. Hegel's point simply is that the criminal's actions, if "universalized" in (roughly) Kantian terms, would have these various implications for rights.

finally, crime is an attack not simply on rights but on the concept of Right itself, since at this early, primitive level Right is composed exclusively and entirely of the right to own property.

Clearly, then, something must be done about crime. The stance that the criminal implicitly adopts, that there are no rights, must be rejected and annulled if rights are to have actuality and force. For Hegel, punishment is precisely this annulment. Its function is to erase, at least symbolically, the criminal act, and thereby to reaffirm and restore the right to own property. In dialectical terms, it is the negation of the negation. By negating crime, by declaring the criminal to be in the wrong, punishment serves the interest of freedom and Right. Its purpose is to reaffirm the right to own property, reestablish the possibility of freedom's actualization, and recover thereby the (at least partial) truth of the concept of Right.

There are a number of implications here that are especially worth noting. To begin with, Hegel refuses to justify punishment on grounds of deterrence. Deterrence theories view punishment as a necessary evil, the justification of which is essentially utilitarian: the benefits of punishment outweigh its very real costs. For Hegel, on the other hand, deterrence is utterly beside the point. In the remark to section 99, he says that "the precise point at issue is wrong and the righting of it. If you adopt a superficial attitude to punishment, you brush aside the objective treatment of the righting of wrong, which is the primary and fundamental attitude in considering crime" (99; cf. *EG* 500). Again, the restoration or reaffirmation of Right is the sole purpose of punishment. Presumably, even if it failed to deter crime, punishment would still be required in order to "right the wrong." Similarly, if something other than punishment could be shown to provide better deterrence, that something would still not be a suitable surrogate for punishment. The implication is certainly not that deterrence is bad, simply that it is beside the point. Mere deterrence fails to "erase" the crime that has already been committed, thus fails to negate the negation.[4]

---

4. It should be clear by now that negating the negation does not simply restore the status quo. For punishment in fact improves and elevates the concept of rights; it explicitly introduces *into* that notion the idea that any violation will be punished and that the active and vigorous protection of rights is therefore a fundamental task of society.

Similarly, punishment cannot be supported on the ground that it rehabilitates the criminal. Its purpose is not to teach the criminal a lesson or to reform him; presumably other things could do that as well or better. Rehabilitating the criminal may certainly be a good thing, but it is separate from the issue of punishment.

Finally, we must make note of Hegel's famous view that by being punished the criminal "is honored as a rational being" (100). Hegel's point here is actually rather straightforward. To punish a criminal is necessarily to hold him responsible for his action; someone who is not responsible, who could not have chosen to act otherwise, would not deserve to be punished. Indeed, lunatics or children or animals, lacking the capacity to act rationally, cannot be criminals; they may do bad things, but those things cannot be crimes, cannot stand as negations of right as right. The criminal is thus, by definition, a free individual. Punishment confirms this by identifying the transgressor as a "criminal."

Of course, true punishment, as opposed to mere revenge, only comes on the scene with the advent of Civil Society in which the principles of law have been firmly established (220). But the full justification for punishment is already present in the section on Abstract Right. As the negation of the negation, punishment is in effect a statement, a declaration that the act of a criminal is a crime and that Right, though apparently annulled by crime, is in fact universal and eternal.

Hegel's theory of punishment, then, must be seen in the light of his logical method. Punishment is precisely part of the analysis of property whereby property—qua "third" concept—ceases to be merely the negation of the negation and begins to acquire positive content. Specifically, the concept of property is said to entail the necessity of punishment. The demonstration of this, and the further analysis of the implications of punishment itself, constitute the material on the basis of which we come to understand concretely— that is, in a more fully mediated way—the proper behavior of humans toward external items of value.

Apprehending the full significance of punishment also requires reference to the dialectic of individual and society, as outlined in chapter 1. This aspect will be treated more fully below. For now, it is enough to note that property and punishment are said to resolve at a certain level the apparent tension between unlimited individual acquisition on the one hand and social patterns of mutual respect and recognition on the other, thereby standing as an important first step in the overall perfectionist project of the philosophy of Right.

2

The purpose of punishment is to right the wrong, hence to stand as a statement that crime is crime. But why is punishment the only thing that can perform this function? Merely to show that punishment cannot be supported on grounds of deterrence is by no means to show that policies aimed at deterrence cannot equally perform the function of "annulling" crime. One might say much the same for restitutive or rehabilitative responses to crime; perhaps they too can negate the negation. But indeed, we can ask further why coercion of any sort is necessary. Why not a simple assertion or declaration to the effect that a particular action was a crime? Cooper raises precisely this last possibility: "let us admit that the existence of rights is only established if some action is taken against those who infringe putative rights. But why should this action take the form of punishment? Why should it not take the form of public denunciation, for example?"[5] Cooper's answer is based on an empirical judgment, viz., the "*empirical* fact, that only punishment possesses the required strength" to "establish the paradigmatic existence of rights." But such an answer seems utterly to misrepresent the very nature and strength of Hegel's argument. For I wish to show that empirical facts are entirely beside the point, and that Hegel's argument is based on, and can only be defended in terms of, purely logical or conceptual considerations.

Let us begin with the simplest possible illustration. Person X has some object in his possession: Person Y comes along and, without the free consent of Person X, appropriates that object and declares it to be his own. This might be what we call an act of theft; Person Y has stolen something to which Person X has a right, i.e., his property. Or it might be an act of restoration; Person Y is reappropriating something that Person X had originally stolen. Or again, it might be a mere skirmish in Hobbes's war of each

---

5. Cooper, "Hegel's Theory of Punishment," p. 166.

against all; each has a right to everything, hence there can be no question of theft.

Now it would seem that there are a number of ways in which society could respond to such an act. One would be to adopt a policy designed to deter Person Y, and other persons, from performing such acts in the future. This might involve imposing some penalty—i.e., inflicting some pain—on Person Y and holding up that penalty in the future. But it might also involve any number of other things: brainwashing Person Y, and other persons, so that they would not be motivated to perform such acts; making objects, such as Person X's object, invulnerable by hiding them or guarding them closely; providing Person Y, and other persons, with adequate surrogates for the objects in question. All such policies could be aimed at, and justified in terms of, deterrence. I know of nothing in Hegel's theory that would rule out such policies or such a justification; presumably Hegel would be happy to see certain actions deterred. The point, however, is that for Hegel none of these policies—including those involving penalties—would be examples of *punishment*. In this regard, two specific points must be stressed:

1. The imposition of penalties, if justified solely in terms of deterrence, is in large part indistinguishable from other forms of deterrence. The purpose of such penalties would not be to punish but to deter; and the decision to impose penalties would thus be based on the purely contingent, hypothetical claim that doing so would provide more deterrence than would other possible and acceptable courses of action. We can, of course, distinguish among the various kinds of deterrence policies (e.g., those involving penalties, persuasion, the imposition of obstacles, etc.). But the goals they share, and the fact that they are all necessarily based on the same contingent, hypothetical claim, suggest that their qualitative similarities far outweigh their differences. And thus, from the standpoint of deterrence, none of these policies is intrinsically more appropriate than any of the others; all things being equal, the one that works best is the one that should be adopted.

2. More importantly, policies aimed at deterrence need not be concerned with criminal acts alone. Indeed, there are many inconvenient and undesirable activities that are perfectly legal and that governments nevertheless seek to deter. The government raises fees at a campground to discourage overuse; it warns con-

sumers about the hazards of cigarette smoking; it removes dangerous lunatics from society for fear that they will cause some harm. In all such cases, deterrence policies are adopted in order to deal with utterly noncriminal acts. Deterrence itself thus fails to distinguish qualitatively the various kinds of acts with which it is concerned. Some of these might be criminal acts, others not; there is, in terms of mere deterrence, no way to tell. All one can say is that deterrence policies are aimed at preventing actions that society has, for whatever reason, deemed undesirable.

On these two grounds, then, we can see the necessity of punishment. Punishment is necessary for logical or conceptual reasons. Its purpose is to help distinguish certain undesirable acts (i.e., crimes) from other such acts (noncrimes) by declaring that, while both may be deterred, only the former deserve to be "punished" on their own account, regardless of deterrence. Crimes are acts which deserve punishment in a way that the overuse of a campground, smoking cigarettes, or the acts of a lunatic do not. Deterrence cannot help to make such a distinction; it can only distinguish undesirable acts (criminal and noncriminal alike) from desirable or neutral acts. Punishment, on the other hand, does do the former by specifying certain acts as punishable regardless of deterrence, acts which it thereby identifies as "criminal."

To return to our simple illustration, then, Person Y may or may not deserve to be punished. For example, if he is shown to be a lunatic, or if the object he took was really his own, then it is unlikely that he has committed a crime. Therefore, it would make no sense to punish him, though we may nonetheless wish to lock him away or impose some penalty designed to prevent him from acting in that way again. If, on the other hand, he is found to be capable of rational choice, and if the object he took is determined to have been the property of Person X, then he may well have committed a crime. But for his act to be *marked* as such, for society to *identify* it as a crime, he must be punished. Only in this way can society distinguish his act from other kinds of acts, identify it publicly as a crime, and thereby restore the rights that the act had, in effect, negated. Failure to punish the criminal would be to suggest that his action is qualitatively *similar* to other, noncriminal acts. And failure to punish anyone would thus make the category "crime" very dubious indeed.

Clearly the necessity of punishment assumes that we are interested in distinguishing crimes from other socially undesirable acts. Not all would be willing to do so. The theories of B. F. Skinner, for example, would seem to deny such a distinction. For Skinner, socially undesirable acts are essentially of a piece; all such acts ought to be deterred, but none ought to be punished. Skinner does favor the imposition of penalties, but only for deterrent, *not* punitive, purposes.

In contrast, Hegel is interested in distinguishing crimes from other socially undesirable acts. He does so in two ways. First, crimes are committed by free individuals, individuals with a capacity for rational choice. Again, lunatics, children, and animals may do things that have bad consequences, but they do not deserve to be punished for them. Penalties imposed on such creatures may well be admissible, but only if justified in terms of deterrence, rehabilitation, education, and so on. Second, crimes are defined as violations of personal rights, hence of Right itself. There are many socially undesirable acts that do not violate any property or other rights; such acts may be inconvenient, unpleasant, even disastrous to society, but they do not of themselves stand as denials of some other person's freedom.

There is perhaps no necessary reason for accepting this distinction between crimes and noncrimes, though it seems both sensible and useful. The distinction itself is rooted in certain Hegelian premises concerning the nature of the Will that are beyond the scope of this book. However, *if* we find the distinction to be a plausible one, then Hegel's theory of punishment would seem to follow as a virtual logical necessity. There can be no crimes unless crimes are somehow distinguished from noncrimes; mere deterrence fails to make such a distinction; hence, the idea of punishment as the distinctly appropriate response to certain actions becomes conceptually necessary. Indeed, crimes can be identified in part as those things which merit punishment, not simply deterrence; and because punishment alone can define crime as crime, it alone can negate the negation and reestablish the truth of right.

Of course, this conceptual argument does not, in and of itself, provide a *moral* reason to punish. But assuming the necessary link between punishment, crime, property, freedom, will, and person, if we want to have "persons" then we must have punishment. The question of whether or not to have persons appears to be a moral one, and our answer should not be prejudged. If, however, we have an adequate and persuasive moral reason for wanting persons (which Hegel presumes elsewhere to have provided), then we would thereby have a moral reason for punishing criminals.

But what of the possibility of a "public denunciation" as mentioned by Cooper, for example, an official edict or decree to the effect that taking the object from Person X without his free consent is a crime? (Of course, I assume here a public denunciation that would cause no real harm to the criminal, that would attach no painful stigma to him or cause him to suffer in any way. Without such an assumption, the denunciation would not be a substitute for punishment but merely another form of punishment). We are now in a position to see why this option must be ruled out on conceptual grounds rather than the empirical grounds invoked by Cooper. I should like to begin my argument with a brief and perhaps homely analogue drawn from our national pastime.

Let us consider two baseball plays. In Play 1, the batter hits a routine ground ball to the shortstop. The shortstop, seeing that he has an easy play, saunters over nonchalantly, takes his eye off the ball, bobbles it, and then kicks it accidentally with his foot; the ball rolls free, thereby permitting the batter to reach first base safely. In Play 2, another batter hits a sharp ground ball up the middle, apparently on its way to the outfield. The second baseman, however, makes a superhuman effort. He moves quickly to his right, lunges, and then finally stretches the full length of his body in a dramatic swan dive. Miraculously he is able to nick the ball with his glove, slowing it down; but the ball nevertheless rolls away freely, and the batter is again able to reach first base safely.

Let us now turn to the official scorer. Bear in mind that the *defining* function of the official scorer is to decide what is a "hit" and what is an "error." At the end of each season, such decisions are straightforwardly summarized to determine the official batting champion, fielding champion, earned-run-average champion, and the like. Returning, then, to our two plays, let us consider two hypothetical outcomes. In the first instance, the official scorer scores each play a "hit." When incredulous onlookers ask him about this after the game, he responds honestly by saying that he saw no real difference between the plays. In his opinion, both involved difficult chances for the fielders, plays that we would not normally expect a competent fielder to make. Hence, it would be unfair to penalize the fielders by putting "errors" on their records; it would be equally unfair to penalize the batters by taking away their "hits." Now, I argue that in such a situation the official scorer's position would be entirely coherent. We might vigorously disagree with him; indeed, we would surely question his judgment, his knowledge of the game, his eyesight, etc. But given the fact of his particular judgment, we must agree that his decision was the only logically acceptable one.

In the second instance, a different official scorer again scores each of our two plays a "hit." When asked about it after the game, this scorer admits the obvious; the first play was routine and should have been easily executed, while the second play was an impossible one in which the fielder had no realistic chance. Nonetheless, the scorer insists on scoring each play a "hit." Presumably he does so for some extraneous reason: perhaps he likes the shortstop personally and does not want to jeopardize their friendship; or he has a wager on who will win the batting championship, and lets his decision be determined accordingly; or he simply does not believe in the system of hits and errors, hence refuses to make such discriminations. In any case, the scorer's position would seem to be utterly incoherent. Of course, it may well be that his extraneous reasons have merit and that they should indeed outweigh his judgment regarding the two plays. But in his role as official scorer, it seems impossible to make sense of his position. Our dispute with him is not a question of judgment, knowledge, or eyesight; rather, we simply question his ability to think coherently.

It might be argued that this second scorer's postgame *assertions* regarding the two plays would suffice. It seems to me that this would be precisely analogous to Cooper's suggestions regarding crime and punishment. The scorer, by telling us how he judged the two plays, has in essence issued a declaration to the effect that one play was an error and the other was a hit. Perhaps, then, there is no need for him actually, officially, to score the two plays in that way. We all know what he thinks of the plays, hence that's all that counts.

This seems to me mistaken for a number of reasons. In the first place, the decision to score the plays identically means that, in the decisive sense, the two plays are to be regarded as identical. The official scorer—qua official scorer—is saying that, yes, the two plays are different but that, no, in another, more important sense, the plays are similar. In effect, he is defining and marking things in two different ways. His postgame declaration indicates that the plays are different, and this view is supported by a clear and definite judgment. But his official scoring decision indicates that, for all official intents and purposes, the two plays are to be regarded as identical. There appears to be absolutely no meaningful or relevant judgment behind this scoring decision. Still, this decision must be considered definitive; for the making of such decisions is precisely the defining function of the official scorer. Thus, the scorer is ultimately *identifying* and *marking* each play a "hit," thereby creating a reality which would seem to suggest that the differences between the two plays are secondary; yet his very judgment— his declaration—denies precisely that.

Further, the scorer's decision, if generalized, would make the very categories "hit" and "error" suspect. Assuming that his postgame declaration implied no official sanction, it wouldn't really matter whether one had made a poor play or a great play, at least from the standpoint of the record book. Of course, the definitional consequences of this would be extensive. For example, the scorer's decision, again if generalized, would in effect define the shortstop to be as good a fielder as the second baseman; it would also define the batters to be equally good at batting. We would then have a very strange definition of "fielding champion" and "batting champion"; ultimately, we would have to wonder about the purpose of keeping records at all.

But even more decisively, the official scorer, by refusing to let his scoring reflect his judgment, would undermine his very position as an official scorer. To be an "official scorer" *means* to make judgments regarding such plays and then let the "record" reflect such judgments. An "official scorer" who refused to do that would simply not be an official scorer in any meaningful sense.

Similarly, to respond to a crime with a mere declaration is, in effect, to make two statements. In one statement—the express declaration—the distinction between crimes and noncrimes is acknowledged. But in another, more decisive statement—the decision not to punish—the distinction is denied. For according to the second statement, crimes and noncrimes are identical to the extent that they fall into the class of actions that are not to be punished. Hence, they must share something very deep and substantial, i.e., some common characteristic which overrides their differences and requires that they be treated in the same way. Yet, assuming the conceptual distinction between them to be valid—as must be the case if we in fact have an express declaration to that effect—it is hard to see what that characteristic might be. The decision not to punish creates a reality, a definition of the two acts, which utterly contradicts the only salient judgment regarding the two acts that we have.

We can look at this in another way. Presumably, all societies have the capacity to punish; indeed, on some influential accounts (Weber's, for example) this capacity is a defining characteristic of the political state. Of course, the power to punish can and does involve a wide range of different institutions. It may involve a complex process that includes police, prosecutors, juries, judges, and probation officers; or it may involve a despot, a democratically elected assembly, a council of church elders, etc. But presumably for each society there is some such entity, a "criminal justice system," the essential purpose of which is to determine how the capacity to punish will be used. This entity would be the analogue of our official baseball scorer. Now, failure to punish a crime, and reliance instead on a mere declaration, would mean that, from the perspective of its distinctive function, the criminal justice system is refusing to discriminate between the crime (say theft) and noncrimes (say reappropriating one's own rightful property). In the absence of any overriding argument in this regard, the result would be—as in the baseball case—gravely incoherent. Specifically:

—The very judgment contained in the express declaration that a crime is fundamentally different from a noncrime would be flatly contradicted by the decision not to punish. This latter decision would thus be made in spite of the only salient judgment that we have.

—But the conceptual muddle would extend well beyond this. By denying, in the decisive sense, any real difference between (say) stealing someone else's property and reappropriating one's own property, the criminal justice system would be calling into question that very notion of property itself. If theft and nontheft are ultimately the same, then theft means nothing. And if that is the case, what could it possibly mean to own property? Of course, on Hegel's account, this would in turn undermine such notions as freedom, will, and person, ultimately rendering the very notion of Right itself at best trivial, at worst nonsensical.

—Finally, a criminal justice system that refused to punish crimes would become, like our official baseball scorer, mired in hopeless self-contradiction. For again, the purpose of such a system is largely to decide who will and who will not be punished. But if a system refuses to punish crimes, then its role becomes utterly senseless. It is, in effect, undermining its own task of deciding who will and will not be punished by ruling out one of the alternatives altogether; for if it does not punish crimes, then presumably it punishes nothing. The task of deciding how to use society's capacity to punish, like the task of keeping baseball records, would thus fall by the wayside. Indeed, there would then be no need for a criminal justice system. And if there were no real criminal justice system, then from the standpoint of society, the categories "crime" and "noncrime" would become gravely suspect.[6]

Consider finally a young student who makes an error on his arithmetic exercise. We might respond with a simple declaration: "This is wrong because . . . ", in which the words following "be-

6. I believe that the above arguments apply not only to Cooper's declaration but to any nonpunitive response to crime, for example, a public ritual of some sort. We can imagine our official scorer responding to the error by (say) dancing around his desk in some prescribed manner. But it is hard to see how such a ritual would solve the problem; for insofar as the official record failed to reflect his judgments, the official scorer—qua official scorer—would still not be acting coherently, and our notions of batting champion, fielding champion, etc., would still be ludicrous. Similarly, a criminal justice system that treated crimes solely in terms of some nonpunitive ritual would undermine its own definitive function of deciding how society's capacity to punish will be used.

Of course, one can imagine an alien culture in which something like "crime" would be handled by relying on some such ritual. In Hegel's account, though, such a culture could not have notions equivalent to our notions of the will, person, freedom, property, and the like; hence, its notion of "crime" would necessarily be very different from ours. More generally, a culture that could coherently respond to crime without resorting to punishment would simply be suffering from some deeper, more primary incoherence.

cause" would contain some judgment as to the nature of the wrong. We might respond in the same way to a lunatic who has just committed homicide; of course, in this case, the judgment contained in the words following "because" would be quite different. But if such a declaration were our only response, then we would in effect be assimilating the two cases in ways we must regard as incoherent. We would be saying that in each case the wrong can be corrected simply by explaining to the wrongdoer the nature of his mistake. Presumably, such an assimilation would be contradicted by the very judgments contained in our two declarations. Given those judgments, we will be coherent only if we *treat* the two cases in appropriately and fundamentally different ways, e.g., explanation for the student, therapy and isolation for the lunatic. Only in this way will we be defining and marking the lunatic's action for what we judge it to be.

Thus, the criminal must be punished for conceptual rather than empirical reasons. As we have seen, this has several aspects. To assimilate crimes and noncrimes is to undermine the very concept of crime, thereby calling into question a range of other morally significant concepts. Further, the punishing agency—the criminal justice system—can maintain its coherence only if its actions faithfully reflect its own best judgments. Thus, the need to distinguish crimes from noncrimes, combined with the need to act coherently, requires that the criminal be punished.

Of course, none of this tells us anything about the nature and extent of particular punishments for particular crimes; it is to this question that we now turn.

3

Must the punishment fit the crime? Hegel insists it must, though there appears to be some exegetical confusion in this regard. On the one hand, he clearly rejects the idea of punishing all crimes with equal severity:

> The Stoic view that there is only one virtue and one vice, the laws of Draco which prescribe death as a punishment for every offense, the crude formal code of Honour which takes any insult as an offense against the infinity of personality, all have this in common, that they go no further than the abstract thought of the free will and personality

and fail to apprehend it in the concrete and determinate existence which it must possess as Idea. [96]

On the other hand, he also appears to suggest that the question of particular punishments is one that philosophy cannot meaningfully address: "How any given crime is to be punished cannot be settled by mere thinking; positive laws are necessary" (96 *Zusatz*). Thus, he seems willing to let others decide questions regarding the severity of punishment, while at the same time censuring certain specific answers to such questions. The analytic tools developed in the previous section can help resolve this apparent contradiction. Indeed, I hope to show that Hegel's position is both consistent and, in conceptual terms, quite plausible.

As indicated above, for Hegel crime is (in part) an attack on someone's rights. Clearly such an attack can occur in any number of ways. For example, it might involve stealing a relatively trifling item such as a fountain pen or a tennis racket or a hair dryer. Or it might involve defrauding someone out of his home or his life savings. Or, again, it might involve taking someone's life. On Hegel's account, such acts deprive the victim of a certain capacity for freedom, but they do not do so in the same way or to the same degree. To steal someone's tennis racket is indeed to compromise that person's freedom, but in a rather limited way. Presumably the victim has other, more substantial pieces of property that permit him to become conscious of his freedom. Some of these, in turn, may contribute materially to the maintenance of his ability to own property. Thus, being deprived of a tennis racket is, on the whole, not likely to affect seriously one's ability to have property in general. Being deprived of one's life savings, on the other hand, might well have such an effect. It would certainly make it far more difficult to obtain other pieces of property; it would likely suggest to the victim the vulnerability of all property, even the most significant, thereby compromising for him the notion of property itself; and to the degree that it represents a larger "investment" of his stock of freedom, it can be said to undermine that freedom to a greater degree. Of course, in this last regard the paradigm case would be murder. To be deprived of one's life is to be denied altogether the capacity for freedom.

All crimes are thus alike, yet different. They are alike in

that each involves an attack on rights and on Right itself, i.e., a "negatively infinite judgment" that does not, in principle, discriminate between this or that particular victim or this or that particular piece of property. For this reason, then, all crimes must be punished. Of course, to punish all crimes is to suggest that they are, in some basic sense, alike; and at this level that is precisely what we would want to suggest. As negations of Right, crimes must therefore be assimilated as acts all of which alike merit punishment.

Implicit in Hegel's position, however, is the notion that those who have rights in fact have different kinds of rights. These rights appear to differ in a number of ways. Some contribute to an individual's happiness and well-being more than others. Some perhaps appeal to our cultural sensibilities more than others. But, most importantly, some rights contribute more than others to the preservation of freedom and personhood. The right to life makes a greater contribution in this regard than the right to one's tennis racket. This is essentially what Hegel seems to be saying in the following passage:

> It is only the will existent in an object that can suffer injury. In becoming existent in something, however, the will enters the sphere of quantitative extension and qualitative characteristics, and hence varies accordingly. For this reason, it makes a difference to the objective aspect of crime whether the will so objectified and its specific quality is injured throughout its entire extent, and so in the infinity which is equivalent to its concept (as in murder, slavery, enforced religious observance, etc.), or whether it is injured only in a single part or in one of its qualitative characteristics, and if so, in which of these. [96]

The difference in rights is very important.[7] For if we are serious about encouraging the development of freedom and personhood, we must be interested in differentiating those rights which are closely tied to freedom and personhood from those which are not.

---

7. Cooper is on the right track here. He sees that there are different rights. However, he merely asserts that "this difference should be reflected in the punishments meted out by a rational legal system" without showing exactly why this is the case. As a result, he fails to identify the kind of conceptual necessity that Hegel is after.

In other words, we will want to distinguish *crucial* rights, the violation of which would seriously compromise freedom and personhood, from less crucial rights.

It is for this reason that the punishment must fit the crime. To punish crimes differently is to *mark* them as different from one another. And to do this is, in turn, to mark a difference in the rights which have been violated. For, clearly, the difference between one crime and another is, in large part, the difference between the rights they respectively violate;[8] hence, to mark the former difference is also to mark the latter.

Thus, for example, murder violates a more essential right than petty theft. To punish these two crimes identically would be to identify them as equivalent, hence to suggest that the rights they violate are in a crucial sense alike. But if we believe that there is a basic difference between the two rights, then we shall indicate as much by punishing the murderer more severely than the thief.

We can now better understand Hegel's teachings on these questions. On the one hand, his fundamental concern is to show that crimes are punished. Thus, he is uninterested in presenting for us an explicit typology of crimes; indeed, as a historicist, he is implicitly willing to admit that different societies may coherently define the "same" crime in different ways, depending on contingently (i.e., historically) generated conceptions of property and the like. And so, Hegel refuses to specify particular punishments for particular crimes. This is clearly a matter for "positive law", i.e., for legal codes that reflect particular sociohistorical circumstances.

And yet Hegel insists that, however different crimes are understood in particular historical settings, punishments should be scaled to reflect those differences. One society may regard Crime X as being much more serious than Crime Y, whereas another society might think just the reverse. Presumably, Hegel would accept such differences with equanimity, as products of historical accident. What is important is that each society scale its punishments so as

8. Exceptions would involve differences in the particular status of the criminal, e.g., his intentions, capacities, etc. Such differences would distinguish (say) first-degree from second-degree murder.

to distinguish clearly and definitively one crime from another in the manner it sees fit. Failure to do so would be to lapse into conceptual incoherence, to say that things which are in fact dissimilar are nonetheless to be treated as though they were identical, to say (again) that a society should ignore its own explicit judgments.

<h1 style="text-align:center">4</h1>

Is insanity an acceptable defense? The issue is largely ignored by Hegel. Yet I believe we now have sufficient materials to reconstruct a Hegelian approach to the problem of crime and insanity. Such a task is important, for we can no longer consider adequate a theory of punishment that fails to deal with the insanity plea.

It seems clear that Hegel would view insanity as a perfectly adequate defense. For again, a crime is by definition the act of a free and rational agent; hence, although lunatics may do bad things, they cannot commit crimes. However, Hegel gives us little help in applying this distinction to actual cases, and this is precisely the issue upon which contemporary criminal justice systems have foundered. The deep problem here does not really concern psychoanalytic theory and expert testimony. Rather, it appears to involve more abstract questions of personal identity and responsibility.

Typically, criminal justice systems ask the following question: "At the time of the event, was the perpetrator able to distinguish right from wrong?" A negative answer would count as a considerable defense; unable to distinguish right from wrong, the defendant presumably cannot have been a free and morally responsible agent. Despite this, however, conventional opinion seems unwilling to accept such a judgment for at least two reasons. On the one hand, we seem unwilling entirely to excuse crimes of passion, acts of blind rage, etc., even though the perpetrator may well have been morally "paralyzed" by his passion or rage. Such occurrences are often the most heinous and offensive of events; to excuse them thus seems somehow wrong. On the other hand, and somewhat paradoxically, we increasingly seem to regard many, if not most, "criminal" acts as being somehow irrational, as being "caused" by social or personal pathologies of one sort or another.

Hence, to take the insanity plea at all strictly would be to narrow considerably the range of true criminal acts. Of course, not all subscribe to this latter view; observers such as James Q. Wilson and Ernest van den Haag are quite willing to see the average perpetrator as a rational and self-interested utility maximizer.[9] But the very intractability of the dispute between those positions itself suggests the difficulty we have had in dealing with the insanity plea.

At this point, it may be useful to refer to Derek Parfit's recent and important essay on "Later Selves and Moral Principles."[10] Parfit describes two views we might hold concerning the identity of persons and personal responsibility. According to the "Complex View," a person's life is best understood to be in fact a "series of successive selves." These selves may be quite different from one another, and the connections among them may vary considerably. Thus, we often say such things as, "He wasn't himself when he did that." In so doing, we appear to take seriously the possibility that a person may actually change and become, in a substantial sense, a truly new person.

Of course, the moral implications of such a view are profound. For example, some years ago I may have solemnly promised to perform a specific deed at some time in the future; but in the interim, I underwent a radical change—i.e., I have become a "new person"—and now find my promise to have been morally repugnant. Presumably, the Complex View would tend to reduce my obligation to fulfill the promise, since the "person" who made the promise no longer exists. The consequences for, say, notions of contract are obviously grave.[11]

It is perhaps in reaction to such possibilities that we may be attracted by the "Simple View." On this account, a person has one and only one self throughout his life; and thus, while he may well change in some respects, his basic identity—hence, the degree to which he is responsible for his actions (including past actions)—

9. James Q. Wilson, *Thinking about Crime* (New York: Vintage Books, 1977); and Ernest Van den Haag, *Punishing Criminals* (New York: Basic Books, 1975).

10. Derek Parfit, "Later Selves and Moral Principles," in A. Montefiore, ed., *Philosophy and Personal Relations* (London: Routledge and Kegan Paul, 1973).

11. Cf. Plato, *Republic*, 331c–d; also, Robert Paul Wolff, *In Defense of Anarchism* (New York: Harper & Row, 1976).

remain undiminished. Such a view considerably simplifies the problem of identity and responsibility, and seems to jibe with traditional and everyday notions of the self. And yet, it is difficult to deny that we do change in ways that appear to produce a succession of (more or less different) selves, and that some such changes are so substantial as to make the connections between the "old self" and the "new self" seem tenuous indeed.

An extreme, yet pertinent, case might involve a criminal act. An individual—say, Jean Valjean—commits a serious crime, is tried and convicted, but escapes from jail and assumes a brand-new identity. Only much later is he found out, by which time he has been completely and radically reformed and is no longer dangerous. Should he now be held responsible, tried, convicted, and punished? Presumably one who believed in the Complex View would be tempted to say no; for the reformed individual is, in some sense, not the same individual who committed the violation. An advocate of the Simple View, on the other hand, would probably say yes: the individual, though changed, is still *that* individual, hence must pay the price for what *he* did.

Such a conceptual impasse—two attractive and plausible but apparently contradictory approaches—seems ideally suited to a Hegelian solution. Now I do not claim to be able to render Hegel's views on the identity of persons; indeed, it is by no means clear that he held explicit views on the subject. I think we can, however, reconstruct a Hegelian approach that is plausible and that may help us deal with certain moral problems, including problems of crime and insanity.[12]

Unsurprisingly, a Hegelian approach would be dialectical and would regard the contradiction between the Complex and Simple Views as being merely apparent, not substantial. Each view is, as it stands, abstract and one-sided. As such, each contains a kernel of truth: the truth of the Complex View may be described as change; the truth of the Simple View, continuity. A Hegelian view would seek to annul yet preserve these two in a higher, more

12. Of course, the literature on personal identity is vast, and I am far from claiming that Hegel's solution is definitive. For an introduction and bibliography, see Amelie Oksenberg Rorty, ed., *The Identities of Persons* (Berkeley: University of California Press, 1976).

concrete unity. On such an account, a person is in fact a rich and substantial composite of change and continuity. The individual changes, but this change is shaped and conditioned by continuity; he continues, but this continuity is qualified and modified by change.

Importantly, the exact mix of continuity and change would likely vary from person to person, depending on contingent and accidental circumstances. Some people change more, some less. But the fact of continuity would suggest (what even advocates of the Complex View presumably would not deny) that a succession of selves are indeed related to one another in such a way that one self in some sense leads to (produces, or, at least, facilitates) its successor self, which in turn leads to *its* successor, and so on. A further implication, then, is that earlier selves are at least indirectly related to later selves insofar as they have led to one or more of the intermediate selves without which the later selves would not have developed.

Such an account seems to jibe reasonably well with Hegel's view of historical development as a gradual and dialectical series of transformations. It may also be helpful in explaining and justifying certain of our morally implicated practices, including those involving punishment. Consider the case of an individual who kills his neighbor while deeply under the influence of alcohol. Presumably, we would want to say that such an individual is somewhat less guilty than a cold-blooded and calculating murderer. For, having been roaring drunk, he simply was not himself, hence should not be punished quite so severely. On the other hand, he seems to be more guilty than our Jean Valjean, whose deed was done many years earlier and whose character has undergone a dramatic and salutary change.

Our Hegelian view of personal identity seems well suited to justifying such different judgments, especially in terms of the continuity and change of selves. At one extreme, the cold-blooded murderer seems to be characterized by a high degree of continuity; the self that we would punish is hardly different from the self who committed the crime, hence we are justified in holding the former responsible. At the other extreme, Jean Valjean has undergone a radical change; the self who performed the deed seems largely discontinuous with the self whose fate we are considering, hence the latter would appear to be guiltless.

But what of the drunken killer? We do now seem to have two selves, one sober and harmless, the other drunk and potentially lethal. But is the connection sufficiently close that we should punish the former? A Hegelian account would suggest a more precise and useful way of posing this question: is there sufficient continuity such that we may suppose a causal connection between the two? Is the sober self somehow *responsible* for the drunken self? May we plausibly identify the sense in which one self had "led to" (produced or facilitated) the other? In the present case, we might well presume a high degree of continuity: after all, it was the sober self who started drinking in the first place. The sober self is thus not a murderer, but he is directly responsible for the existence of a killer. Hence, while perhaps we would not want to punish him for first-degree murder, we would want to punish him for his somewhat lesser but still grave offense (132R).

As regards insanity, then, we would not simply ask if the perpetrator were able to distinguish right from wrong at the time of the incident. For if our answer were 'no," we would also want to ask why this was the case. Specifically, a Hegelian approach would require that we look into the sources of irrationality and attempt to determine the degree of continuity between the irrational self, its predecessors, and its potential successor. We raise, that is, the possibility that some underlying rational self was partly responsible for the onset of insanity, a self that could—in some form—re-emerge after suitable therapy.

Admittedly, this presents an unappetizing prospect. Should we really blame an individual for having become insane? But perhaps we need not go quite so far. A Hegelian account would suggest that the reasons why a person changes are complex and probably impossible to pin down. Again, a virtually infinite number of accidental/contingent factors affect all of us in incalculable ways. However, to trace the development of character entirely to such external factors is to fall into what we might call the Skinnerian trap. If insane individuals have no responsibility for their condition, then neither do sane individuals. To adopt such a view, of course, is ultimately to compromise notions of freedom and will, crime and punishment, and the like. As indicated much earlier in this discussion, we might well want to do so. But if, on the other hand, we wish to retain such notions, then we must accept the possibility that individuals—including insane individuals—may bear *some* responsibility for their condition.

Thus, if the perpetrator did not know right from wrong, we would also want to ask how he got that way. Of course, such a question would be extremely difficult to answer with any precision. But, presumably, if the individual's upbringing, life history, biochemical makeup, etc. were at least roughly "normal" as judged by society's standards, then society would seem to be well justified in holding him at least somewhat responsible—i.e., in finding at least some small degree of continuity between his preinsane, insane, and putative postinsane selves. And to *that* small degree, an appropriate and corresponding punishment would seem to be fully justified. Insanity, then, is a considerable defense, but not a complete one.

5

At this juncture, three further observations need to be made.

First, Hegel's theory of crime and punishment is not simply retributive, at least not in the traditional sense. Traditional retributivism is based on notions of desert: "punishing a person is morally justified if and only if the person committed an offense for which he deserves punishment."[13] Hegel would agree with this but find it incomplete. For Hegel, the criminal's guilt makes him morally eligible for punishment; we certainly commit no moral offense when we punish a guilty person. But this does not, in and of itself, *require* that we punish him. As we have seen, the necessity of punishment is based rather on logical or conceptual considerations such that a failure to punish is to compromise the very concept of crime. Thus, Hegel's theory does retain the element of moral desert (characteristic of retributivism) without embracing the principle of revenge; and it does so without recourse to added utilitarian considerations.[14]

13. James P. Sterba, "Retributive Justice," *Political Theory* 5 (August 1977): 350.

14. Cf. H. J. McCloskey, "Utilitarian and Retributive Justice," *Journal of Philosophy* (1967): 91–110.

Second, Hegel's theory is by no means airily abstract or irrelevantly metaphysical. Rather, it provides materials for explaining, justifying, and perhaps reshaping a number of our morally implicated practices. The account of crime and insanity, for example, shows how we can give considerable credence to sociopsychological theories of criminal behavior without forfeiting our moral right to punish transgressors.

Finally, the concepts of crime and punishment provide a crucial introduction to the general theme of "accommodationism" and "perfectionism." Of course, at this point we get nothing like an adequate or satisfying Hegelian approach to the problem of individual and society. Nonetheless, Hegel's arguments here are particularly revealing of the issues between accommodationists and perfectionists, and serve to foreshadow, in important ways, the nature of his full and mature solution.

In holding to the necessity of punishment, the appropriateness of particular punishments, and the legitimacy of the insanity defense, a Hegelian view emphasizes the rationality and self-consciousness of the individuals involved. The criminal is, by definition, a rational being, capable of apprehending in some sense the truth of Right; were this not the case, he could not be a moral agent, hence could not be held responsible for his actions. But indeed, it seems that this must also be true of those individuals who participate legally in the institution of property and who engage in the practice of property rights. As law-abiding citizens, as potential criminals who have eschewed a life of crime, we must in principle ascribe to them this same capacity for knowing, and acting according to, the maxims of Right.

Thus, the most primitive social institution of Right—the institution of property—cannot exist without individuals who are, in some sense, reflective and rational. If individuals were incapable of conscious thought and action, then the institution of property, considered as a set of social rules and patterns, would surely be an absurdity. As we have seen, punishment would be never justified since crimes could not be committed; and without the possibility of crime, the very idea of property would be rendered incoherent. But again, the individuality of the individual appears to be equally dependent on property, insofar as an awareness of the capacity for free choice depends precisely on property ownership. To emphasize once more, Hegel's claim is that the individual qua individual is fundamentally characterized by the freedom of his will; but this freedom amounts to nothing unless he is able to recognize and exercise it; and such recognition in turn presupposes that he possess property, i.e., some external object that is rightfully his in which he can witness the effects of his freedom.

In this formulation, Hegel seems to be approaching the problem of individual and society from the perspective, roughly, of modern accommodationism. There is an inherent tension between society's rules with respect to possession and property and those claims which emerge from the acquisitiveness of the individual. The tension is resolved with the realization that punishment is a necessary conceptual consequence of property. In punishment, that is, Hegel shows how the rules of society and the needs of the individual can in fact be balanced. The individual can indeed be freely and openly acquisitive, but only within those constraints or limits imposed by the law. Many things that the individual might ordinarily want to do—take something that is not his, for example—are denied him in the interests of those rules or patterns that make society possible. Society, on the other hand, makes enormous allowances for individual desires by merely placing formal constraints on individual action. Within those constraints, the individual may act as he sees fit or, perhaps more accurately, as his desires take him. At this level, then, Hegel's philosophy of Right appears to be straightforwardly accommodationist.

We should not be surprised by this, since the discussion of Abstract Right is linked up in quite obvious ways with certain standard currents in modern liberal thought, hence is most obviously presented as a viewpoint that is abstract, unmediated, and ripe for sublation. But even at this quite preliminary stage, a strong element of perfectionism has begun to intrude itself and to foreshadow the general direction that the philosophy of Right will take. This element is present precisely in the claim that crime and punishment require, or are conceptually bound up with, free and rational individuals. As we have seen, Hegel presupposes of individuals that they are rational and that they have free will. In some respect, these are seen to be essential determinations, as discussed, for example, in chapter 2 above. At the least, they are a part of what makes individuals essentially what they are.

According to Hegel then, the individuality of the individual is related to or composed of his capacity for freedom and reason. Fully exercising this capacity is, in turn, related to and dependent upon the institution of property, hence also on the institution of punishment (since, speaking conceptually, property requires crime which requires punishment). Thus, satisfying the requirements of individuality is shown to be contingent upon the successful establishment of certain rules and patterns of a social or legal nature. Similarly, those rules or patterns depend upon the full development of individuality. For as we have seen, punishment presupposes, and can only be imposed upon, persons who have a capacity for choice and who, we must presume, have reflectively and self-consciously elected either to obey or disobey the law. To the degree that individuals are unable to, or are systematically prevented from, acting in a free and reflective manner, the institution of punishment—hence of property—loses its legitimacy.

Thus, the rules and patterns of society and the individuality of the individual must come to fruition together. It is only in virtue of the other that each can, in Hegel's term, attain its "actuality" (*Wirklichkeit*). To approach them in their discreteness is to treat them abstractly, to miss the sense in which society and individual are in fact concrete elements of a concrete whole. In the theory of crime and punishment, we get a first inkling as to why this might be so—an inkling limited by, among other things, the rather feeble content of the concept of Right at this stage. Nevertheless, this selfsame emphasis on the *mutual* dependence of social institutions and human individuality is characteristic of Hegel's philosophy of Right in general. Indeed, I believe that it is the central theme of his political thought, a theme which defines Hegel as perfectionist rather than accommodationist and which begins to emerge with genuine clarity in the Hegelian critique of Kantian morality.

4

A Note on the Moral Standpoint

If Kantian philosophy establishes the immediate context for the development of Hegel's metaphysics, this is at least equally true for Hegel's ethics. The second part of the philosophy of Right, entitled "Morality," provides the fundamental transition from a liberal-individualist conception of Right to a more complete Hegelian conception rooted, as we shall see, in an organic theory of the state. Because of the nature of this transition, the defects of Abstract Right and the subsequent necessity for a fuller notion of Ethical Life cannot be comprehended without attending, at least briefly, to the discussion of Morality. But Morality itself is, in Hegel's account, virtually a synonym for Kantian ethics. Thus, it is Kant who provides the key arguments whereby we come to appreciate the deficiencies of (essentially) Hobbesian moral theory and also come to see, if only dimly at first, what kind of thing the complete concept of Right must be.

This emphasis on Kant should not surprise us. As John Toews has persuasively demonstrated, the generation of German philosophers who came of age in the late eighteenth and early nineteenth centuries was, at least in its formative years, deeply committed to the idea of perfecting and actualizing Kant's philosophy of freedom.[1] The Kantian "Copernican revolution" spoke to an intellectual community eager to dispel the dualisms of the Age of Reason, to reaffirm the unity of human existence in the world, and to establish at the pinnacle of that unity human rationality understood as a kind of immanent divinity. And if the pursuit of Kant's critical

1. John Edward Toews, *Hegelianism: The Path toward Dialectical Humanism, 1805–1841* (Cambridge: Cambridge University Press, 1980), pp. 34ff.

system soon revealed new, equally serious dualisms, this only changed the task from one of fleshing out Kantianism to one of determining how its truths could be preserved while its defects were being overcome.

A great deal of attention has been devoted to Hegel's critique of Kant's morality, and I have no intention of rehearsing these arguments at any length. There is a sense in which Hegel's position in this regard cannot be adequately treated and evaluated without a quite substantial exposition of Kant's ethical writings. On the other hand, the importance of Hegel's critique for an understanding of *his own* moral theory is, in fact, fairly straightforward and easily summarized. Thus, in this chapter I wish to make only two central points, and to make them rather briefly. Philosophically these points are perhaps not especially obscure, and my treatment of them will not be particularly novel. I have nonetheless chosen to devote a separate chapter to them in order to emphasize their importance in the unfolding of the concept of Right and in the development of my own argument.

1

As is well known, Hegel criticizes Kantian morality for being "an empty formalism." According to Kant, the morality of an action largely depends upon its being sanctioned in terms of the categorical imperative whereby the deed is rendered "universalizable." Specifically, an action would be morally right if one could rationally will that it be reformulated as a universal principle or maxim of action. In part, the goal here is to replace impulse and desire with rational choice as the basis of moral decision; in part, it is to ground morality not in the particular features of this or that individual but in considerations of a more general, transpersonal nature.

In Hegel's view, the categorical imperative describes an essentially superficial application of the principle of noncontradiction. It operates at the level of the Understanding which fails to comprehend the dialectical nature of contradictions. One aspect of this is that the idea of the categorical imperative is merely formalistic in that virtually any action can satisfy the criterion of noncontradiction. Thus, whereas Kant claims that certain putative maxims are inherently contradictory, hence insupportable, Hegel denies this. For example, Kant argues that one could not universalize the maxim of breaking a promise; the principle "It is morally acceptable to break a promise" is logically contradictory, or at least leads necessarily to logical contradictions. But Hegel wonders why this is so, why one could not simply do away with promising, hence break promises with perfect consistency. If Hegel is right in this regard—I happen to think he is not—then Kantian morality is indeed merely formal, because virtually any action might be compatible with it, provided that the action is performed in the right way. This kind of argument has been made against Kant by a host of other writers, including Mill and Bradley, but it is by no means self-evidently correct. Kant himself insisted that the categorical imperative has clear substantive implications, and others have attempted systematically to support this claim.[2]

For our purposes what is important is that Hegel's ethical theory is framed in terms of this critique. Above all, Hegel insists that the rightness or wrongness of an action is not merely a matter of form—not simply a question of how the action is performed, on the basis of what motives, whether impulsive or rational, and the like—but also a matter of content, i.e., what is actually done. Ethical theory must focus not only on how we do things but on the deeds themselves; and it must, as a result, generate a fairly explicit set of rules or laws. Whereas Kant seems to define moral theory as a search for the nature of moral action per se, Hegel understands it as including also, and more importantly, an effort to generate a clear code of conduct.

It is in this sense, then, that we must understand Hegel's famous distinction between a theory of Morality (*Moralität*) and a theory of Ethical Life (*Sittlichkeit*).[3] Morality, as a fundamentally Kantian endeavor, is indeed concerned with the nature of moral action as a personal, internal thing, a feature of individuals taken more or less in isolation; the focus is, roughly, on the way in which persons make decisions with regard to conduct. Stated somewhat differently, Morality is largely a matter of moral psychology. Now the

2. For example, Patrick Riley, *Kant's Political Philosophy* (Totowa, N.J.: Rowman and Littlefield, 1983), pp. 38ff.

3. For a helpful treatment, see Joachim Ritter, *Hegel and the French Revolution: Essays on the Philosophy of Right* (Cambridge, Mass.: MIT Press, 1982), pp. 151–82.

first central claim I wish to make with respect to Hegel's critique is simply that he rejects this standpoint as a complete account of what is Right. In Hegel's philosophy, a theory of Morality is, in effect, supplanted by a theory of Ethical Life, the purpose of which is to identify rules of action, and concrete practices based on those rules, which ought to govern the conduct of individuals. As Ritter suggests, Hegel's goal is to reestablish as a basic task of moral philosophy the essentially Aristotelian project of describing the laws, institutions, and practices of a moral society.

Thus, Hegel begins his description of Ethical Life as follows: "Ethical Life is the Idea of freedom in that . . . self-consciousness has in ethical existence its absolute foundation and the end (*Zweck*) which actuates its effort" (142). That is, to provide an account of Ethical Life is to describe the concrete end or object of the moral person qua actor, an end which constitutes, so to speak, that person's actual ethical existence. This end, however, cannot be understood simply as some higher purpose or motive but, rather, in terms of clear rules of conduct: "The objective ethical order . . . posits within itself distinctions whose specific character is thereby determined by the concept, and by means of which the ethical order has a fixed content—necessary and independent—and an existence elevated above subjective opinion and choice. These distinctions are absolutely valid laws and institutions" (144). Ethical Life thus describes a "fixed" content. The justification of this content, moreover, depends not on the pyschology of authentic moral agents; rather, its basis is quite "independent" and rooted in "necessary" considerations of, presumably, a philosophical nature. That is, the right rules of conduct are not simply those rules chosen by well-meaning persons acting out of a genuinely moral motivation. Rather, they are derivable on their own account and are discoverable through reason. Thus, the laws and institutions of Ethical Life are "absolutely valid" not because of consent, not because they owe their existence to the best of intentions, not because they are selected by virtuous persons, but rather because they have in some sense been philosophically demonstrated.

Thus, Hegel's entire approach to the problem of Right is quite different from Kant's. But it is impossible adequately to account for the theory of Ethical Life without recognizing that, although clearly based on a certain denial of Morality, in another sense it absorbs, hence accepts, the Moral standpoint. This is the second central claim I wish to make regarding Hegel's critique of Kant. What Hegel denies is the *exclusivity* of Morality, the idea that a theory of moral sentiments and moral psychology can provide a full and complete account of Right. But Hegel also insists that such a theory is indeed a necessary and indispensable component of Right. Kantian *Moralität* must be a part of, though it cannot be the whole of, a theory of Right.

In particular, what Hegel finds central and entirely correct in Kant's moral theory is the notion that conduct must be freely willed, that it must be chosen by an autonomous moral agent; and further, that this requires action to be based not on some kind of arbitrary decision, nor on impulse and caprice, but rather on a rationally discovered and justified principle. Kant's insight is that freedom is indispensible to Right and that freedom itself is a matter of choosing according to, and on the basis of, human reason. In effect, what Kant—following Rousseau—has done is to elevate the modern principle of individuality by demonstrating that capricious behavior, being heteronomous, is in fact inimical to genuine freedom and subjectivity.

For Hegel, this insight manifests itself above all in the claim that moral action, as rational action, must be undertaken self-consciously. Indeed, it seems that the very concept of rational action implies at least a certain degree of self-reflection. To act freely is to act on the basis of self-legislated principles, on the basis of principles one has discovered and imposed upon oneself. But this very act of discovery and imposition suggests some significant element of self-consciousness; for insofar as the agent has gone through a process of reasoning whereby a particular course of action is found to be morally justified, he is certain to be somehow conscious of the nature of the endeavor itself. To be truly free, therefore, the person must be at least dimly aware of the fact that he is engaging in a distinctive process of moral deliberation. This certainly seems to be the case of someone who invokes Kant's categorical imperative; how could one construct a universal maxim without in some sense knowing that that's what one is doing? For Kant, then, moral action is fundamentally self-reflective, and on this score Hegel is in full agreement: "Since this unity of the concept of the will with its embodiment—i.e., the particular will—is knowing, consciousness of the distinction between these two moments of the Idea is present. . . . " (143). The "concept of the will," which is the notion of the will as rational and free from impulse and caprice, must be embodied in the particular wills of individual persons. But this embodiment can occur only if persons are aware of the sense in which their freedom and subjectivity demand it. One cannot thoughtlessly or unreflectively become a self-legislating, rational agent; it can happen only self-consciously. Thus, the unity of the principle of freedom (the concept of will) with its manifestation in the individual (the particular will) is "knowing," i.e., fundamentally a matter of rational self-awareness.

My two claims, then, are as follows: (1) for Hegel, a complete theory of Right must include a description of legitimate and independently justified laws and institutions, what Ritter calls an Aristotelian project; but (2) it must also be responsive to the basic Kantian insight that moral action is free in the sense of being rational and self-conscious. In this sense, then, the critique of Kant brings to bear something that is only implicit in Hegel's theory of punishment and in his philosophy of Abstract Right as a whole. As we have seen, the problem of crime and punishment raises the fundamental question of individual and society so that claims implicit in the one seem to contradict those implicit in the other. In his theory of punishment, Hegel's position on this problem appears to be deeply ambivalent with respect to the accommodationist and perfectionist strategies. By insisting on the reflective rationality of the criminal, Hegel seems to be pointing toward a perfectionist solution; but the perspective of Abstract Right, rooted in modern/liberal and legalist notions of property rights, is itself compatible with and suggestive of accommodationist strategies.

With the critique of Kantian morality, this ambivalence dissolves. In *Moralität*, we encounter an apparent contradiction between individual autonomy on the one hand and independent, obligatory rules and principles on the other. Kant's failure adequately to account for such rules and principles prompts Hegel to demand a recommitment to objective ethics, to the so-called Aristotelian project. But Hegel's overriding demand is that this recommitment must be accomplished without causing any violence whatsoever to Kant's crucial insights regarding freedom and moral personality. Hegel insists on having it both ways, and the critique of Kant thus exposes, for the first time, the perfectionist roots of Hegel's political philosophy. That is to say, the philosophy of Right must embrace in a full and uncompromised form both the Kantian account of the moral self and the Aristotelian demand for substantive moral laws.

Indeed, the entire structure of Ethical Life is based on the confluence of these two elements. But what is the nature of this confluence? In what way does the concept of Right bring together objectively valid rules and subjective moral freedom? For Hegel, the answer seems to lie in the distinctive relationship between such rules and those who obey them. Briefly, this relationship is a matter of mutual dependence. Absolutely valid laws cannot take effect in the world unless they are freely and consciously assented to by the individuals involved; similarly, subjective moral choice cannot be genuinely free unless it is guided by a rational appreciation of that which is objectively Right. Each side of the equation depends upon the other.

It is easy to see why rules that are objectively valid are, for that very reason, indispensable. Free participation, on the other hand, is necessary for at least two reasons. To begin with, objective laws and institutions, if they are not to remain simply the property of philosophers, must have authoritative force in the real world of human affairs. But in order for them to be "actualized" in this way, their validity must be recognized by the ruled. Hegel writes that "the ethical order is . . . a circle of necessity whose moments are the ethical powers which regulate the life of individuals. To these powers individuals are related as accidents to substance, and it is in individuals that these powers are represented, have the shape of appearance, and become actualized" (145). The rules of Ethical Life do indeed "regulate" the conduct of individuals. They are, to this extent, laws in the conventional meaning of that term. But if they are seen as something external and illegitimate, then their actual effectiveness can only be a matter of chance, dependent upon accidents of history which determine whether the powers that be happen to uphold them or not. Thus, the laws can be truly established in the real world only through the conscious recognition and choice of the governed: "The substantial order, in the self-consciousness which it has thus actually attained in individuals, knows itself and so is an object of knowledge" (146). Again, the *validity* of laws does not depend on their being actualized in this way, and Hegel notes that "from the objective standpoint, we may say that in [Ethical Life] we are ethical unselfconsciously" (144 *Zusatz*). But if ethical laws, no matter how valid, are not *consciously* assented to, then they can only remain prescriptions, not yet fully actualized in the world—not yet "actually attained"— hence ultimately inefficacious.

Moreover, if the laws are imposed against the choices of the individuals they are meant to govern, then the great Kantian insight that freedom is necessary to Right will have been frustrated. In order truly to preserve the moment of subjectivity, in order to move beyond the primitive unity of the premodern world and incorporate the modern concept of the individual, absolutely valid laws and institutions must be consciously understood to be such by those whose conduct they regulate. In the absence of this, Ethical Life would lack the element of individual freedom without which, as Kant has shown, morality ceases to be a distinctive category of human conduct.

In the translator's footnote to 145, T. M. Knox captures nicely the two sides of Ethical Life, the objective side which discovers and justifies the rules of society, and the subjective side according to which those rules are freely assented to: "[T]he might of the ethical order is actualized in and through the conscious and deliberate volition by individuals of universal ends; what the state's compulsive power exacts, the individual also wills, so that freedom is at the same time a 'circle of necessity' ".[4]

In sum, the concept of Right necessarily includes individual freedom; and, borrowing from Kant, freedom is understood in terms of the individual's capacity to act according to rules prescribed by reason. But further, such rules must be rules in the full sense, derivable not simply from your reason or mine but from reason per se, hence independently and, in principle, philosophically demonstrable. Thus, Ethical Life is essentially a matter of individuals freely choosing to obey rules whose Rightness is quite absolute. Indeed, we may say that Ethical Life is nothing but that "third" concept on the basis of which the apparent contradiction between

4. T. M. Knox, "Translator's Notes," in G. W. F. Hegel, *Hegel's Philosophy of Right* (Oxford: Oxford University Press, 1971), p. 348.

Kantian and Aristotelian ethics—between individual moral freedom and the objective, absolutely valid rules of society—is to be
overcome. To a substantial degree, the third part of the philosophy
of Right, *Sittlichkeit*, may be understood as an elaborate analysis
of this third concept, whereby its positive content is deduced and
specified. This analysis is, of course, extremely complex, and includes the three central moments of family, civil society, and state,
each of which engenders particular dialectical tensions and reso-
lutions of its own. Nevertheless, on such an account we may say
that Abstract Right presents for us in simple form the problem of
individual and society; Morality establishes both the complexity
of that problem and also the need for a perfectionist solution; and
Ethical Life provides an analysis of the nature of that solution by
discovering in the negation of the negation—in the sublation, the
simultaneous annulment and lifting up of Kantian and Aristotelian
ethics—a positive content.

Some further implications of this account bear mentioning:

1. The critique of Kant as described here already conveys at
least a part of Hegel's specific strategy for overcoming the contradiction of individuality and society. The rules and patterns of society, whereby the community's needs are satisfied, are sanctioned
and justified through reason; but reason is also seen to be the
essence of individuality, i.e., the capacity to act not out of impulse
and caprice but on the basis of self-legislated and rationally demonstrable principles. This shared basis in reason seems to be part
of what Hegel has in mind when he refers to the "identity" of laws
and subjectivity:

> [The laws] are not something alien to the subject. On the contrary,
> his spirit bears witness to them as to its own essence, the essence in
> which he has a feeling of his selfhood, and in which he lives as in
> his own element which is not distinguished from himself. The subject
> is thus directly linked to the ethical order by a relation which is more
> like an identity than even the relation of faith or trust. [147]

It seems that the "essence" which unites the laws and the individual
can only be reason itself. Rationality is the basis of selfhood, of
human freedom and subjectivity in the full sense, and the proper
basis also of society's institutions and practices. Thus, the link
between law and subject, between community and individual, is

more substantial than, say, bonds either of faith or trust; for these latter typically involve choices and judgments which are somehow incapable of being proven, which defy rational demonstration and which, as a result, could well turn out to be insupportable (whereby the bond itself would shatter).

2. Focusing for a moment on the subjective side of this linkage between law and individual, Hegel seeks to distinguish between virtue and rectitude: "virtue (*Tugend*) is the ethical order reflected in the individual character so far as that character is determined by its natural endowment. When virtue displays itself solely as the individual's simple conformity with the duties of the station to which he belongs, it is rectitude (*Rechtschaffenheit*)" (150).[5] Virtue is, it seems, a characteristic of the individual which develops, or has relevance, mainly in opposition to particular natural and social forces that tend toward immoral or nonmoral behavior. It is, in short, the achievement of an individual who has been able to overcome the influence of a social setting conducive to impulsive or capricious choice. Rectitude, on the other hand, is simply a matter of harmonizing oneself with, and acknowledging the authority of, social rules and patterns that have proven to be ethically sound. There is nothing self-evidently courageous or difficult about rectitude: it does not have the appearance of an "achievement." Nonetheless, for Hegel it represents a considerable advance over individual virtue. Indeed, "[T]alk about virtue . . . readily borders on empty rhetoric, because it is only about something abstract and indeterminate . . . and is addressed to the individual as to a being of caprice and subjective inclination" (150 *Zusatz*). In effect, the member of Ethical Life has internalized the rules of society; he understands and acknowledges their Rightness, hence follows them because it is his duty to do so. It is, in a sense, natural for him to obey—although this is, as Hegel says, a "second nature," something attained through rational, self-conscious reflection.

The language of virtue seems to assume that the individual is fundamentally a creature of caprice and inclination; thus, it counsels a heroic struggle to overcome these traits. But the struggle is, in some sense, directionless, since it remains unclear exactly what laws should be obeyed and what actions should be performed. For

5. On the translation of *Rechtschaffenheit*, see ibid., p. 349.

Hegel, this is why the language of virtue often approaches an "empty rhetoric." He finds that virtue is an important concept mainly in primitive societies whose institutions lack philosophical justification, whereas in Ethical Life the individual "has simply to follow the well-known and explicit rules of his own situation" (150 *Zusatz*).

3. But again, this rule-following must be free in the sense of rational and self-conscious. For otherwise, rectitude degenerates into a merely habitual kind of behavior. Now it is true that Hegel does describe the "second nature" of ethical action in terms of habit: "But in the simple identity of individuals with the actual order, Ethical Life appears as their general mode of conduct— i.e., as custom (*Sitte*)—while the habitual practice of ethical living appears as a second nature which, put in place of the initial, merely natural will, is the permeating soul, significance and actuality of custom's existence" (151). But this habitual obedience should not be understood in the usual sense as something unreflective or automatic. For, as Hegel is at pains to remind us, "[i]t is true that a man is killed by habit, i.e., if he has once come to feel completely at home in life, if he has become mentally and physically dull, and if the clash between subjective consciousness and mental activity has disappeared . . . " (151 *Zusatz*). Thus, when Hegel says that obedience to the laws of Ethical Life is habitual, he means not an unconscious and unreflective kind of behavior but, rather, something like self-disciplined action. Indeed, it is rather similar to the discipline of philosophical thought itself, "since such thought demands that mind be trained against capricious fancies, and that these be destroyed and overcome to leave the way clear for rational thinking" (151 *Zusatz*). Just as the discipline of a philosophical education can hardly have as its goal the stupefaction of pupils, so the "habits" of Ethical Life cannot be said to aim at mindless conformity. Quite to the contrary, the goal in each case is to train the individual so as to prepare him for a life in which he freely and self-consciously abides by the rules and principles of reason.

4. It is only in Ethical Life, then, that we come to appreciate the true nature of freedom. The free individual is the individual who acts rationally; his conduct must not simply accord with, but must be chosen explicitly in the light of, human reason. But it is reason that also generates and sanctions objectively valid laws and

institutions. Thus, to obey those laws—knowingly, not unconsciously—is, in effect, to obey oneself—to be, in Hegel's phrase, in "possession of one's own essence" (153). Indeed, in Ethical Life the individual

> recognizes as the end which moves him to act the universal which is itself unmoved but is disclosed in its specific determinations as rationality actualized. He knows that his own dignity and the whole stability of his particular ends are grounded in this same universal, and it is therein that he actually attains these. Subjectivity is itself the absolute form and existent actuality of the substantial order, and the distinction between subject on the one hand and substance on the other, as the object, end, and controlling power of the subject, is the same as, and has vanished directly along with, the distinction between them in form. [152]

Subjectivity (free choice) and the substantial order (absolutely valid laws and institutions) are thus shown to be rooted in the same essential soil, in universal reason which ultimately manifests itself in self-conscious human action.

At this juncture, it is important to reemphasize the fact that, for Hegel, the individual comes to *recognize* this unity of subject and substance, and that he *knows* about the necessary relationship between particular ends and universal principles. Many commentators on Hegel's politics, including some of the most sympathetic, seem to overlook or lose sight of this crucial element. It is hard to account for this, since Hegel's discussion in this regard is quite clear. The fact is that the ethical order simply cannot be fulfilled, it cannot be actualized in a complete and satisfactory way, unless the particular individuals who are a part of that order come to recognize and understand the sense in which it is rationally justified, the sense in which it is Right.

To this point, of course, Hegel's argument is itself rather abstract. He has provided a preliminary account of the kind of thing Ethical Life is but has not yet provided a description of its specific content. Again, Ethical Life may be understood as the negation of the negation whereby the claims of both Kantian and Aristotelian ethics to exclusivity are denied while, at the same time, the importance of each in the context of the other is affirmed. In effect, Ethical Life is defined as individual moral autonomy "together with" objective and absolutely binding moral rules. Hegel's task is to flesh out this as yet merely formal concept, to describe some of its necessary positive content so that we may have a sense as to what Ethical Life might actually be like and how it resolves the dialectic of individual and society. Such a description is offered, of course, in the three main divisions of the section on *Sittlichkeit*, and it is to a discussion of these that we now turn, focusing especially on the institution of marriage and on the constitution of the rational state, each considered as an objectively valid practice to which free individuals have knowingly and rationally pledged their obedience.

5

Marriage

One of the characteristic figures of modern literature is the dissatisfied spouse. Emma Bovary may well be the model case. A person, average in most ways, finds himself or herself in a marriage that has, for any number of reasons, gone bad. The individual is thus torn in at least two directions. On the one hand, he wants simply to be happy—romantically, sexually, financially, or whatever—hence comes to judge the marriage in terms of personal contentment. Such contentment, in turn, is identified with the individual's well-being as an individual, which involves personal growth, fulfilling one's capacities, and the like. Thus, in deciding how to deal with his situation, the person comes to employ criteria that we may call egoistic in the broadest and most benign sense. If, on balance, the marriage makes him happy, then he should stay married; if not, he should get out of it, either in the legal or psychological sense. This is a most plausible view, since we typically regard the decision to marry in the first place as a matter of choosing for happiness and individual well-being.

But, of course, rather different considerations emerge from outside the individual, so to speak, and also appear to be important in judging the relationship. Specifically, the marriage has claims of its own. There are the sacred vows in which one has pledged one's word; the contractual obligations, freely assented to; the interests of society in seeing to it that an important social practice continues to thrive. There are the children, the needs and feelings of the other spouse, the interests of the extended family, the question of the estate—all things which the marriage, directly or indirectly, gave rise to, and which appear to exert moral claims of their own. The force of such claims, frequently, is to devalue considerations of an egoistic nature and to emphasize instead the importance of a particular social institution.

Our typical individual thus faces seemingly contradictory imperatives. Assuming his dissatisfaction to be both deep and abiding, such considerations may impel him to dissolve the marriage, to seek contentment elsewhere. Only in this way, perhaps, can the individual honor and attain his own individuality. Institutional considerations, however, may require that he sacrifice his own personal feelings—or his individuality—in the name of duty. We are well aware that this kind of conflict may, in fact as well as in fiction, have consequences of a most unfortunate nature.

It may be that any interesting philosophy of marriage will have to deal with this apparent conflict. But in any case, I am quite certain that it provides a basic problematic for Hegel's account and that, as such, it continues and deepens the basic Hegelian theme of individual and society. Specifically, our initial sketch suggests that the ordinary understanding of marriage is somehow self-contradictory. On the one hand, we conceive of marriage as a device for securing the individual satisfaction and well-being of both marriage partners as they, in their individualities, understand it. One the other hand, we also think of marriage in terms of its important social functions. We feel that both conceptions are in some way essential; yet we also see that between them exists an ever present tension which, in not unusual circumstances, manifests itself as a straightforward contradiction. Again, to assign privilege to the social function of marriage is often to undermine the satisfaction and individuality of the partners, and vice versa—or so it seems.

We seek, then, some third concept of marriage that may subsume the first two and show the contradiction between them to be merely apparent. Such a concept is by definition nothing but the first two taken together, each regarded now as a necessary but insufficient feature of marriage properly understood. The burden of Hegel's theory is simply to elaborate this third, higher concept—to specify its positive content—so that we see how the well-being and individuality of the marriage partner cannot contradict but must, in fact, be bound up with and depend upon the social function of the institution. This elaboration will, in turn, require reexamining and enriching our understanding of the two constituent elements, viz., the partner in marriage as a seeker of satisfaction and the marriage itself as a social institution. That is, the full concept of marriage, as the negation of the negation, will reflect upon and alter the way in which we understand both of its constituent elements. These latter will cease to be for us abstract, unmediated, and discrete, and will become, instead, concrete parts of a fully mediated whole. In this respect, the discussion of the partner seems to me especially important in Hegel's scheme, and will receive particular attention in the pages that follow. For, as we shall see, Hegel's account of the partner in marriage depends upon a more general treatment of the nature of the human self, and this will have substantial bearing on the overall perfectionist project of the philosophy of Right as a whole.

Our goal, then, is to reconstruct Hegel's analysis of the concept of marriage, considered as the concrete complex of our two ordinary conceptions. In pursuing this goal, it will of course be necessary to explicate the specific arguments of the theory of marriage,[1] which are several and include controversial positions concerning love, the marriage ceremony, sexuality, and the like. My own judgment is that these arguments, taken together, do provide a systematic analysis of the concept of marriage, and that this concept can indeed offer a basis for overcoming the dialectical tension inherent in the very nature of connubial relations. That is, the apparent contradiction between the claims of the partner qua individual and those of the marriage qua institution does dissolve when marriage is properly conceptualized in Hegelian terms. In at least two important respects, pertaining to the indispensability of marriage and to the role of women, Hegel's account seems to me deficient or unpersuasive. But in each case, I shall claim that his formulation is, in fact, incongruent with the other, more central aspects of marriage as Hegel himself describes it, hence can and must be rejected as, in effect, logically mistaken. On the whole, then, the Hegelian concept of marriage appears to perform quite

---

1. I use the word *theory* here in the loosest sense, to include Hegel's concept of marriage, his justification of that concept, and his analysis of the role of marriage in the dialectic of individual and society. Of course, the reader should also note that marriage itself is only one-third of Hegel's treatment of the family, the other sections dealing with family capital and the education of the young.

well its role within the larger structure of the philosophy of Right, especially insofar as it exemplifies and contributes to the perfectionist project.

The basic features of the theory of marriage are easily summarized. For Hegel, marriage is the distinctive and appropriate relationship between the sexes. It is a relationship of love, but one based on spiritual or rational bonds rather than bonds of inclination and physical desire. It is a matter not of romance but of reason. As such, it involves the mutual renunciation of independence, of "selfish isolation," and the consequent awareness of mutual unity. Through marriage, the individual ceases to be "an independent person" and comes to recognize himself as first and foremost a "member" of some larger entity (158, 158 *Zusatz*; cf. *EG* 519).

Further, Hegel insists that marriage, like the state, is not a contractual relationship (163). This is so despite the fact that marriages arranged by parents may well be more firmly grounded than any others (162). Moreover, Hegel regards the marriage ceremony itself as absolutely crucial. Indeed, to treat the ceremony as merely "an external formality" is to subvert the marriage relationship, to introduce into it "an alien intruder" that will threaten the very substance of the union (164). Beyond this, Hegel requires that marriage be monogamous (167) and that it involve no incest (168). He claims that it can subsist and thrive in the absence of sensuousness and romance (164, 164 *Zusatz*), and that while divorce ought to be possible, it is nonetheless a violation of the very principle of marriage (163 *Zusatz*). Finally, he argues that marriage, though ultimately rooted in free choice, is not simply an option for us but is in fact an ethical obligation: "Our objectively appointed end and so our ethical duty is to enter the married state" (162).

All of this amounts to a traditional, bourgeois picture of marriage which many of us at first blush will regard as simply quaint. Modern culture, at least in certain of its moods, accepts virtually without question a more romantic view. For many, a marriage lacking in romance and sensuality is a sad and barren affair. And yet, perhaps paradoxically, most people also seem to be convinced of the essentially contractual nature of marriage. Indeed, the elaborate marriage contract, in which not simply financial arrangements but also the division of domestic labor are negotiated in rich detail, is still enjoying something of a vogue. Of course, divorce is now a way of life. The marriage ceremony frequently means little more than a few minutes before a justice of the peace. Arranged marriages seem to be for older, more primitive cultures. Casual physical liaisons are often taken for granted. The notion that we have a duty to marry may strike many of us as particularly absurd. Indeed, the unmarried household is apparently becoming the rule rather than the exception. Thus, if some of us can sympathize with those who would find Hegel's views attractive, many people seem quite happy to have progressed well beyond them. It may be that we genuinely lament the casualness of contemporary connubiality; but we are at a loss to see how its defects can be rectified without incurring much greater costs. A Hegelian account of marriage seems to speak to a simpler time, a time long past.

Hegel's views, however, can hardly be attributed to the historical period in which he wrote. The contractual interpretation of marriage was, as Hegel well knew, propounded above all by Kant (75); in arguing against the sensual and romantic view, Hegel explicitly rejects the emergent approach embodied in Schlegel's *Lucinde* (164 *Zusatz*); and indeed, the conjugal biography of (say) Hegel's one-time friend Schelling certainly suggests the currency of "progressive" ideas among German intellectuals of the time. It seems more plausible, then, to view Hegel's account of marriage not simply as a historical artifact but as that which it claims to be, viz., a matter of conceptual analysis.

1

The theory of marriage, and all of the arguments of the philosophy of Right, are based in part on a particular theory of the self. I say this despite the fact that the philosophy of Right does not seem to offer an explicit treatment of the human self, i.e., a systematic account of how humans differ from nonhumans and how one human differs from another. Of course, it may be argued that we can find such an account in the introduction to the philosophy of Right, especially in its treatment of the concept of the will. Now there can be no doubt that Hegel's theory of the self is importantly dependent on such passages. The single most fundamental characteristic of the human self is the free will. To be human means being able to abstract from all external things, to enjoy the "unrestricted possibility of abstraction"; yet, at the same time, to be

able to posit oneself as something distinct and particular, something "determinate," hence restricted in certain important ways;
and finally, to become aware of both of these capacities and to
understand that freedom involves a process of *self*-restriction or
self-determination (4–7). In a sense, this is what it means to have
a human self; the capacity to reflect upon one's impulses, and
thereby to evaluate them so that they become the "rational system
of the will's volitions." (19).

But this by itself cannot entirely satisfy us as an account of the
human self. For while it outlines in general terms the philosophical
bases of selfhood, it fails to show us any of the self's identifiable
traits as manifested in thoughts and attitudes, in cognitive processes, in what we normally refer to as personal characteristics,
and also in their related social institutions. Hegel tells us in the
introduction that, at base, humans qua humans have a capacity
for self-legislation; they attain freedom, hence fulfill the requirements of selfhood, only when they choose to act on the basis of
rational principles which they themselves have discovered. But we
need to know in addition something about those principles, and
something about the process of discovery, if we are to have an
adequate account of the human self. In my view, this requires
some retrospective attention to the overall threefold structure of
the philosophy of Right: Abstract Right, Morality, and Ethical
Life.

A basic unit of analysis in each of these three sections is the
individual. However, Hegel's "individual" undergoes several
changes as the argument of the philosophy of Right advances, and
these changes may be understood as the unfolding of the concept
of the human self. Thus, we begin in the section on Abstract Right
with the individual as Abstract Person (35–38).[2] This Abstract
Person is essentially a legal entity; he is a bearer of rights simpliciter. His rights permit him to seize, utilize, and dispose of his
possessions as a matter of Right, i.e., de jure, which thereby turns
his possessions into property. Now, the Abstract Person has a
variety of desires, needs, and impulses that determine how he

2. In the relevant passages, Hegel typically uses only the German word *Person*.
However, the phrase "Abstract Person" is a convenient and accurate way of distinguishing this early *Person* from the *konkrete Person* of later passages (eg., 182).

chooses to use his property. But while this fact is essential, the particular desires, needs, and impulses he has are only contingent and accidental, hence play no necessary role in the definition of his self qua Abstract Person. To put it otherwise, the individual's mind at this stage must have *some* psychological content, but this is solely a formal requirement; the precise nature of the content is unimportant. The Abstract Person is thus abstract in that his selfhood is comprised entirely of the generalized capacity to utilize property in conjunction with other Abstract Persons, for example, in contractual relations. The self is this and nothing more. A further implication, then, is that the various empirical selves, though quantitatively distinct from one another, are qualitatively identical. They differ only in terms of their particular desires, needs, and impulses; hence, they differ in nothing essential.

We should be clear as to what Hegel is doing when he describes the Abstract Person. His description is not intended to be arbitrary or fanciful. Rather, his goal is to describe the necessary and sufficient properties of the human self from the standpoint of one particular sphere of human activity, viz., the sphere of law or "abstract right." It seems to me in this regard that Hegel's account is largely persuasive. In the Western legal tradition as we typically understand it, individuals are to be treated only in the abstract, i.e., as formally identical entities whose various particular qualities are not a subject for law. The focus of law is not on this or that particular person, characterized by this or that set of desires, needs, and impulses, but rather on the generalized individual. Implicit in the legal tradition, then, is a concept of the human self which is roughly as Hegel describes it.

Such a concept of the self, however, seems to be deficient in at least two ways. To begin with, it contradicts our general intuition that human selves are in fact qualitatively, not just quantitatively, different from one another. While we might agree that there are traits which all humans possess, the very notion that you and I are qualitatively identical strikes us as ludicrous. More specifically, the very concept of self, by singling out the individual for special attention, seems to imply that the differences between individuals are absolutely crucial. Indeed, if individuals were fundamentally identical, then it is hard to see why we would have or want to have the concept of self at all. We can, for example, quantitatively distinguish the various bees in a hive from one another, but we do not attribute selfhood to each of them at least in part because we judge their differences to be only secondary; that is, the concept of self would not in any way clarify or comport with our understanding of bees. The fact that we have and use a concept of the human self, on the other hand, suggests that we regard the differences between individual humans as being much more essential. By denying this, the concept of the self found in Abstract Right appears to be seriously inadequate.

Second, and relatedly, this legalistic view makes it difficult to distinguish human selves from nonhumans. Abstract Persons are possessed of desires, needs, and impulses; but this seems to be true of animals also. Abstract Persons do communicate with one another, formulate plans, carry out tasks in which possessions are utilized, recognize one another; but again, so do some animals, at least as far as we can tell. And to repeat, Abstract Persons, like animals, are different from one another in only inessential ways. Hegel would not want to attribute rights to animals (47, 47 *Zusatz*), but others would,[3] and it is not clear that Hegel is correct in this regard, given his description of the Abstract Person. Thus, Hegel should not be satisfied with this initial account of the human self, and in fact he is not.

With the development of the concept of Morality, as discussed in the previous chapter, the individual has ceased to be an Abstract Person and has become instead what Hegel calls a Subject (105, *EG* 503). In large part, this change is reflective of a difference in the concept of the self. For as Subject, the self is no longer simply a bundle of desires, needs, and impulses. Rather, it now also includes a conscience, a self-legislated purpose, and a notion of itself. It is, in short, *self-conscious*. The implications of this are absolutely crucial. For to begin with, it means that the self is fundamentally reflective, i.e., its psychological content includes not simply desires, needs, and impulses, or the consciousness of these, but also the consciousness of that consciousness. We might say that the latter is composed of "second-order thoughts."[4] A

3. See Peter Singer, *Practical Ethics* (Cambridge: Cambridge University Press, 1979).

4. I borrow here from Harry G. Frankfurt, "Freedom of the Will and the Concept of a Person," *Journal of Philosophy* 68 (1971): 5–20.

second-order thought would be a thought not about some non-thought but rather about a different thought. For example, when a feeling of pain registers as a thought in my consciousness, we may say that its content is provided by the damage done to the nerves of my finger by the hot iron; but when I reflect on this thought, the content of my new thought is no longer the physical fact of iron-on-finger but rather the original consciousness of that event.

It may be observed here that the capacity to have second-order thoughts is already attributed by Hegel to the Abstract Person. For example, Hegel writes of "the self-conscious but otherwise contentless and simple relation of itself (i.e., the free will) to itself in its individuality... "(35). We might assume that to be self-conscious in this way is to have second-order thoughts, and that this capacity is thus not unique to the Subject. I doubt that such a view can be correct. Hegel does indeed attribute self-consciousness to the Abstract Person, but this self-consciousness is "contentless." The notion of a contentless awareness is certainly curious, but what Hegel seems to have in mind is the view that the Abstract Person simply has a sense of himself as an entity which is somehow distinct from all other entities, an unencumbered and self-contained identity. As T. M. Knox puts it in his footnote to section 35, the self-consciousness of the Abstract Person is merely the knowledge that "I am I." Such crude self-awareness can hardly count as consciousness of consciousness. For as Hegel remarks, the phenomenal mind is "*only* self-consciousness" whereas "mind fully explicit... has itself, as the abstract and free ego, for its object and aim"... (35). This, then, seems firmly to distinguish a kind of brute self-awareness from the "*explicit* awareness of (self)-identity" (105) that we associate with a creature who is truly conscious of being conscious.

My suggestion, then, is that the self of Morality—the Subject—is distinctive in its capacity to generate second-order thoughts. But is this concept of the self therefore free from the defects we found in the earlier legalistic view? Specifically, does the new concept help to distinguish humans from nonhumans and from one another?

One way to approach this might be to think about the kinds of thoughts we call second-order. Clearly, many of these will be quite primitive and, as it were, unimpressive. When I simply think today about a particular thought that I had yesterday, this will qualify as a second-order thought. But even this crude kind of self-awareness does not seem to describe the mental activity of nonhuman animals. The point is crucial. For the ability to form second-order thoughts seems to provide a nice dividing line, beyond which lies a rich and varied realm of consciousness. If we can have even primitive thoughts about thoughts, then it seems plausible that we can have thoughts about those thoughts about thoughts, and so on; the possibilities thus seem to be endless, and the result is the opportunity to engage in various kinds of complex discourse, all of which are distinctively human.

Two such kinds of discourse are especially worth mentioning. The first might be called "human communication," by which I mean a distinctively human capacity to use language.[5] Now it seems certain that some animals can use language. Consider the famous description of "Washoe," a chimpanzee who had been taught to use American Sign Language:

> By the time she left Reno in 1970, Washoe had a vocabulary of around 140 signs. The Gardeners [her teachers] observed her to use 294 two-sign combinations such as "more food," "give me a drink" and "come open."... Washoe picked up a few signs without being taught them, for example, "smoke"; the scientists were always asking each other for cigarettes.... I interviewed Washoe through the bars of her cage.... Washoe asked me for a cigarette, always the first request on prison visits. She made the sign "smoke" which is two fingers held to the mouth....[6]

Clearly, to say that Washoe could use language means that she had learned to perform acts that had in the past been successful in eliciting desired responses. To say that she knew the word *smoke* means that she had learned how to get a cigarette from her interlocutors.[7]

5. I do not mean to imply that language is the only form of human communication. Many of the arguments made here would apply to nonverbal forms of communication as well.

6. Peter Jenkins, "Teaching Chimpanzees to Communicate," in Tom Regan and Peter Singer, eds., *Animal Rights and Human Obligations* (Englewood Cliffs, N.J.: Prentice-Hall, 1976), pp. 86–87.

7. See Herbert S. Terrace, *Nim* (New York: Alfred Knopf, 1979), pp. 210–21.

We may well count this as one way of using language. But it seems to be different from the way humans often—perhaps even typically—use language. In this regard, it may be helpful to consider Grice's famous arguments on "meaning." For Grice, "non-natural meaning" involves the following kind of situation: *A* (an utterer) must intend to induce by *x* (an utterance) a belief in an audience, and he must also intend his utterance to be recognized by the audience as so intended.[8] But further, *A* must also feel that the latter recognition is itself necessary in order to induce the belief. That is, to induce a belief in an audience, the utterance must be recognized by the audience as being intended to induce that belief. We can illustrate by distinguishing three cases derived from Grice's essay:

a. Salome discovers on her own the severed head of Saint John the Baptist.

b. Herod presents Salome with the severed head of Saint John the Baptist.

c. In the absence of any severed head, Herod simply tells Salome that Saint John the Baptist is dead.

In each case Salome comes to believe that John is dead, but she does so for different reasons. In (*a*) Salome's belief is based not on some meaningful communication but rather on a simple "natural" observation. In (*b*) Salome knows not only that John is dead but also that Herod intends her to know this; however, her recognition of his intention is entirely irrelevant to the production in her of the intended effect. Thus, there is something unique about (*c*) which seems to involve a peculiarly human mode of meaningful communication; for in (*c*) the intended effect occurs without any direct, "natural" observation and requires that Salome recognize Herod's intention to use his utterance in order to make her believe that John is dead.[9]

---

8. H. P. Grice, "Meaning," *Philosophical Review* 66 (1957): 383.

9. Of course, it requires more than this, including Salome's belief that Herod knows what he's talking about, is not lying or play-acting, and the like. Brian Barry, *Political Argument* (New York: Humanities Press, 1965), pp. 20ff., has suggested that Grice's account is incomplete and requires some attention to the conventions by which particular expressions acquire meaning. This suggestion seems to be an entirely friendly and persuasive amendment, and in no way changes the present

In (*a*) there need be no second-order thoughts; Salome thinks only about the physical fact lying before her. In (*b*) the case is less clear. As stated, Salome seems to be thinking about Herod's intentional thought; Herod seems to be thinking about Salome's putative belief. But it surely does not have to be this way. For Salome might entirely disregard Herod's intention—may, for example, think of him as a zombie incapable of having anything we might call an intention—and yet still see that John is dead. Similarly, Herod may intend not to induce a belief in Salome but simply wish to see her scream, faint, or become ill. Thus, cases such as (*b*) need not involve second-order thoughts, though they may. Case (*c*), on the other hand, is unintelligible without second-order thoughts. Herod thinks (i.e., intends something) about Salome's thoughts (beliefs) about Herod's thoughts (intentions); Salome thinks (believes something) about Herod's thoughts (intentions) about Salome's thoughts (beliefs). In each case, the individual thinks about the other person's thoughts and about his own thoughts as well.

Now, our intuitions strongly suggest to us that such complex Gricean intentions are not attributable to animals.[10] Indeed, the above description of the chimpanzee gives us absolutely no reason to believe that it was capable of having second-order thoughts. It seems most plausible to say that though some animals may be able to use language, they can do so only as a tool in order to elicit certain desired responses, e.g., affection, being handed a cigarette or a banana, and the like; in so doing, they may also be taught to attach names—words or signs—to particular objects, including their own bodies; but nowhere is there any reason to believe that they can have thoughts about thoughts or could employ what might be called Gricean language. It would seem that the opportunity to communicate in this way is distinctively human.[11]

Another kind of discourse based on second-order (or *n*th-order)

---

argument. See also, J. R. Searle, "What is a Speech Act?" in J. R. Searle, ed., *The Philosophy of Language* (Oxford: Oxford University Press, 1977), p. 46.

10. Jonathan Bennett, *Linguistic Behavior* (Cambridge: Cambridge University Press, 1976), p. 14.

11. Ultimately, Bennett appears to disagree with this conclusion (ibid., pp. 110–12), but he presents virtually no evidence in support of his position.

thoughts would involve moral principles. It seems clear that animals, being thinking creatures with desires, needs, and impulses, can certainly engage in decision processes where they often decide that one alternative is "better" than another. On some influential accounts, this would suffice as evidence of moral thinking, and it may well be. But there seems to be another kind of moral thinking which involves second-order thought and which animals seem unable to do. To use Frankfurt's term,[12] while a chimpanzee may in some sense want to do X, only a human self could "want to want to do X." Let us take the case—Frankfurt's case—of a heroin addict who chooses to cure himself. He may do this because one of his desires, the desire to avoid death at all costs, is simply stronger than another of his desires, the desire for heroin. In this case there need be no second-order thoughts; the addict simply satisfies the stronger urge. But we can imagine another scenario; the addict chooses to cure himself not because of some overwhelming fear or impulse, but because he rationally decides that his desire for heroin is somehow untoward, immoral, undignified, or evil—i.e., he decides that he does not want to have the desire for heroin. Such a choice would have to involve a second-order thought, a thought concerning (say) the moral worth of another thought. The agent would have to reflect critically upon his own thoughts, and on some accounts this is precisely what makes moral reasoning possible.[13]

A paradigm case of this kind of reasoning would be the categorical imperative, something that nonhuman animals presumably cannot invoke. Along these lines, it is important to note that Frankfurt finds our notion of the free will to be rooted precisely in our capacity for second-order volitions. In his words: "It is in securing the conformity of his will to his second-order volitions, then, that a person exercises his freedom of the will."[14]

A related view is argued by Taylor, who claims that the capacity for second-order thoughts is basic to our notion of personal moral

12. Frankfurt, "Freedom of the Will and the Concept of a Person," pp. 8ff.

13. See, for example, Vincent C. Punzo, "The Normative Function of Reason as Reflectivity: An Alternative to Hare's Prescriptivism," *Review of Metaphysics* 33 (1980): 593–614.

14. Frankfurt, "Freedom of the Will and the Concept of a Person," p. 15.

responsibility.[15] The implication, then, is that this capacity is at least part of what *qualitatively* distinguishes one human self from another; the possession of a free will, and the ability to engage in what Taylor calls "strong evaluation"—"where desires are classified in such categories as higher or lower, virtuous or vicious, more or less fulfilling"—suggests that the differences between persons are often deeply moral, hence by no means secondary or inessential. To call one person evil and another saintly is to differentiate them in a way that does not apply to bees in a hive.

This kind of second-order thinking seems to be in part what Hegel means when he says that the Subject exists "for itself." He writes of the "reflection of the will into itself" (105), of the "single individual aware of itself" (106), in virtue of which "the subjective will determines itself as objective too" (106) and thus becomes "aware of its [own] freedom" (107, 110). Kant says something similar in the *Foundations of the Metaphysics of Morals*: "But here [in morality] it is a question of objectively practical laws and thus of the *relation of a will to itself* so far as it determines itself only by reason" (emphasis added).[16] This latter should not surprise us since, as we have seen in chapter 4, Hegel explicitly understands the Subject to be, as it were, Kantian man. In any case, the notion of consciousness having itself as an object, or of the rational will reflecting upon itself, appears to presume the existence of creatures having the capacity to form second-order thoughts.

The above arguments strongly suggest, then, that the concept of the self as Subject is well suited to distinguishing human selves from nonhumans and from one another. It suggests further that earlier notions regarding the "individuality of the individual," as manifest for example in the perspective of Abstract Right, will likely provide an unsatisfying basis from which to treat the problem of individual and society. However, Hegel is still not completely satisfied. For reasons that can only be touched on here, he finds it necessary to go beyond the Subject to what he calls the Concrete Person of Ethical Life. In the Concrete Person we discover the

15. Charles Taylor, "Responsibility for Self," in Amelie Oksenberg Rorty, ed., *The Identities of Persons* (Berkeley: University of California Press, 1976).

16. Immanuel Kant, *Foundations of the Metaphysics of Morals* (Indianapolis: Bobbs-Merrill, 1976), p. 45.

concept of the self in its full articulation. The Concrete Person differs from the Subject in that his selfhood is deeply shaped and determined by the social, institutional, and ultimately cosmological contexts in which he finds himself. We might say that the Concrete Person is *situated*. Unlike the Subject of Morality, who is conceived as being radically unfettered and self-defining, the Concrete Person actualizes himself only by accommodating himself to, and being integrated with, the inescapable facts of the world about him. It is in this kind of integration that one finds genuine human freedom. Exactly what being so situated entails is a complex matter that will be treated in the next chapter.[17] Suffice it to say for now that Hegel envisions the concept of the self to include the *Lebenswelt* of which the particular individual is a part.

The theory of marriage stands as the first phase in the development of Ethical Life. Thus, with reference to Hegel's concept of the self, two conclusions emerge: (1) marriage is the initial step in the process by which the self becomes "situated"; and (2) marriage therefore presupposes the concept of the self as embodied in the Subject. At this point, we should now be able to see the full significance of the fact that the theory of marriage appears so late in the overall plan of the philosophy of Right. The family seems to us the most primitive and basic of social organizations, as Hegel surely knew, and it may strike us as odd that it should be included only after the treatment of topics such as property, contract, crime and punishment, the categorical imperative, and the like. But, in fact, Hegel's point is that the full concept of the family presupposes the (nearly) full development of the self; and thus, the family, though historically and sociologically prior, is—when fully actualized—a very advanced kind of social institution.

But on what, then, is the theory of marriage based? In my judgment, it is best understood as a logical derivation from the concept of the self. That is, marriage must be seen as the rationally necessary form of conjugal relations between individuals whose selves are those of Subjects beginning to emerge as Concrete Persons.

17. See Kenneth L. Schmitz, "Embodiment and Situation: Charles Taylor's Hegel," *Journal of Philosophy* 73 (1976): 710–23.

2

We may summarize the argument thus far by saying that the self has essentially three characteristics. First, the self is rational, by which is meant not means-to-end rationality (presumably Abstract Persons and nonhuman animals have that) but, rather, the kind of reflective rationality attributable only to self-conscious human beings. Second, the self has a will that is presumed to be free in the sense of being self-determining. Finally, and as a result, the self is to be regarded as a moral entity having the capacity to act in terms of rational and self-legislated principles. In what follows, I hope to show that the major features of marriage as Hegel understands it—viz., love, sexuality, the marriage contract, and the marriage ceremony—can be understood and justified precisely in the light of these premises.

1. For Hegel, marriage is above all a relationship of love. Exactly what he means by this is not immediately clear. Love is variously described as "a feeling," "the consciousness of [one's] unity with another," "ethical life in the form of something natural," and "the most tremendous contradiction" (158, 158 *Zusatz*). One writer, Joan Landes, has interpreted such passages to indicate the essentially "sentimental" nature of the Hegelian concept of marriage, but this does not seem to explain Hegel's formulations very well.[18]

The key to understanding these formulations is to focus on the central distinction between what we may call love-as-feeling and what Hegel calls "ethico-legal love" (*rechtlich sittliche Liebe*—161 *Zusatz*). His account here is sketchy but, I believe, easily enough reconstructed. Love-as-feeling is simply a matter of taste and inclination, of purely subjective caprice. As such, it involves the peculiar and transient kind of attitude that we associate with infatuation. It is acute and overpowering but also somehow mystical and inexplicable; trying to explain it would be like trying to account for one's taste in food or clothes. Love-as-feeling thus lacks any rhyme or reason, and the romantics among us will count this in its favor. But Hegel does not. For a clear consequence is that any marriage based on such feelings must be purely accidental,

18. Joan B. Landes, "Hegel's Conception of the Family," *Polity* 14 (1981): 5–28.

grounded not on an explicit rational principle, but on a purely fortuitous coincidence of inclinations which may or may not endure.

I do not think it is infatuation per se that concerns Hegel; I see nothing in his thought that would rule it out, or even relations based upon it, given their proper time and place. But marriage based on love-as-feeling, on infatuation, is a perversion, for Hegel emphasizes that the implications of marriage go well beyond the satisfaction of subjective preferences. Among other things, marriage involves the division of domestic labor in society (165–71), the breeding and rearing of children (173), the ultimate responsibility for education (174–75), and the fate of private property as determined by inheritance (179, 180, *EG* 520). All of these are functions of social and ethical consequence; they directly affect not merely the original two parties, but many others besides. Hence, they should be rooted in some kind of rationally defensible decision. That is, in view of their moral implications, we would sensibly demand that they be undertaken in a manner that can be known, evaluated, and justified in terms other than the satisfaction of the particular and transitory desires of two individuals. It is for this reason that society explicitly confers on married people the peculiar right and responsibility to perform such functions; but to marry out of mere inclination, out of love-as-feeling, is to claim that right and responsibility without offering any rational justification. If society asks such a pair of individuals why their union should earn them the right to raise children, manage family capital, etc., their only response could be something like "Well, we feel like it."

Marriage should thus be based on ethico-legal love. In ethico-legal love, "the decision to marry comes first and the inclination to do so follows" (162). There is, then, feeling and sentiment in marriage—"in the actual wedding both decision and inclination coalesce"—but this comes only after the fact. For Hegel, one does not "fall" in love; rather, one rationally decides to love. Presumably, this means deciding to respect and honor the other person, to value his or her opinions and abilities, to bestow affection, to offer comfort in times of need, and the like. An implication here is that only ethico-legal love is free; when one "falls" one is not free (young Werther would seem to be a fine case). A second implication is that the decision to marry is based not on some whim, but rather on the judgment that this union is well suited to performing social and ethical functions such as rearing children, managing family capital, etc. Presumably, judgments of this sort can be closely considered, debated, challenged, even refuted; such is not the case with mere inclination (162 *Rand.*).

We may think that Hegel is being too strict here, that the inclination to marry might actually precede any rational judgment, and that this would be acceptable provided such a judgment actually comes to pass. This is probably correct, but it can hardly stand as a model for what Hegel intends. In his view, reasoned choice must be, so to speak, sovereign; rather than providing a post hoc test of our feelings, it should instead give rise to them. Our inclinations should develop out of a knowledge of what is right, rather than of their own accord; in this way, they may be thought of as "spiritual" through and through. Thus, the marriage that starts in passion and only later obtains rational justification would seem to be, for Hegel, the exception rather than the rule.

It would appear that ethico-legal love nicely describes the kinds of relationships we would attribute to fully developed selves, Subjects-becoming-Concrete Persons. Such selves are self-conscious and rational, are aware of their capacity for free choice, and thus are able to act in terms of self-legislated moral principles. To base marriage on love-as-feeling would be to deny virtually all of these traits. For rather than being rational, principled, and free, marriage would become capricious, accidental, and ultimately slavish.

2. Hegel approaches the sensual aspect of marriage in similar terms. Of course, he emphasizes time and again his view that marriage is not fundamentally a physical relationship, and that sensual pleasure—a fleeting and contingent thing—of itself lacks any genuine ethical content (161, 163, 163 *Zusatz*). Yet he also insists that marriage "contains first, the moment of physical life" and that it must play a central role in the propagation of the species (161, 162 *Rand*).

It seems plain enough that relations between Subjects cannot be purely or even predominantly sensual. For if they were, then there would be no difference between Subjects and animals or Abstract Persons. Stated positively, Hegel argues that relations between Subjects are fundamentally spiritual (*geistig*) rather than sensual, meaning again that they are based on a capacity for reflective reason which is peculiar to Subjects and Concrete Persons. However, whereas Subjects are different from Abstract Persons in the various respects outlined above, they nonetheless do retain the basic traits of Abstract Persons, albeit in altered form. The notion of Abstract Person has been "annulled, yet preserved"; we no longer think of humans as Abstract Persons, yet humans are still characterized in part—though only in part—by the traits of Abstract Persons. The fact that Subjects are rational, self-conscious, and free does not mean that they cease to have desires, needs, and impulses. Subjects do have bodies, there is an animal side to their nature; and thus, they cannot be simply indifferent to sexual pleasure.

The Subjects of marriage therefore are not purely ascetic; they do enjoy physical gratification. But this enjoyment is entirely ruled by reason. The following is the key passage:

> Marriage's specific ethical character . . . consists in this, that the consciousness of the parties is gathered out of its physical and subjective mode and brought to the thought of that which is substantive; and instead of continually reserving to marriage the capriciousness and arbitrariness of sensuous desire, it takes the union out of this arbitrariness. . . . It subordinates the sensuous moment as something conditioned by the true and ethical character of the relationship and by the recognition of the union as an ethical one. [164]

The sensual thus thrives in marriage, but only as it is "spiritualized" by the rational will of the Subject. Indeed, the above passage suggests not merely that physical desire is tamed and channeled by reason, but in fact that reason comes to determine what is and is not desirable. In this way, "the sensuous moment, the one proper to physical life, is put into its ethical place as something only consequential and accidental" (164). The fact that marriage is spiritual rather than sensual does not imply that the sensual is abjured altogether, but only that it operates strictly under the rule of reason.

3. To view marriage as a contract is, for Hegel, an "infamy" (*Schändlichkeit*) (75). In large part, this is because contract "arises from the arbitrary will" rather than the rational will, hence is rooted entirely in impulse and inclination (75; also 15–17). Further,

the union established by contract is only "posited by the parties," i.e., it is something external, artificial, and temporary; for Hegel, marriage is a much more substantial tie. Finally, the object about which a contract is made can only be "a single external thing," i.e., a piece of property rather than an entire mode of existence. Thus, conjugal relations between Subjects cannot be predominantly contractual; they must be principled rather than arbitrary, substantial rather than superficial, ethical rather than material.

It is at this point that we can begin to sketch some of the specific dialectical work that marriage accomplishes. In contract, the agreement entered into creates a new will, a "common will," based on the conjuncture of the particular wills of the parties involved. The contract is thus expressive of a unity of two different wills regarding the contracted items, a unity which is distinct from its constituent wills, hence may itself be regarded as a different, artificial will (73–74). I may wish to buy a particular item and you may wish to sell it to me; but only in a contract—tacit or otherwise—can we embody and observe our joint intention to carry out the exchange.

But for Hegel, the creation of this new will leaves the original wills largely untouched. In part, this is what he means when he calls contractual relations "external." This new artificial will, embodied in the contract, is essentially a sum of the particular wills (so to speak), an aggregation of them in which their basic character is unaltered. This is shown by the fact that contracts can be successfully completed without either one of the parties changing significantly his mode of acting in the world.

Let us consider this more closely. A contract between two parties can be regarded as a simple convenience in virtue of which each individual uses some feature of the other in order to obtain something he wants. The contract per se, then, has no particular moral content; it is merely an expedient. The parties can enter into such an arrangement solely out of some particular desire or interest and out of the simple observation that a contractual arrangement offers a useful way of satisfying that desire or interest. There need be no additional sense of obligation in this, no element of responsibility or duty. The parties, that is, can successfully complete the contract without ceasing to be Abstract Persons, i.e., creatures of desire, need, and impulse. They can emerge from the contract largely unimproved. The fact that contract is frequently discussed in terms of some higher moral principles, i.e., by Kant and ultimately by Hegel himself (79), only means that something besides contract has been added to the analysis, presumably an understanding of the human self that goes beyond the Abstract Person.

Thus, contract, as a fortuitous and contingent relationship, need produce no special awareness in the individual regarding his own will or its interrelationship to the other's will. To be sure, contract does contribute materially to the (self-)unfolding of Right. In particular, the individual does come to see himself as a property owner, and to recognize this quality in the other person (71). But this fact does not directly affect the nature of his will. The individual in contract does not cease to be an Abstract Person (81); hence, contract does not directly elevate the parties involved.

Marriage also seems to create a new will: "The identification of personalities, whereby the family becomes one person . . . , is the ethical mind" (163). The process here is very different, however; for in marriage the individual wills themselves must come to recognize the exact nature of the union they have formed. Consider passages such as the following: "In a family, one's frame of mind is to have self-consciousness of one's individuality within this unity as the absolute essence of oneself" (158); "love means in general terms the consciousness of my unity with another" (158 *Zusatz*); "in self-consciousness the natural sexual union . . . is changed into a union on the level of mind, into self-conscious love" (161); "the ethical aspect of marriage consists in the parties' consciousness of this unity as their substantive aim" (163); "[in marriage] the consciousness of the parties is crystallized out of its physical and subjective mode and lifted to the thought of what is substantive" (164; see also 170 *Rand*).

It is clear from such passages that marriage is bound up with significant changes in the consciousness of the individual. Marriage requires that each individual become aware of the interdependence implicit in marriage and of the kind of will necessary to make such interdependence work. Further, the individual naturally begins to think of his own will in this light. The marriage stands before him, as it were, a symbol and embodiment of his own capacity to unite with another. In this way, he comes to see that he is no longer independent and alone, but has become, instead, a self-conscious "member" of a larger entity (158). He sees finally that the marriage bond cannot subsist unless it is composed of individuals who have mutually willed to join with one another, and who have done so on rational grounds; and he sees that his own participation in marriage—and that of his partner as well—thus requires such an act of will, one that must be based on an explicit, justifiable, and binding principle of reason. Through this process of recognition, the individual will changes, is elevated, and comes to see its mutual dependence on another.

Of course, it is perfectly possible to think of this not happening, to think of individuals "getting married" without acquiring the kind of self-consciousness just described. But this would simply not be marriage as Hegel understands it, i.e., a rational, principled, and free partnership based on "ethico-legal love." Again, we can certainly conceive of conjugal relations being contractual; but we should also be able to see now that conjugal relations based on marriage are conceptually different and seem much better suited to describing the kinds of relationships we would ascribe to Subjects-becoming-Concrete Persons.

4. At this point, Hegel's insistence on the marriage ceremony should be easier to understand. As a rational endeavor, marriage must be based on an explicit principle of one kind or another; that is, the decision to marry demands a reasoned justification. But since marriage is also a reciprocal endeavor, and further has ethical implications for the larger society, it demands a justification that is not simply reasoned but also public, i.e., subject to refutation. We may say, only somewhat metaphorically, that the decision to enter conjugal life requires an argument of the following form: "We—man and woman—believe that our union is rational, and is such that our right to raise and educate children and to own and dispose of an estate ought to be recognized by society; and we believe this for the following reasons . . . ". Clearly then, there must be some forum in which such an argument is made, and that forum is quite simply the marriage ceremony.

We must assume that Hegel would be largely indifferent to the particular features of the ceremony, provided that it were based primarily on reason. The following passage is central: "Marriage is made ethical only through the ceremony which is the achievement of the substantive through signs, i.e., language as the most mental embodiment of mind (*das geistigste Dasein des Geistigen*)"

(164). It is the use of words, written or spoken, that ensures that the decision to marry is formulated as an argument which can be evaluated in terms of rational criteria. These words may be of various kinds, but without them the rationality of the conjugal bond can only be implicit rather than "actual" (*wirklich*— 164).

3

Prior to marriage, two individuals—one male and one female— confront each other as independent and unconnected creatures. Each has his or her own peculiar and distinctive set of desires, needs, impulses and (qua Subject) moral sensibilities; these will likely conflict at some points with those of the other individual. At the very least, there is no good reason to believe that there will not be conflict, the absence of which would be purely fortuitous. In the face of such conflict, then, the following question arises: how can these individuals enter into a relationship without compromising their particular desires, needs, impulses, and sensibilities, i.e., those things that mark their individuality?

A number of possibilities present themselves. The relationship can be fleeting and superficial, satisfying mutual impulses and simply circumventing conflicting ones; but as we have seen, such a relationship would be no different from relationships entered into by lower creatures. Alternatively, the relationship might be asymmetrical, with one individual forced to sacrifice his desires, needs, impulses, and sensibilities to those of the other, a kind of updated version of the master/slave dialectic; conflict is suppressed, but again neither individual emerges fully as a Concrete Person. Finally, some third party—custom, opinion, the law—may force both individuals to give up what they would otherwise freely choose and submit to a conjugal life; once more, though, the very unfreedom of such an arrangement disqualifies it as a mode of ethical existence. In the first case, neither individual accepts any limitation, but their union is not a real union in any substantial sense. In the second and third cases, a lasting union of sorts is effectuated, but only by depriving one or both parties of the capacity for full human selfhood.

In marriage as Hegel sees it, these various contradictions are *aufgehoben*, i.e., they are sublated or annulled while their constituent elements are at the same time preserved and elevated. That is, each party retains his distinctiveness and identity, yet the union between them is substantial and enduring. The mechanism by which this occurs—and this is the crucial point for Hegel's larger, perfectionist project—is that each of the parties becomes aware, or is conceived of as being aware, of the nature of marriage—i.e., aware of the sheer possibility of a union that is deep and yet fully responsive to the requirements of individuality. Specifically, each party comes to understand the meaning of genuine love, to see the futility of love-as-feeling, and to realize further that his very selfhood depends upon making a rational, ethical commitment to another, an act of free self-limitation. This realization thus involves a change in the consciousness of the individual; by reflecting intelligently on his own nature and on the possibilities of conjugal life, he—as the vehicle of *Geist*—has moved to a higher stage of development. He has become more purely "spiritual"; to put it more conventionally, but no less accurately, he has become more rational. Nothing very mysterious is intended here; the individual has simply learned something important about himself, and this is a kind of learning which most of us will find very familiar. But without this process of consciousness-raising, of ethical enlightenment, it is hard to see how marriage in Hegel's sense could occur.

The direct implications here are twofold. First, by virtue of this process of enlightenment, the conjugal bond is perfected. It is now based on love and on a rational principle, and it is therefore both strong and well justified. But second, by virtue of this same process, the individual is uplifted and has moved that much closer to the ideal of the Concrete Person. He has become conscious of the fact that his subjectivity must be freely situated in a relationship with another, and in this consciousness he finds his fulfillment and indeed, in Hegel's word, his "liberation" (*Befreiung*—162). Thus, the two basic elements in the equation—on the one hand, the relationship, on the other, the individual—are jointly perfected. Ethical life depends upon the spiritual growth of the individual, which itself depends upon the actualization of ethical life. In this sense, then, the theory of marriage exemplifies, and contributes substantially to, the perfectionist goals of the philosophy of Right. Indeed, I would offer here the perhaps radical hypothesis that the theory of marriage, more than any other single passage in Hegel, provides a key to understanding the entire philosophy of Right. As we have seen in chapter 2, much of Hegelian philosophy involves the analysis of some "third" concept on the basis of which an apparent contradiction between two prior concepts can be overcome. Such an analysis proceeds in part by treating the two prior concepts in their necessary "concrete" connections with one another, thereby deepening and elaborating our understanding of each. Presumably, those connections come to light precisely in the analysis of the third concept. Thus, by pursuing that concept, the first two, though retaining certain aspects of their original distinctive character, themselves come to be transformed and enriched so that the contradiction between them dissolves and the part of the world they are meant to describe can emerge with newfound clarity.

With respect to marriage, we encounter an apparent contradiction between the spouse qua individual and connubial relations qua social institution. This contradiction dissolves through an analysis of a "third" concept—marriage, properly understood—an analysis which forces, and is also responsive to, a new, deeper understanding of the two constituent concepts, individuality and social institution. Specifically, the apparent contradiction is shown to rest entirely on a shallow understanding of those two basic entities. We originally thought of individuality with respect only to Abstract Persons, and we thought of connubial relations in either contractual or romantic terms. Given such understandings, the problem of the dissatisfied spouse—the problem of Emma Bovary—does indeed appear to involve a hopeless, tragic contradiction. Abstract Persons involved in a contractual or romantic marriage will, in not unusual circumstances, be forced either to sacrifice their individuality or to compromise the social function of marriage.

But in pursuing the concept of marriage, Hegel shows that individuality properly understood pertains not to Abstract Persons but to Subjects-becoming-Concrete Persons, i.e., individuals who have the kind of reflective rationality attributable only to free, self-conscious, self-legislating beings. The concept of individuality is thus thought to be substantially deepened and enriched. Similarly, marriage as a social institution comes to be seen not in contractual or romantic terms but as a relationship of ethico-legal love based upon and entirely responsive to the demands of reason. A marriage properly arises not out of convenience or inclination but because something about it makes rational sense, and demonstrably so. With the constituent elements thus refined and elevated, the problem of individuality and society—with respect to marriage, at least—simply disappears. The individuality of the rational Subject-becoming-Concrete Person is in fact fulfilled and perfected precisely in virtue of his membership in and self-conscious commitment to a relationship or institution which is itself rooted in rational, clearly justified ethical claims.

It is in the theory of marriage, then, that we can come truly to appreciate for the first time the fundamental intersection of substantive and methodological materials as outlined in part 1 of this book. In chapter 2, we encountered certain features of the dialectical method whereby an apparent contradiction between two concepts is overcome by the introduction and analysis of a third. In chapter 1, we outlined a particular, historically important problem concerning individuality and society and described a strategy—labeled strategy (C) or perfectionism—for dealing with that problem, whereby the constituent concepts are enriched so as to demonstrate their mutual compatibility and dependence. Hegel's theory of marriage is a precise embodiment of these two themes. In this theory, warring concepts are enriched, the dialectical opposition between them is dissolved, and the result is the apprehension of an institution in which the claims of individuality and those of society are jointly perfected.

This is the pattern of the entire philosophy of Right. Indeed, in the theory of marriage we find all of the basic methodological and thematic resources of Hegelian political thought—the Concrete Person, social institutions as structures of freedom and rationality, the dialectic as a deductive enterprise aimed at conceptual elaboration and enrichment. The remainder of the philosophy of Right is, then, simply a matter of further developing these materials and applying them not just to the isolated practice of marriage but to the complete structure of social institutions, including and especially the rational state.

4

Before turning to the rational state, two final issues merit our brief attention, the first concerning the necessity of marriage, the second, the role of women.

This chapter has sought to present and defend Hegel's concept of marriage. It has also sought to demonstrate the role played by marriage in the unfolding of *Geist* as manifested in individual consciousness. None of this, however, proves that marriage itself is a *necessary* stage in Hegel's dialectic. To describe the role played by marriage is not to show that something other than marriage— say friendship—could not play this role equally well. We thus face the following question: why is *marriage* the institution that begins the transition from Subject to Concrete Person?

As far as I can tell, Hegel does not offer an explicit answer. However, we can briefly and plausibly reconstruct one, based on premises that are at least partly suppressed in Hegel's work. One such premise is that humans possess a natural urge to procreate, to perpetuate themselves in their offspring, thereby contributing to the survival of the species. Another is that humans also possess an innate sense of sociability and a need to share life's experiences with another person. A third is that much of the moral education of children necessarily occurs in the family and that parents therefore must play a crucial role in ethical life.[19] Of course, we can all think of countless apparent exceptions to these premises—celibates, confirmed bachelors, homosexuals, and the like. Such exceptions, however, do not prevent us from accepting the premises as largely plausible. Taken together, they suggest the necessity of conjugal relations which, as shown above, must take the form described by Hegel.

Still, it seems that all of these premises would be consistent with relationships that might be very different from Hegelian marriage. For example, we can imagine certain communal living arrangements that would satisfy procreative and other social urges, provide children with sound moral instruction, and be based upon the free and rational decision to join with others in a self-limiting union based on ethico-legal love. It is clear that Hegel would not approve of such arrangements (167), but I cannot see the strength of his argument against them. I would suggest, then, that Hegel has provided a plausible account of marriage, has shown further that *something like* marriage is necessary to the unfolding of Objective Spirit, but has failed to prove that *only* marriage can do the job.

19. The first and second of these premises are more evident in the last section of Hegel's *Encyclopedia*, the *Philosophy of Spirit*.

I believe that he has also failed to provide a consistent and persuasive account of the role of women in marriage. His analysis in this regard is notorious, and deservedly so. Among numerous assertions about women that may strike many of us as pejorative, most famous is Hegel's refusal to accord them full participation in the rationality of *Geist*:

> Women are capable of education, but they are not made for activities which demand a universal faculty such as the more advanced sciences, philosophy, and certain forms of artistic production. Women . . . cannot attain the ideal . . . . [W]omen regulate their actions not by the demands of universality but by arbitrary inclinations and opinions. Women are educated—who knows how?—as it were by breathing in ideas . . . . The status of manhood, on the other hand, is attained only by the stress of thought and much technical exertion. [166 *Zusatz*]

By thus far overlooking this aspect of Hegel's account, I have implicitly taken the position that it plays no central role in the theory of marriage, and that the latter is fully coherent without the former. But, more strongly, I would suggest that the two—the theory of gender and the theory of marriage—are in fact flatly contradictory. For, if my earlier account is correct, then the success of marriage depends upon the full and mutual spiritualization—i.e., rationalization—of the parties; both must attain to the kind of reflective enlightenment required of Concrete Persons. But the theory of gender would make this simply impossible, since, according to Hegel, women could never achieve such rationality. Thus, either way we must scrap one or the other of Hegel's arguments, or else there is a way of reconciling the two that I have been unable to discover.

In any case, we should note finally that Hegel frequently, if paradoxically, demands that each party, male and female, enter the marriage bond out of a free, rational, and principled choice, and that—against Landes's apparent interpretation[20]—he seems to regard marriage as an ethical duty for both sexes (162).

Marriage, then, describes conjugal relations appropriate to Subjects-becoming-Concrete Persons and also provides an important analysis of how this "becoming" might in principle occur. Still, from the viewpoint of Right, marriage remains quite preliminary. For the nuclear family itself is an evanescent thing, coming apart

20. Landes, "Hegel's Conception of the Family," p. 22.

as the children grow up and move out into civil society; further, the marriage relationship retains an unsatisfying element of particularity insofar as it excludes very real interdependencies of a much more inclusive nature. It is, therefore, only with the rational state, with the complete development of the ethical community, that we can come to comprehend fully the concept of the Concrete Person.

6

The Constitution
of the Rational State

The philosophy of Right culminates in a description of the rational state. In a sense, it is only natural that this should be the case. Hegel's political thought is aimed at deducing, from specific premises pertaining to the human will, certain conclusions regarding the concept of Right; and Right itself is understood to include the sum total of our morally implicated practices and institutions, properly conceived. Ultimately, then, the concept of Right pertains to our ways of living with one another insofar as they raise issues of a moral nature; and these ways are, in turn, subject to and perhaps reflective of the determinations of political society. As we have seen, Hegel's arguments lead him to identify Ethical Life as that way of living on the basis of which the problem of individual and society is to be resolved. In describing a rational state, then, his task is to show just what Ethical Life is, considered from the perspective of its broadest and most inclusive aspect, i.e., the political.

The importance for Hegel of politics is based on certain conceptual claims which, unfortunately, can only be asserted here as premises. Briefly, according to these premises political society is, by definition, that realm of human interaction which governs all others; it is "sovereign," it reserves to itself, so to speak, the right to regulate the remaining varieties of human interaction and, in principle, its reach can be as extensive as practicality allows. Wherever humans live together there is likely to be some such ultimate practice, in terms of which particular forms of social life are, according to the fashion, either actively regulated or generously allowed to operate without overt interference, and where the decision actively to regulate or not is itself subject to review and revision. This practice—however formulated and instituted—is the practice of politics conceived in the broadest possible terms and, as such, is the defining characteristic of political society. It follows, then, that all of our ways of living together are, at least in theory, subject to the claims and judgments of politics.

Indeed, if a particular political society is, for some historical or theoretical reason, explicitly denied (or if it denies to itself) the opportunity actively to regulate a certain sphere of human inter-action—as, for example, through constitutional protections of in-dividual rights—this says only that the society has chosen to legislate that sphere by leaving it alone. To adopt, say, an absolute right of free speech is to "regulate" speech—to determine, in ef-fect, its potential range and content—by declaring that all speech will be allowed. Thus, the relationship of political society to the rest of social life as one of regulation, either intrusive or permissive, is by definition necessary and unavoidable. Of course, it may be that some aspects of social life are difficult or even impossible to control reliably. This only asserts a practical limitation, however; it in no way denies the fact that the purpose of political society is to determine, either through active interference or through benign neglect, the ways in which we live together.

But all of this pertains to the concept of "political society," whereas the term Hegel uses, the "state," has narrower conno-tations.[1] In brief, the state typically refers to a particular form of political society characterized, among other things, by the presence of institutions having the authority to coerce. The concept of po-litical society certainly allows for the possibility of legitimate coer-cion, but it does not seem to require it. That is, we can imagine forms of political society regulative of our ways of living together which are nonetheless based on a rejection of coercion and which

1. For an account, see Z. A. Pelczynski, "Political Community and Individual Freedom in Hegel's Philosophy of State," in Z. A. Pelczynski, ed., *The State and Civil Society: Studies in Hegel's Political Philosophy* (Cambridge: Cambridge Uni-versity Press, 1984), pp. 55ff. Although sketchy, Pelczynski's essay provides an interpretation that is similar in many respects to the present account. His views are now much closer to my own than they were in 1971. Still, he continues to resist the appeal of Hegel's philosophical method, for example, at p. 63; as a result, I believe that he cannot account for the most distinctive features of Hegel's political thought.

embrace, for example, decision making only through perpetual unanimous consent. Thus, to say at the outset that the concept of Right necessarily culminates in a "state" is, perhaps, to prejudge the issue. It is by no means clear that Hegel has done this. But we must be careful not to assume that the state is the proper form of political society, and we must be alert to the possibility that Hegel may indeed have made this assumption.

Of course, Hegel's focus on the state is understandable in the light of history. Indeed, it may be that, just as Hegel saw Plato's greatness in his ability to sum up the experience of the Greek polis, so too he saw his own task as the summing up of the experience of the modern nation state. Philosophy comes on the scene too late to do anything but record and comprehend that which had already occurred; to have written about something other than the nation state would, perhaps, have been to engage in a kind of crystal-ball gazing which, for Hegel, had nothing to do with philosophy. Still, the fact that the nation state was in some sense the dominant form of political society in the early nineteenth-century does not seem to be philosophically decisive; for it may have been that the materials were already available to construct a different, perhaps preferable form of political society and that the failure to do so was simply a matter of historical accident.

In this respect, Hegel describes his own task with customary, if sometimes underappreciated, clarity:

> But if we ask now about the *historical* origin of the state in general; or still more if we ask what the laws and regulations [*Bestimmungen*] of a particular state are or have been; or if that state originally arose out of patriarchal circumstances, out of fear or trust, out of corporations, and the like; or if its laws are consciously conceived and established in terms of positive divine right, or contract, custom, etc.—all these questions are no concern of the Idea of the state. Rather, we are here dealing exclusively with scientific knowledge, and from that point of view all these things are mere appearances and therefore matters for history. So far as the authority of any existing state has anything to do with reasons, these reasons are culled from the forms of the law taken to be valid within it. [258]

By this time, we should be quite familiar with passages such as these and understand that Hegel's project is a matter not of empirical description but of conceptual analysis. The concept to be analyzed, however, is ultimately the concept of Right, and our question concerns the particular nature of political society within, or according to, that concept. Whether this society will prove to be akin to what we normally call the state remains to be seen; but the issue is absolutely crucial for an understanding and evaluation of Hegel's political thought. It may be, for example, that Hegel has correctly deduced the nature of the state, yet has failed to describe the true nature of political society as prescribed and required by the concept of Right.

Ultimately, our task is twofold. First, we must inquire to what extent Hegel's deduction of the state as the conceptually correct form of political society is based on, and follows soundly from, premises available to him. Second, we must also ask to what extent those premises might be historically particular in the sense that we today could not adopt them without significant emendation. In effect, then, we shall be addressing the following kinds of questions: To what extent did Hegel correctly deduce the concept of the state? Does that concept complete, or contribute to, the deduction of the concept of Right as Hegel himself required? Are Hegel's successes and failures, such as they might be, related to conceptual materials that continue to be authoritative for the modern, indeed contemporary, mind? In short, does the rational state succeed in terms of criteria set forth and adopted by Hegel himself?

There is, it should be noted at the outset, a certain peculiarity in Hegel's picture of the state. On the one hand, and as mentioned in chapter 1 above, this picture appears to represent a fairly standard modern, liberal conception of political society. Specifically, the state described by Hegel seems far closer to the emergent practice of politics in modern times than would those images provided by the other great political writers of the tradition, say, the *kallipolis* of Plato, Aristotle's mixed regime, Rousseau's General Will, or even—arguably— Hobbes's Leviathan. While Hegel's rational state certainly describes no political society existing in his day, many if not most of its features existed or were approximated in the Western world.

Thus, again, we encounter a constitutional monarchy featuring certain elements of representative government and characterized by an emphasis on written law; a separation of governmental power between legislative and administrative "branches"; a bicameral legislature representing different segments of society; a modern bureaucracy; official religious toleration and a separation of church and state; substantial provisions for free speech; a comparatively unregulated economy; and the like. Certainly in his account of the state Hegel could hardly be considered a radical democrat; but it is equally difficult to see how he could be identified with the extreme forces of the nineteenth-century reaction. Of course, in the German politics of his day, he himself was caught quite in the middle.

But this rather conventional, moderately liberal picture of political society seems not to sit very well with two other, equally characteristic elements of the rational state. First, Hegel presents his state explicitly in terms of an organicist model. The state is an organism, a single, integrated whole composed of elements or constituents whose role is, in a non-Hegelian way of speaking, functional. Thus, Hegel rejects any notion of the state as an aggregate or collection, much less as a device or an instrument; and in so doing he distances himself quite dramatically from the modern liberal tradition either in its Hobbesian or republican modes.

Second, it is not entirely clear to what extent the monarch in Hegel's state is really a "constitutional" monarch in any meaningful sense. To be sure, he is part of an elaborate and specified system of governmental institutions and therefore plays a role in a constitution. But Hegel's monarch appears not to operate under the usual constitutional limitations. He has no contractual obligations to which his actions must conform. He does not seem to be subject to the law; indeed, the law may be simply what he says it is. While Hegel's is, in some sense, a parliamentary system, the parliament does not appear to possess anything that can be familiarly called a "right" against the monarch. To be sure, it may be that the monarch ought to be constrained by that which Right—and reason itself—prescribe, but there is absolutely no suggestion that the monarch is a peculiarly rational, enlightened, or philosophical individual in the sense of Plato's philosopher-king. Thus, there is, at least at first glance, an absolutist element in Hegel's account of monarchy that appears to be at odds with, and perhaps to nullify, its more conventional, liberal elements.

This conflation of modern and seemingly premodern elements may not present a historical mystery. We find in much of romanticism, for example, an effort to recapture an older spirit of human integration and wholeness while retaining at least some of the achievements of an Enlightened culture. In this sense, though perhaps only in this sense, Hegel's political theory may be thought to be, if not quite typical, then at least familiar. But even if this is historically true, the philosophical problem remains. How can an organicist account of political society, a seemingly absolutist account of monarchy, and a rather conventional, liberal account of political institutions be mutually coherent? In answering this question, we shall examine these three features in turn, each considered in the light of the deduction and analysis of the concept of Right.

It will be useful, however, to preface this discussion by traversing some old ground in a new way, briefly considering once again Hegel's accounts of punishment, morality, and marriage explicitly in the light of one another and as comprising premises from which to derive a conception of political society.

1

As we have seen, the philosophy of Right pursues the apparent contradiction between individual and society and, in the concept of Right itself, seeks a truly comprehensive account of moral life properly understood. Such an account would have to show how the claims of the individual and those of society can both be fully satisfied. It must do this by developing conceptions of individuality and of social rules or patterns such that the full embodiment of one can be seen to depend upon the equally full embodiment of the other.

Thus, in the discussion of crime and punishment, we saw how Hegel sought to establish a basis for social order rooted in the rights of property-holders and in the rationality of persons. For Hegel, the individuality of the individual—that which makes him an individual and distinguishes him from other creatures, human and otherwise—is largely based on the freedom of the will. This is the fundamental premise of the philosophy of Right, a premise said to be itself derived from certain arguments of the *Phenomenology of Mind*. Insofar as Right describes the full embodiment of individuality, it must acknowledge and be responsive to this premise. It does so by deducing, from the freedom of the will, a human right to private property, and by deducing from this latter a theory of crime and punishment. Thus, in defining and marking criminal actions, one ratifies thereby certain essential and inescapable features of human individuality, including especially subjective freedom.

Further, the theory of crime and punishment also expresses the view that subjective freedom is a matter of rationality. It does so in part by claiming that the criminal legitimately can be held responsible for his crime. Hegel seeks to show that the free will is, in fact, a rational will; to be free, the will must be responsive to the rules of reason so that the individual acts not in terms of impulse and caprice but according to principles which are in some way demonstrable and which he has legislated to himself. Thus, the individuality of the individual, which is a matter of subjective freedom, is also a matter of rational action. Of course, the concept of Right must recognize and be responsive to this fact, and it does so by asserting and justifying the claim that punishment "honors" the criminal as a rational being. To punish is to affirm the rationality of the criminal which, in turn, is to define individuality in terms of reason. In this way, the practice of punishment institutionalizes the claims of the individual qua individual.

In the theory of crime and punishment, then, Right comes to include in an especially forceful way the individuality of the individual, understood in terms of freedom and reason. But clearly, at this juncture we also have the beginning of the process whereby the legitimate claims of society are asserted and defended. For with the notion of punishment, the concept of Right expresses further the idea of an ordered way of living together enforced by social institutions rather than by individuals. To be sure, in the section on Abstract Right these institutions are hardly even sketched. Nonetheless, it is quite evident that the subjective freedom of individuals is in some way bound up with rules or principles that govern interactions among persons, and that those rules and principles will be part of an entity which is distinct from particular individuals, either taken alone or in the aggregate. Of course, this entity will itself be dependent upon rational principles; for if this were not the case, its rules would lack any clear justification. But from this we must conclude that *both* subjective freedom and social authority are rooted in, and expressive of, reason. The individual qua individual must acknowledge the claims of reason when deciding (for example) whether or not to commit a crime; society must acknowledge those same claims when deciding whom to punish and how. In a rather primitive and unspecified manner, then, we have discovered at the outset a basis for dissolving the apparent contradiction between individual and society.

This general theme is pursued further in the critique of Kantian morality. As we saw, for Hegel the freedom of the will suggests that the individual is fundamentally a moral entity, i.e., a creature responsible for his actions. Thus, the individual is distinguished from other creatures, human and otherwise, not simply by virtue of his subjective freedom but also, and relatedly, by his moral personality. In this respect, Hegel's view comports with an old and established tradition of Western thought and, especially, with Kantian ethics. But in finding the categorical imperative to be merely formal, Hegel takes perhaps more seriously than Kant himself the idea that the free will must be a rational will. Specifically, Hegel views reason as capable of generating objectively correct conclusions. Whether *objective* here means "true from a God's-eye point of view" or simply humanly irrefutable may yet be unclear, but for present purposes the difference does not matter. For in either case, reason produces claims that must be assented to, and the individual—whose will is a rational will—must act in accordance with those claims. Thus, morality has, at least in principle, a definite content which can be discovered and proved.

But again, this true rational content is authoritative not simply for individual conduct but for institutional practice as well. In particular, the rules or laws of political society must conform to that which reason prescribes; if they fail to do so, they lose their justification. But this means further that the legitimate claims of the individual (ultimately based on the free will) and those of society (insofar as they can be justified) are derivable from a single source, human reason, which, in turn, is governed by the requirement of internal consistency. We may say, perhaps metaphorically, that reason generates a single, consistent set of judgments to which assent must be given; and further, that the principles of conduct appropriate to the individual and the rules and patterns appropriate to society, insofar as all are drawn from that set of rational judgments, must be mutually coherent. If we discover a contradiction between the claims of the individual and those of society, it can only be because we have made a philosophical error.

The discussions of Abstract Right and Morality thus establish some of the premises upon which the concept of Right is based. In the section on Ethical Life, this concept itself is elaborated in terms of a series of institutional recommendations. The accounts of the family, civil society, and the state are designed to show the specific social consequences of the earlier arguments. That is, given certain premises regarding individuality, society, and human reason, Hegel seeks to deduce in general terms the conceptually correct forms of our living together. These forms include intimate and private varieties of human interaction (the family), economic and "social" relations (civil society), and the established practices and institutions of political life (the state).

In our treatment of marriage, we saw how two distinct and autonomous individuals, each having a free will, come together on the basis of a joint rational decision to create a new entity having, so to speak, a will of its own. The constituent members of this entity continue to be distinct and free, yet they are now bound to and limited by their participation in the marriage. What makes this conjunction of freedom and bondage coherent is simply the fact that both sides of the equation—the individual free will and the corporate will of the family—are rooted in human reason. Each, that is, is governed by a single, internally consistent set of rational principles.

Moreover, in marriage persons come to *see* that their individuality and freedom are a matter of rationality; this insight is in itself a crucial step in attaining or, more accurately, fully embodying their individuality and freedom. They see, further, that reason requires conjugal relations in which the sensuous, natural element, though by no means extirpated, is nonetheless entirely at the service of the spiritual or rational element. In this way, marriage is the first step in which the premises of Abstract Right and Morality receive an institutional expression. Whereas those premises demonstrated human reason to be a common denominator on the basis of which the individual/social problem can be resolved, in marriage we begin to see how this might actually manifest itself in social life. Above all, marriage, properly understood, involves a "spiritual" change on the part of the individuals in question. It literally raises their consciousness, prompting them to see that in fulfilling the claims of reason they perfect, thereby, both the marriage relationship and also their own respective individuality.

Of course, in Hegel's formulation the family is philosophically succeeded by the institutions of civil society, including a "system of needs" understood in largely economic terms. It is widely held that Hegel's concept of civil society is essentially a description of the modern world as envisioned and prescribed by the theorists of classical liberalism and the bourgeois political economists. This is largely correct, though it requires certain emendations. Specifically, it must be understood that the creatures of civil society are not simply economic beings—isolated from one another, unencumbered by the sway of culture, and engaged in an unalloyed, self-interested quest for competitive advantage. Rather, civil society is composed of people who live in families and who have, in principle and to some extent in fact, the kinds of self-conscious ties and commitments described in chapter 4 above. Moreover, these individuals also find themselves embedded in any number of "corporate" entities—townships, guilds, and clubs, to mention but a few—which function as "second families" and to which the individual is attached in ways that involve far more than competitive advantage. Civil society is, thus, not simply a marketplace. It is a world rich with various kinds of normative and institutional social structures. Indeed, it is the modern Western world roughly as we know it, and as the liberal political economists knew it also, some of their more conventional interpreters notwithstanding.

Still, taken as a whole—viewed dimly from a distance, so to speak—civil society does look like a realm of fundamentally economic beings. For at this stage in the development of Right, the ties to family and corporation do not generally extend to society itself. The individual, upon entering the larger world outside of his various families—the world beyond his constitutive social connections—encounters others as strangers with whom he many be involved simply and solely as a matter of convenience or economic necessity. There is, in short, no self-conscious *substantive* relationship among such individuals. They are alien to one another, and are liable to look to each other simply with a view toward personal gain. As a result, the state itself—the public power—appears merely as an external instrumentality designed to order and regulate the practices of competition. From this perspective, the state is characteristically, in Hegel's term, the Police power.

It must be emphasized that civil society is not to be understood as a regression, a step back from the sublime unity of the family. Rather, in civil society the individual comes to see even more clearly than before the degree to which his freedom and individuality depend upon rational self-awareness. Specifically, he comes to see that in pursuing selfish ends, he finds himself necessarily enmeshed in "a system of complete interdependence wherein the livelihood, well-being, and legal status of one man is interwoven with the livelihood, well-being, and legal rights of all" (183). In confronting this web of relationships, the individual is finally aware that not only marriage but all forms of social life—all varieties of living together—need to be rationally justified. Just as our decision to marry must be based on ethico-legal love, so too must our other economic and social relations be structured in a way that accords with reason. But again, the establishment of a rational society would, in virtue of its very rationality, comport with and, indeed, nurture the claims of the individual, rooted as they are in the rationality of the individual's will.

This task, the formulation of social institutions on the basis of reason, is the task of political society. But political society itself needs to be rationally constructed, and it is with this effort that the philosophy of Right concludes. Given our discussion of philosophical method, we shall say that Hegel seeks to discover the concept of political society as it must be in the light of those concepts which precede it—concepts of will and individuality, of morality and social order, of family and civil society, and the like. These concepts, that is, provide the premises from which to deduce the concept of political society. Obviously, the premises are numerous; but we may nonetheless say that, at a minimum, the concept of political society should be responsive to the following considerations.

1. It should describe institutions which do indeed represent *the complete overcoming of the apparent contradiction between individual and society*. In the family, the contradiction is dissolved with respect to two individuals living a conjugal existence. But in civil society, the inadequacy of this resolution for public life is revealed,

as distinct and autonomous individuals are thrown together in that web of interdependence. With political society, then, we seek some conception whereby the unity of the family can be replicated in a more comprehensive fashion in such a way that the claims of the individual and those of society are jointly and definitively satisfied.

2. By implication, political society must also be *a realm of free action*. For insofar as it satisfies the claims of individuality, it must include the notion that individuals have free wills. But, further, the policies of any particular political society—its decisions and laws—must themselves be seen as issuing from some kind of subjective freedom. Political society cannot be a purely natural entity whose patterns are established through a kind of unthinking and instinctive necessity; rather, its unity must be seen to have a "spiritual"—i.e., rational and free—basis.

3. Finally, political society must in some sense be *sovereign*. As the ultimate manifestation of right, and the final determinant of our ways of living together, political society is by definition that source of rules and patterns above which there is no other. But this means that the claims of political society need to be legitimized explicitly in such terms. That is, its authority over the countless other institutions of social life—familial, economic, cultural, and the like—must be justified on the basis of some concept of sovereignty, so that its peculiar position in society can be clarified and defended.

Again, I believe that these requirements derive largely from the analysis of Right up to and including the discussion of civil society. They provide premises from which to deduce the concept of political society or, in Hegel's term, the concept of the state. Thus, the state must describe an entity that resolves the problem of individual and society, embodies the notion of free action, and can be understood and justified as sovereign. We turn now to a closer examination of political society in the light of these requirements and with respect to three basic themes of Hegelian political philosophy: the organic theory of the state, the necessity of the monarch, and the structural integrity of a modern, "inwardly differentiated" constitution.

2

In a most rudimentary sense, the state is simply a synonym for the dissolution of the tension between individual and society. As we have seen, the principle of the individual implies certain imperatives that often appear to contradict those implied by the principle of society. Deductively then, we seek a concept which is nothing other than the noncontradictory conjunction of such imperatives, and the state is that concept. Thus, the state may be described simply as "the mutual coherence of imperatives deriving from the principle of the individual and the principle of society, respectively."

But, of course, this does not tell us very much. Our task is to analyze the concept of the state in the light of this purely formal requirement, to determine in particular the kinds of practices and institutions it implies so that the apparent contradiction is indeed shown to be only apparent. Hegel proceeds in two ways. First, he examines one common account of the modern nation-state and seeks to show how it necessarily fails to meet these deductive requirements. Second, he presents what seems to be the only plausible alternative account and claims that it does indeed describe the necessary mutual coherence of imperatives we are seeking.

As to the first, then, he argues against what we may call the "external state." This theme is present throughout the political writings, as, for example, in the following passage: "If the state is confused with civil society, and if its specific end is laid down as the security and protection of property and personal freedom, then *the interest of the individuals as such* becomes the ultimate end of their association, and it follows that membership of the state is something optional. But the state's relation to the individual is quite different from this" (258; cf, 75, 100, and 260). Here and elsewhere, Hegel seems to be simply acknowledging a basic feature of what we have called accommodationism. According to the latter, the purpose of political society is to serve the independent interests of individuals whose connections with one another are purely contingent. Typically, it does so by establishing rules or patterns over against those individuals. As we have seen in chapter 1, although society's rules and patterns may ultimately be aimed at maximizing individual freedom or the satisfaction of personal interests, they still often imply imperatives that contradict possible and, indeed, quite plausible imperatives deriving from the principle of the individual. Thus, the state understood in this way is "external" to the individual. The relationship between state and individual is rather like the relationships among individuals, or groups, in civil society; each defines its interests and needs as being independent, apart from, and often in opposition to, those of the others, yet each finds itself caught up with them in a complete system of interdependence.

It is most evident that Hegel is rejecting here a conventional, liberal account of political society, and that the political philosophy of Hobbes—as well as the political practice of the nineteenth-century Anglo-Saxon world—would preeminently qualify. But indeed, Hegel would similarly reject virtually all varieties of modern social contract theory, including Rousseau's, in which the individual is treated fundamentally as an "individual in isolation" (258). As we have seen, the particular case of Rousseau is especially difficult, and it may be that Hegel's reading of the *Social Contract* is not quite right; nevertheless, the criticism of Rousseau, whether fair or unfair, reflects again the formal/dialectical requirements of the concept of the state as presented by Hegel.

But while we can see easily enough the sense in which accommodationism fails, it is also important to understand exactly why it fails. An important difficulty with accommodationist theories is that they take appearance for reality and confuse empirical observation with conceptual analysis; and this is an error which can lead not only to modern contractarianism but also to a might-is-right doctrine such as that of von Haller (see the footnote to 258). As should be clear by now, the issue here is not a matter of descriptive versus prescriptive theories of the state but, rather, one of conceptual integrity. Our concept of the state must be consistent with our prior concepts; and while it must also be consistent with empirical observation, this turns out to be not a very exacting standard. In general, empirical observation sets certain clear and important limits—trees cannot talk, the sun rises in the east, humans often disagree, and the like—within which an extremely large number of conceptions may be possible. Which of these conceptions is to be preferred is, again, a matter of conceptual analysis, i.e., examining the necessary implications of our other, presently uncontested concepts.

As regards the state, then, it seems that the problem pertains to the conception of the individual and that of society as they appear in most modern, liberal theories. Briefly, the accommodationist account of the individual (or, more accurately, of the individuality of the individual) fails to comport with certain key premises that Hegel regards as well established and, indeed, proven. One such premise is that the individual free will is not the "natural will," not the will of impulse and arbitrariness (see 14 and 15); the latter is in fact unfree and fails, moreover, to distinguish human action from, say, animal behavior.[2] Another premise is that individual rights and individual duties coalesce, and that each has for its content the principles and conclusions of human reason (see, for example, 261).

Similarly, the accommodationist account of society as a merely contingent or convenient concatenation or juxtaposition of individuals again belies certain well-founded premises. For one thing, it fails to see that the identity of individuals is strongly influenced by their (largely unavoidable) participation in a web of interrelationships, so that the latter is, in some substantial sense, constitutive of the former. Further, it ignores the fact that the spiritual life of individuals—the form and content of their consciousness, the truths they hold, the very language they speak—is, roughly in Wittgenstein's sense, bound up with their "forms of life." As a result, it overlooks the sense in which society, properly conceived, cannot be merely external to, and only protective of, the individuals that comprise it. Just as the logic of the Understanding overlooks the necessary interconnectedness of otherwise finite forms of thought, so the political theory of accommodation fails to see that society cannot be a mere aggregation of discrete atoms.[3]

As we have noted, the unfolding of the concept of Right from Abstract Right to Morality to Ethical Life is associated with a similar development in the concept of the individual from Abstract Person to Subject to Concrete Person. With this latter development, Hegel has attempted to supersede the accommodationist account of individuality. He has sought to show that our sense of what makes the person a truly human individual involves his embeddedness in a web of relationships with other persons, each of whom can think rationally and, thus, can have access to that

2. Patrick Riley, *Will and Political Legitimacy* (Cambridge, Mass.: Harvard University Press, 1983), pp. 33–37.

3. Charles Taylor, "Atomism," in Charles Taylor, *Philosophy and the Human Sciences: Philosophical Papers 2* (Cambridge: Cambridge University Press, 1985).

body of truths and principles which is the necessary content of reason. The liberal, essentially Hobbesian account of the individual simply fails to comport with our other, currently uncontested concepts pertaining to the will, freedom, thought, reason, and the like. Similarly, the very notion of individuality-as-embeddedness implies that the relationship between the individual and society must be much more intimate than Hobbes and the others suspected. We cannot conceive of society as merely an artificial and convenient aggregation of discrete individuals, since the very notion "discrete individual" is difficult to sustain. Thus, our concept of political society must reflect and express the idea that the individuality of the individual and the rules and patterns of society have, analytically, some direct bearing upon one another.

For Hegel, the clearest way to articulate this concept of political society is to accept an organic metaphor. Political society is an organism. The identity of the parts is dependent upon their relationship to the whole; the well-being of the whole is dependent upon the proper constitution of the parts. In a crucial passage, Hegel argues as follows:

> Much the same thing as this ideality of the moments in the state occurs with life in the physical organism. Life is present in every cell. There is only one life in all the cells and nothing withstands it. Separated from that life, every cell dies. This is the same as the ideality of every class, power, and Corporation as soon as they have the impulse to subsist and be independent. It is with them as it is with the belly in the organism. It, too, asserts its independence, but at the same time its independence is set aside and it is sacrificed and absorbed in the whole. [276 *Zusatz*; cf. *EG* 541]

Of course, the organic account of political society is very old. We encounter something like it in both Plato and Aristotle, and it is an important part of the medieval and early modern theory of kingship.[4] However, Hegel's formulation is different in at least two respects. First, as the above passage implies, and as is elsewhere made explicit (for example, at 272), each part of the organic whole contains in some meaningful way elements of the whole

4. John Neville Figgis, *The Divine Right of Kings* (Cambridge: Cambridge University Press, 1914).

itself. Nothing very mystical or portentous is intended here. All that is meant is that the fundamental nature of the organic entity must be reflected in our understanding of each of its parts. To alter Hegel's anatomical metaphor just a bit, consider the relationship between a human hand and the human organism of which it is ideally a part. All organicists would agree that the hand in isolation from the organism is deficient, and that its identity, its function, and ultimately its meaning are in some substantial measure dependent upon its relationship to the whole. Of course, when we encounter a hand in isolation—a severed hand, a picture of a hand, a plastic model of a hand—we can identify it easily enough, but this is only because we are familiar with normal hands. Thus, our knowledge of what a hand is, is deeply bound up with our knowledge of the role it plays in the organism. But Hegel wishes to go just a bit further than this and say that the hand, properly understood, is expressive of the entire nature of the organism. When we see a hand in isolation, we should regard it not simply as performing certain unique and specifiable functions, as a particular constituent in some larger entity; we should also view it explicitly in the light of the other elements of the organism. Thus, for example, the hand is part of an organism that sometimes runs, though the hand itself is not absolutely necessary to running; it is part of an organism that cooks its food, though one can surely cook without hands; and it is part of a rational organism, though obviously it does not think. Hegel wants to say that the hand cannot be completely understood unless we see it as something that not merely clenches, but clenches while the organism is running; that does not simply grasp, but sometimes grasps pots and pans; and that can perform its various operations in conjunction with, or at the behest of, a human will which is by definition rational and free.

Thus, when Hegel says that "life is present in every cell" this means, for example, that rational life is present in the human hand. We must attend to the fact that the hand not only performs certain physical motions, but that these motions often have a decidedly spiritual or moral weight—i.e., a caress, a handshake, a punch, and the like. As regards political society, then, for Hegel the characteristics of the state must in some way be reflected in our understanding of the individuals who comprise it. Their identity as individuals will derive not simply from the functions they perform in society but also from the nature of the society itself.

Second, Hegel's political organism differs from most others in that the individuals who comprise it must be understood as free. Now, while it is clear that our concept of the hand is deeply influenced by the hand's relationship to the organism, we can also see that the hand's particular, independent features will themselves play a role in our concept of it, in that a hand is different from a claw or a paw despite certain functional similarities. In the same way, while our concept of the individual must indeed reflect his role in political society, so too must it reflect the particular features of the individual per se. Since the individual is above all a free subject, a creature of free will, we must continue to see him in this light even while viewing him as part of a larger organism. But how can this be? How can the individual be bound, so to speak, by the functional exigencies of the state while yet remaining free? Is not organicism fundamentally a denial of autonomy? If the hand and the other parts of the body were truly to operate freely, in utter independence from one another, surely the organism would be destroyed and the parts along with it.

Of course, pre-Hegelian organicism fully realizes this and, thus, denies to the individual the kind of freedom and subjectivity which is a hallmark of modern political thought. To my knowledge, a satisfying study of the organic theory of politics remains to be written. Still, it seems that in the medieval and early modern conception, for example, the organic metaphor was hardly a metaphor at all. For the state was thought to be a genuinely natural and living body, not merely *like* an organism but an organism in fact, in which "every member had his task—not assigned to him by some bureaucratic chief, but naturally his own—upon the fulfillment of which the life of the whole depended."[5] In such a scheme, there could be no question of individual autonomy.

Hegel's view is quite different from this. Imagine, for a moment, a human body in which each of the various major parts were to have a mind of its own. The hand, for example, would have its

5. Michael Walzer, *Regicide and Revolution: Speeches at the Trial of Louis XVI* (Cambridge: Cambridge University Press), p. 25.

own little thinking apparatus distinct from—though, let us say, somehow inferior to—the one located in the head, a small brain that it could utilize in order to think, will, and act, all of the other parts of the body being similarly equipped. (Of course, I ignore here vexing questions regarding the relationship and putative difference between "mind" and "brain.") Certainly, the opportunities for chaos here would be considerable, yet it is still possible to view these various anatomic entities as parts of an organic whole. All that is required is that we regard them as being dependent upon one other so that the very identity of each is determined, at least in part, by its role or function within the larger entity, the body itself. The hand-with-a-mind is, so to speak, free and autonomous; yet beyond that, it is what it is insofar as it functions as part of the body and, indeed, obeys the commands of the mind-in-the-head. A body such as this would differ from bodies as we know them in that the unity of the parts would be a direct result not simply of a natural, physical process but of subjective choice as well. The hand-with-a-mind would do what the mind-in-the-head required, but it would do so not solely out of physical necessity or instinctive compulsion but, rather, out of reflective deliberation and choice. It would recognize that its own identity was such that it should obey the head, and its obedience would follow from this recognition. In this way, the body would be very much an organism, since the parts, if separated from the body, would cease to be what they are, would wither and die. The unity of the body, then, would be based in part on rational rather than simply physical necessity.

I believe that Hegel's political society is an organism in roughly this way. Each individual is a free subject who comes to recognize, nonetheless, that his identity is dependent upon his orderly participation in the social whole. Of course, there must be some glue to keep these various individuals together, and that glue is simply the content of reason. Reason prescribes the nature of political society and the nature of the individuals who comprise it; and each individual, as a rational creature, has the capacity to recognize that which reason prescribes. In fulfilling his capacity for reason, the individual comes to see that his very individuality is dependent upon society, and that only by being integrated into the body politic can he affirm his subjectivity and his freedom.

A clear implication here is that the individuals who comprise the state must be in some sense conscious of its rationality. It is, I think, quite remarkable that this feature of Hegel's political thought has been so persistently ignored or underplayed. For the fact is that he insists, time and again, on the importance of what might be called self-conscious membership in political society. In section 260 of the *Philosophy of Right*, he tells us that "personal individuality and its particular interests pass over *of their own accord* into the interest of the universal" and that they "even *recognize* it as their own substantive mind." Individuals regard the universal interest as "their *own* universal aim and are active in its pursuit" (emphases added). There may be a certain ambiguity in such assertions, for at places Hegel seems to suggest that this self-consciousness is a property not of particular individuals but of the "substantive" or transpersonal Mind. Consider, though, the following passage: "individuals likewise do not live as private persons for their particular ends alone, but in the very act of willing these they will the universal in and for itself and *consciously* have its end as their own"(260, emphasis added). It seems that self-awareness is not simply a property of the transpersonal Mind—though it is that—but is also somehow manifest in the consciousness of particular individuals. They "consciously" pursue the good of the political organism as a whole, "recognize" its interests as their own interests, and will its ends in the light of reason. Indeed, this must be the case if individuals are to emerge truly as individuals. The unity of political society cannot be the product of some unseen hand in which the egoism of individuals, when added together, somehow produces the interest of all. For one thing, this kind of summing of particular interests is explicitly rejected by Hegel as a basis for politics. But, more importantly, it would reduce the individuals of the rational state to mere Abstract Persons, acting in terms of the arbitrary or natural will, failing to participate, except vicariously, in the rationality of the state, hence not truly free in any real sense. Hegel's political organicism thus requires that the individual come to appreciate, however imperfectly, the sense in which his own identity is bound up with the state. He must come to see that "since the state is Mind objectified, it is only as one of its members that the individual himself has objectivity, genuine individuality, and an ethical life. Unification pure and simple is the true content and aim of the individual. And the individual's destiny is the living of a universal life. His further particular satisfaction, activity, and mode of conduct have this substantive and universally valid life as their starting point and their result" (258). In the light of Hegel's theory of the self, the acceptance and *Aufhebung* of Kantian morality, the raised consciousness of the husband or wife and the bourgeois encounter with interdependence in civil society—in the light of all this, we must take "the living of a universal life" seriously as a manifestation of rational, self-conscious freedom.

Hegel's political organicism is thus different both from traditional organicism and from the external theory of the state. Whether these three perspectives comprise the only possible alternatives is not immediately apparent, though it is difficult to imagine some other conception of the relationship between parts and whole. In any case, what does seem clear is that neither traditional organicism nor the external theory can solve the problem of individual and society. According to the first, the freedom and subjectivity of the individual must be denied or repressed in the interest of the whole. According to the second, the claims of individual and of society must each be compromised so as to accommodate the other. In Hegel's formulation, neither of these moves is required. The problem of individual and society is shown to be a nonproblem, and this is achieved by reformulating our concepts of individuality and society, respectively. Specifically, the individuality of the individual is shown to be a matter not of caprice nor of good will, but of free, rational participation in an organic state; it is not merely compatible with, but utterly dependent upon, its role in political society. Similarly, the state itself is shown to be an organic ordering of free, rational individuals; its very identity is utterly dependent upon those individuals. If then we encounter imperatives or claims that are contradictory, those claims must be in some way unacceptable, because irrational. All legitimate claims—those of the individual and of the state—are rooted in the single body of reason, which is internally consistent and authoritative for all of us.

It seems that, with this conception, Hegel has provided an extremely powerful account of the concept of political society. Against it practical objections will be of no avail. To say that very difficult one for Hegel scholars. The majority opinion has

Hegel's political organicism is somehow utopian is, again, to miss the point of philosophy as Hegel understood it. For philosophy's goal is not to dictate policy or even to prescribe particular actions. Its purposes, rather, are conceptual. Hegel is arguing, in effect, that we must conceive of political society in the terms he suggests. If we find ourselves in a situation where existing societies fail to measure up, and where empirical realities are such that radically improving those societies seems to be impossible, this is a comment not on our conception but on our historical circumstance. Thus, for example, it would be perfectly consistent to say that Hegel's view of the state is correct while at the same time maintaining that, for practical reasons, our present political task is to better accommodate the competing and contradictory claims of individual and society.

If Hegel's view is vulnerable, then, it must be on conceptual grounds. Here it seems that to reject the rational state largely requires rejecting the view of individuality upon which it is based. For example, if we feel that the individuality of the individual is indeed a matter of the natural or arbitrary will, as Hobbes surely did, then much of Hegel's political philosophy will fail to satisfy. Similarly, if our view of the individual is in some way atomistic, then again the kind of political organicism we have described here will lose much of its appeal. This is certainly not the place to work through these various positions, which involve the deepest questions of philosophical anthropology. It is, I believe, enough to suggest that Hegel's general viewpoint has affinities with certain important currents in contemporary philosophy, roughly Wittgensteinian in inspiration, that emphasize the sense in which our concepts of human thought and language—and of meaningful action as well—presuppose and depend upon the individual's participation in the practices and institutions of social life.[6]

3

Hegel's political organism operates in terms of a rational constitution that is, in some fundamental sense, monarchical. In this respect, his political theory accords with most other varieties of organicism. Nonetheless, the question of monarchy has been a

---

6. Taylor, "Atomism."

been stated perhaps most clearly by Avineri, who claims that Hegel "divests the monarch himself of any real power." The king is merely "a symbol of the unity of the state" and is, in substantive terms, "ultimately trivial"; his sole responsibility it is to "dot the *i*'s."[7] Indeed, Avineri finds it a "paradox" that Hegel insists on keeping the traditional form of monarchy, and this paradox remains, in Avineri's treatment, largely unexplained. Similarly, Pelczynski sees Hegel's teaching as a serious confusion of limited and unlimited kingship, and concludes that Hegel arrives at "a theory of monarchical absolutism which is contrary to his belief that the rational form of the modern state is a constitutional monarchy."[8] Of course, Ilting reads Hegel as emphasizing in the *Philosophy of Right* an absolutist king who needs no democratic legitimation. This formulation is said to contradict directly Hegel's discussion in the Berlin lectures where, again, the monarch is reduced to a mere formality. On Ilting's account, the problem is best explained by saying that Hegel bowed to political pressures as most evidently manifested in the Carlsbad Decrees, that he compromised his position "in order to be able to assert the conformity of his political philosophy with restoration ideology."[9] Indeed, says Ilting, by beginning the treatment of the constitution with a consideration of monarchy, Hegel unintelligibly inverts the order of the dialectic; and by making the monarch absolute, he sacrifices his own true conception of political society. Along these lines, Henrich claims to show that the lectures of 1819/1820 shed further light on the issue. There again, Hegel insists that the monarch, though an essential moment of the state, is nevertheless a mere formality who functions simply as the symbolic culmination of the decision-making process.[10] All of these scholars thus call into question the im-

7. Shlomo Avineri, *Hegel's Theory of the Modern State* (Cambridge: Cambridge University Press, 1982), pp. 187–88.

8. Z. A. Pelczynski, "Hegel's Political Philosophy: Some Thoughts on Its Contemporary Relevance," in Z. A. Pelczynski, ed., *Hegel's Political Philosophy: Problems and Perspective* (Cambridge: Cambridge University Press, 1971), pp. 230–31.

9. K.-H. Ilting, "Hegel's Concept of the State and Marx's Early Critique," in Pelczynski, ed., *The State and Civil Society*, p. 100; and K. -H. Ilting, "The Structure of Hegel's *Philosophy of Right*," in Pelcyznski, ed., *Hegel's Political Philosophy*, p. 106.

10. Dieter Henrich, "Einleitung des Herausgebers," in G. W. F. Hegel, *Phi-*

portance of what Hegel actually says about monarchy and suggest that his absolutist assertions, while historically understandable, are either philosophically unnecessary or, indeed, philosophically incoherent.

It is easy enough to see the origins of this general view, for the Hegelian concept of monarchy is quite complex. In providing an account, we must be able to specify Hegel's answers to at least three sets of questions: (1) Why must the rational state be monarchical at all? Could not other forms of government, including republican or democratic forms, equally satisfy the requirements of an organic political society? (2) Why does Hegel insist on an hereditary monarch? In the face of his rationalism and his generally modern approach to government and administration, hereditary monarchy seems to be a jarring anachronism. (3) How can we reconcile Hegel's insistence on the monarch's absolute supremacy with other assertions of his that seem to describe the monarch as a figurehead? Exactly what role does the monarch play in the rational constitution?

I believe that Hegel's system can generate quite plausible answers to each of these questions and that, in the light of his political organicism, he provides a challenging and, as far as I can tell, unique defense of monarchical government. I shall deal with these three sets of questions in turn:

1. *Why monarchy?* Ilting speaks, apparently with some derision, about Hegel's "deduction" of the concept of monarchy.[11] Pelczynski's derision is rather clearer: "Apart from an obscure metaphysical argument about the personality of the state being fully actualized only in a concrete, natural person, Hegel can only justify his preference for monarchical sovereignty on the not very strong grounds of expediency."[12] Yet it seems that if we grant certain of Hegel's arguments pertaining to organicism and the role of sub-

losophie des Rechts: Die Vorlesung von 1819/20 in einer Nachschrift (Frankfurt: Suhrkamp, 1983), p. 25. See also, in the lectures themselves, p. 241.

11. Ilting, "The Structure of Hegel's *Philosophy of Right*," p. 106.

12. Pelczynski, "Hegel's Political Philosophy: Some Thoughts on Its Contemporary Relevance," p. 231.

jectivity in politics, then his defense of monarchy becomes neither very obscure nor, perhaps, very unattractive.

As we have seen, for Hegel the problem of individual and society can only be resolved by conceiving of political society as an organism. In this organism, the identity of the parts and of the whole are deeply dependent upon one another in a way that parallels, at least metaphorically, the seamless identity of the infinite world as it must be rationally comprehended. But two further implications of this position should be emphasized. First, political society so conceived is a single thing. It is one entity, not merely a conglomerate of several entities, and thus its various aspects or "moments" are themselves to be understood as developments or elaborations of *it*. This is well presented, for example, in Hegel's brief discussion of sovereignty (278). For Hegel, the state is in some sense an entity of sovereignty; but as the state is, so to speak, a monad, only *it* in its entirety can be sovereign. Of course, sovereignty may *actively* manifest itself in one or another of its members; hence, we can say that decisions come directly from this or that institution. But to say that the monarch or the majority is sovereign over against the rest of the state is to ignore the state's fundamental unity. Again, this unity is quite radical, so that parts and whole are utterly dependent on one another. Thus, if we wish to say that the state acts, we must conceive of this not in terms of one particular part of the state but, rather, the state as a single, irreducible whole.

Second, as we have seen, the political organism is based not on an unreflective, natural kind of necessity but, rather, on rational or spiritual necessity. Unlike the parts of a physical body, the members of the state submit out of reflective deliberation and choice. In this way, the Hegelian state fully recognizes and satisfies the requirements of the modern individual, understood as an autonomous and rational being. But, further, the organic entity composed of these beings must itself act in a free and rational manner. The state is not a herd of animals which moves this way and that depending upon some collective instinctual force. Such a state would itself be fundamentally irrational, mired in a kind of natural necessity that would deny the spirituality of human life. To imagine a political society along these lines is to imagine individuals freely and rationally choosing to submit to an existence of physical compulsion that would, as a consequence, undermine the very freedom and rationality upon which it is based. Freedom requires us to obey reason and, hence, the state itself must act in a free and rational manner.

Thus, we can only conclude that political society is, in some meaningful sense, an agent. This raises certain difficulties, however. Though political society is a single entity, it is—by definition—composed of many individual human beings. This is, in part, what makes the state a distinctive kind of organism; unlike most other organisms, it is made up of free, rational creatures (who, for example, are themselves organisms not composed of free, rational creatures). In view of this, we may still be tempted to define political society, however tightly integrated and unified, as a collectivity. But Hegel wants to claim, further, that there is a sense in which agents—doers of actions—can only be persons, not "fictional" persons or collectivities, but "real" persons. Hence, there is for Hegel a sense in which the state cannot act except in the form of a single person; and, on this score, he seems to be correct.

To see why this might be so, we must consider briefly what it means to perform an action. There is, of course, a quite substantial philosophical literature on this subject, and a great deal of disagreement. Depending on the particular account, actions are said necessarily to involve a desire of some kind, or a combination of desire and belief, an intention, a volition, a reason, or a context in which the ascription of an action to an agent simply seems to be plausible. Each of these accounts has been subject to criticism. For example, there appear to be clear cases of actions in which nothing plausibly identifiable as a desire or a belief or even an intention is present. But assuming that a satisfactory account would include at least some of these elements, it seems quite clear that collectivities can indeed perform actions. Collectivities—say a conventional nation-state or a legislature or a majority—can be said to have wants and desires, beliefs, intentions, and the like. And of course we ascribe actions to collectivities all the time, as when we say that Germany invaded Poland or Congress enacted a piece of legislation or the majority spoke. In each case, an entity composed of many individuals is said to have performed an action in roughly the same way that individuals themselves perform actions.

But there seem to be at least two differences between collectivities and individuals in that individuals can perform certain *kinds* of actions that collectivities cannot perform. The first pertains to the distinction between "basic actions" and other actions, and is attributable largely to the work of Arthur Danto.[13] According to Danto, most actions performed by humans are the effects of some distinct set of causes. Thus, if I hit a baseball, this action is caused by a variety of other actions of mine, including driving to the ballpark, selecting a bat, stepping up to the plate, and moving my muscles in such a way that the bat comes in contact with the ball; further, it might also be the effect of the actions of other persons, including the manager's decision to let me hit and the pitcher's decision to throw me a fat one. Danto claims, though, that not all actions can be caused. For if this were so, the very concept of an action would be incoherent; we would not be able to distinguish actions from mere physical events or bodily movements. On his analysis, then, if there are any actions at all, there must be certain actions that are in some sense uncaused and that we may call "basic actions." The contingent nature of this claim should be emphasized. The argument provides no proof against a strictly determinist or physicalist account of human behavior; rather, it simply claims that if we believe humans can act, then we must believe that they can perform basic actions.

A basic action is self-generating and, since it has no cause, is not amenable to further analysis. To try to explicate a basic action would be like trying to explain to a blind person the color red or trying to get a paralyzed person to understand what it means to move his arm in the way in which a normal person understands this.[14] Thus, basic actions are simply given. Nonetheless, since they are uncaused, we must say they represent that aspect of human behavior which is autonomous and free. If, that is, we choose to accept—as Hegel does—the fundamental autonomy of the person, i.e., the ability to act rather than simply be in motion, then we must attribute to the person the capacity to perform basic actions. In Hegel's account, basic actions would be acts of free will, and

13. Arthur Danto, "Basic Actions," in Alan R. White, ed., *The Philosophy of Action* (Oxford: Oxford University Press, 1968).
14. Ibid., pp. 53–54.

the fact that such acts must be based on reason is not to provide a causal explanation of them.

However, it seems to be quite clear that collectivities cannot perform basic actions. For the actions of a collectivity will always be caused by the actions of the individuals who comprise it. Thus, if we wish to say that Germany invaded Poland, this can only be the result of the actions of persons, some of which will themselves be caused but some of which will be basic. Similarly, to say that the majority passed the referendum requires that we acknowledge the majority's action as being caused by the actions of those who voted. In view of this, then, there is a sense in which the actions of a collectivity cannot be autonomous and free in the way that an individual's actions can. The collectivity's actions cannot be self-generated but, rather, can only be caused by something distinct from itself. Of course, there may be a difference between a collective action that is caused by the members of the collectivity and one that is coerced by, say, some external power. Nonetheless, the distinction between collective and individual action remains; and it seems to be for this reason that phrases attributing actions to collectivities often have an artificial or metaphorical character.

One might try to obviate this difficulty by distinguishing between causing an action and constituting one.[15] Roughly, the action of an individual can be said to constitute a collective action in the sense of standing for it or representing it while, nonetheless, not being a cause of it. David Copp's example, pertinent to the present discussion, is of a prime minister whose official proclamation constitutes his country's act of declaring war on another country. Copp distinguishes here—correctly, I believe—between primary actions and secondary actions, the former constituting the latter. The secondary action, the country's declaration of war, is a different action from the prime minister's issuing the proclamation, and the latter certainly need not be a cause of the former. Nevertheless, the proclamation is, in some sense, an action in that, given certain relevant facts, it must be the case that the country has declared war. Thus, the one action constitutes, although it does not cause, the other.

15. David Copp, "Collective Actions and Secondary Actions," *American Philosophical Quarterly* 16 (July 1979).

But this distinction in no way shows that a collectivity can perform a basic action.[16] For in cases of constitution, it seems that collectivities still will have had to act directly at some point. In Copp's case, the country will have had to communicate in some way with the prime minister or it will have had to establish the relevant facts for the constitution-relationship to be possible in the first place, e.g., it will have had to elect a parliamentary majority, which in turn will have had to elect the prime minister and thus make it possible for him to issue an official proclamation.

Thus, collectivities in general cannot perform free and autonomous actions as individuals can. But there appears to be a second, related difference between collectivities and individuals with respect to action. In a classic essay, H. L. A. Hart argued for the view that to speak of an action is to ascribe responsibility.[17] The view has been very controversial, but has been substantially supported in an interesting way by Joel Feinberg.[18] Against Hart, Feinberg denies that all accounts of action involve ascriptions of responsibility which are defeasible—i.e., prima facie true but rebuttable in principle—"in the manner of certain legal claims and judgments." But he does agree with Hart that such accounts involve ascriptions of responsibility in some sense. Specifically, "to be responsible for one's own complex actions (e.g., closing a door) is properly to have one's simpler actions identified as the cause of an upshot." And further, "to be responsible for one's simple actions is only to be properly identifiable as their doer." In this way, the notion of responsibility seems to be tied to what we have called basic actions. To ascribe responsibility is to identify the performer of a basic action, either for its own sake or for the sake of finding out who caused a complex or nonbasic action.

But clearly, if ascribing responsibility involves identifying basic actions, and if collectivities cannot perform such actions, then one cannot ascribe responsibility to collectivities. Of course, this raises

16. Ibid., p. 185.

17. H. L. A. Hart, "The Ascription of Responsibility and Rights," *Proceedings of the Aristotelian Society* 49 (1949): 171–94.

18. Joel Feinberg, "Actions and Responsibility," in Joel Feinberg, *Doing and Deserving: Essays in the Theory of Responsibility* (Princeton, N.J.: Princeton University Press, 1970). For a caveat, see Feinberg's preface, pp. vii–viii.

venerable problems associated with the law of corporate entities and involving, for example, notions of limited liability. But, strictly speaking, it seems incoherent to hold a collectivity responsible for an action other than in a convenient, metaphorical sense. Ultimately, the responsibility—and the consequent praise or blame—must be ascribed to one or more of the individuals who comprise the collectivity, but this is often very nearly impossible to do. When the government passes a law, to whom should we ascribe responsibility? Would it be the legislature as a whole, or only those legislators who voted in the majority? Would it be the lobbyists who influenced the legislators, or the legislative staffs who did the research? Would it be the executive agency that effectively wrote the bill, or the editorial writers who supported it? Perhaps it would be the constituents of those legislators who voted for it, or perhaps only those constituents who voted in the last election, or perhaps only those who voted for the winning candidate. Indeed, perhaps the responsibility really lies with the Founding Fathers who created a structure of government that enables the legislature to operate in the first place; but then, they had *their* constituents and staffs and the like. Certainly, each of these individuals may be justly held responsible for his own actions. But when it comes to asking who is responsible for this or that collective decision, it seems impossible to say. Such decisions are typically generated by complex systems, things which do not act but are more or less explicit structures of social relationships in which the various discrete actions of individuals somehow come together to produce an outcome.

One might object and say that, in fact, we routinely and plausibly hold collectivities responsible for their actions. But the above formulation suggests that it is always problematic to do so. We say that a particular nation committed an act of aggression and should be punished for it, and one way of punishing the nation would be through some kind of military action. But what if, in the process, we kill thousands of innocent citizens, for example, citizens who actively opposed the original act of aggression or even citizens who condoned it through their inaction but cannot be plausibly said to have fomented it? It surely was not the case that all the residents of Dresden were responsible, much less equally responsible, for the horrors of the concentration camps. This is not to say that the bombing of Dresden was unjustified, only that it cannot be fully justified on the grounds of punishing responsible actors.

The conclusion of the argument seems to be as follows. For Hegel, political society must be conceived of as an autonomous, rational agent, an entity capable of acting in the fullest sense; for otherwise it would merely operate out of some kind of natural principle, thereby failing to fulfill the requirements of freedom, both for itself and for its members. But further, such a society cannot be conceived of merely as a collectivity, for collectivities cannot be actors in the fullest sense; they cannot perform basic actions and cannot plausibly be held responsible for the actions they do perform. If then, political society is to be an actor, it must be conceived of in terms of a single, real human being; and this human being is the monarch. Louis XIV's claim that "L'état c'est moi" is, I believe, adopted by Hegel as an analytically true principle of political society. In a very real sense, the state *is* the monarch; hence, the state is an actor—autonomous and responsible—only insofar as the monarch is too.

This rather audacious doctrine requires, I think, only minor qualification. To say that the state *is* the monarch is not to say that the two are identical, for obviously the state includes many items which cannot be predicated of the monarch himself. Rather, I think Hegel would say that the *will* of the monarch is identical to the will of the state; when the monarch qua monarch wills something, when he decides and acts, then his willing does not merely represent or stand for the willing of the state but, rather, actually *is* that willing. In this sense, the Hegelian doctrine of monarchy is quite literally an absolutist one. Just as an individual human organism can only act in terms of its own unique and autonomous will, so the political organism acts in terms of *its* will, and that will is quite identical with the will of one real human being, the monarch.

Of course, the absolute monarch of Hegel's rational state does not act in a vacuum. In the same way that the will of an individual human is properly informed by the person's desires, experiences, and knowledge, so too must the will of the state—the monarch's will—be exercised in the light of public opinion, legislative recommendations, the advice of knowledgeable councillors, and the like. Indeed, for Hegel the truly free will must be a rational will, and a monarch who acted capriciously and against all relevant advice would, presumably, be deeply irrational. Such a monarch would plunge himself, and the state he ruled, into mindless unfreedom or insanity; indeed, the state would be deeply unhealthy and would, perhaps, even die. Like an individual person who abuses his body with the excesses of the arbitrary will, the capricious monarch would destroy the organism of which he is the head; as such, the capricious monarch is in fact no monarch at all, is a violation of the concept of monarch.

Indeed, it seems clear that the monarch, in order to be free and rational, would have to act only in terms of the input he receives from the other parts of the state. Again, this means that he must respond to the people, the legislator, the experts, and the like. When my body is hungry, I am rational if I eat; though when reason tells me I should fast, then I am rational if I do not eat. Similarly, the monarch should satisfy the express desires of the masses, provided that doing so can be shown to be the rational course of action. The freedom of the monarch, like the freedom of the will in general, requires that he be bound and limited by that which reason prescribes; and it seems certain that reason prescribes actions aimed at promoting the good health of the organism as a whole.

Clearly, such an absolutism will not be absolutist in the conventional sense. In Hegel's rational state, there will be parliamentary government, a separation of powers, broad rights of free speech, the rule of law, and substantial elements of democracy. Indeed, it seems that the rational state could be further democratized without undermining any basic Hegelian principles. But all such practices have as their function and identity the task of communicating relevant information to the monarch who is solely responsible for making community decisions. They should not be understood as independent checks upon the monarch, and he is under no obligation of a legal or contractual nature. If we wish to say, nonetheless, that the monarch is merely a formality who dots the *i*'s, then Hegel is certainly prepared to accommodate us. But to imply by this that the monarch is somehow trivial or inessential is like trying to deny that in any free human action the will must be obeyed. It is in this sense that Hegel's monarch is an absolutist one; the actions of the state are his actions and his alone.

If this argument is correct, then it seems that the monarch is indeed an analytically necessary feature of political society as Hegel conceives it. Of course, contemporary readers will not be happy with the substantive outcome, but it must be clear what the consequences of its denial would be. If we wish to reject monarchy but retain the organic conception of political society, then this seems to entail a denial of freedom insofar as such a society would be unable truly to act and could move only like a herd of animals, driven by some external, natural force. It may be that some premodern societies have existed in this manner, but it is difficult to reconcile it with our modern conception of humans as free and rational subjects. Thus, to reject monarchy requires rejecting the organic conception of the state itself, and, presumably, this has been done by most modern philosophers of politics. For them, political societies move by a kind of systemic inertia. But as we have seen, to reject the organic conception means to forfeit any chance of dissolving the problem of individual and society. For again, only in an organic conception can the claims of the individual and those of society be fully and mutually satisfied. And indeed, to reject this conception seems to require that we view the individuality of the individual in an atomistic way, as a matter of arbitrary willfulness or, at best, an illusory and unreliable kind of reasoning.

In sum, there appears to be nothing paradoxical or confused about Hegel's defense of monarchy, and our explanation of it can rely largely on philosophical rather than narrowly historical or political considerations. Moreover, though different versions of the philosophy of Right do indeed emphasize different aspects of monarchy, all of them appear to be fully compatible with the account we have provided. Finally, it seems certain that the defense of monarchy rests not on grounds of expediency, nor even on an obscure metaphysical argument, but on a relatively straightforward analysis of the concept of political society. This analysis may well be mistaken, but it appears that to reject monarchy requires either rejecting the basic tenets of political organicism or else emending in some substantial manner certain fundamental principles of the philosophy of action.

2. *On hereditary monarchy*. In the light of this argument, we can see more clearly the nature of Hegel's interest in the principle

of hereditary monarchy. Hegel is quite insistent on this principle, and, again, has been severely criticized for it. According to Avineri, the system of hereditary succession is merely "as good as any other,"[19] while Pelczynski complains that "there is nothing in the nature of hereditary monarchy that makes it necessarily independent of the pressures or influences of particular interest."[20] Indeed, Pelczynski seems to suggest that an elected president could accomplish just as well what Hegel wants from a monarch.

Against such views, I think it can be shown that Hegel's preference for a hereditary system is not merely capricious or expedient but is based on rather explicit, albeit arguable, philosophical considerations. To begin with, it should be clear that in defending hereditary monarchy, Hegel is actually arguing against two quite different positions. On the one hand, he is indeed rejecting Pelczynski's suggestion involving an elective monarchy of some kind. On the other hand, and perhaps paradoxically, he is also rejecting a more traditional, divine right conception of the king as emerged most clearly in the early modern period. Naturally, this conception itself is bound up with ideas of hereditary succession. Nonetheless, like elective monarchy, it is said to violate the essential principles of monarchy as implied by the concept of political society itself.

In order to see the nature of Hegel's argument, we need to consider what he calls the "majesty" of the monarch, as in the following passage: "Both moments in their undivided unity—(a) the will's ultimate ungrounded self, and (b) therefore its similarly ungrounded objective existence (existence being the category which is at home in nature)—constitute the Idea of something against which caprice is powerless, the 'majesty' of the monarch" (281). The majesty of the monarch is that which makes him special, which identifies him as being fit for monarchy. But, for Hegel, the fundamental characteristic of the monarch is simply the fact that he has a (free and rational) will. His function is merely to decide, to render the various desires and calculations of the political organism in the form of a free action. This function requires no

19. Avineri, *Hegel's Theory of the Modern State*, p. 188.
20. Pelczynski, "Hegel's Political Philosophy: Some Thoughts on Its Contemporary Relevance," p. 232.

particular insight or ability other than the very common ability to choose. Thus, the monarch is best conceived of as an entity of willing *simpliciter*; the fact that he has a will is his only salient characteristic.

In such a view, then, we must purge from our concept of the monarch all other seemingly salient characteristics. It is in this sense that Hegel's account of monarchy is entirely different from—indeed, essentially unrelated to—the traditional, absolutist doctrine. As Michael Walzer has argued, the traditional view emphasized the peculiar *personal* traits of the monarch: "Throughout society, inequality was radically personal in nature, and it was at least partly explained by reference to the personal attributes of the king. He had been touched by God, singled out as divine deputy; hence he was godlike and living proof that heaven itself intended men to be unequal in rank and privilege. The king was quite simply a different sort of person. . . . "[21] The king was thus uniquely suited to his role by virtue of his particular attributes. As a godlike creature, he presumably was possessed of a special kind of wisdom and moral insight, an elevated capacity to choose well, and far greater opportunities to receive divine guidance. These attributes made it plausible, indeed necessary, that he and he alone should be sovereign.

For Hegel, on the other hand, to emphasize such putative traits is to view the monarch in terms other than pure willing. It is, for example, to invest one person with certain abilities of insight and knowledge that belie our general understanding of human beings. While we might well agree that individuals differ greatly in terms of intellectual capacity and moral insight, we must also agree that no single person is godlike and no particular individual so far exceeds all others that he or she should be the exclusive source of political wisdom and right. Indeed, our strong sense is that political knowledge must spring from the various resources of the community—the desires of the people, the deliberations of legislators, the experience and wisdom of those who have studied history, human behavior, philosophy, and the like. That is, in terms of "knowing" what ought to be done, the combined resources of the

21. Walzer, *Regicide and Revolution*, p. 12.

political organism itself are decisive; hence, all that is needed from the monarch is the pure, unalloyed capacity to will. But further, this capacity, far from being the special trait of a godlike figure, is in fact the most ordinary and regular feature of virtually all human beings. By definition, every one of us has a will that is, again by definition, capable of being exercised in a free and rational manner. Thus, there is a sense in which, for Hegel, anyone could be king. The king need not be particularly intelligent or insightful, saintly or devout. Indeed, the only qualification is precisely that he be viewed apart from his particular personal traits.

It is essentially for this reason that Hegel insists on hereditary monarchy. In such a system, the monarch attains to the crown not through some kind of intellectual or spiritual achievement but, rather, through natural or biological accident. By basing succession on birth, one explicitly denies the relevance of personal traits. The monarch cannot claim to merit his office on the basis of wisdom, accomplishment, divinity, or whatever. As a result, hereditary monarchy makes it absurd to think that the monarch is in some way special or different. It undermines all possible rationalizations for the monarch usurping deliberative or legislative functions, and it renders incoherent the notion that the throne is somehow the "private property" of the king (281). Hegel writes as follows: "The monarch, therefore, is essentially characterized as *this* individual, in abstraction from all his other characteristics, and this individual is raised to the dignity of monarchy in an immediate, natural fashion, i.e., through his natural birth" (280). Thus, Hegel is not troubled if the accidents of birth produce kings whose particular talents prove to be quite modest. For the dignity and, indeed, the majesty of the monarch lie rather in the very purity of his identity as the willing part of the political organism and in his very ordinariness as a human being.

It is for precisely the same reason that Hegel rejects the notion of elective monarchy which, indeed, he regards as the "worst of institutions" (281). For, again, an elected monarch will be defined in terms of traits other than the pure capacity of willing. These traits might include the particular opinions, experiences, rhetorical skills, and abilities of the monarch; or, indeed, they might include the simple fact that he is a "representative," hence is somehow to be understood as a mere receptacle of the particular, "arbitrary" wills of the voters. In any such case, an elective system of monarchy necessarily implies that there is something substantively relevant about the person of the monarch which peculiarly qualifies him for rule. Again, such a monarch would naturally, and quite rightly, come to see his office in terms of his own distinctive personal traits, hence come to regard it as his "private property."

Thus, the majesty of the monarch is, in actual fact, a matter of his pure abstractness from all particular qualities, his "ungrounded immediacy," i.e., the pure and simple fact that he has a will. Again, the function of the monarch is simply to exercise his will, to decide. Just as our own individual will acts on the basis of what our senses and powers of reasoning provide, so the monarch's decisions will be based entirely on the experiences and information provided by the political organism. To invest the monarch with some further quality—be it divinity or representativeness—is to enlarge his function beyond what is called for by the concept of the state, and to usurp the other organs of the body politic.

But if Hegel has shown hereditary monarchy to be philosophically justified, this is not to say that it is philosophically necessary. For it seems that we can think of other selection processes that might work equally well. In particular, the notion of a lottery comes to mind. Selecting the king from the population at random, perhaps presupposing certain minimal and unexceptional qualifications, would seem to fit the philosophical requirements quite nicely. The monarch would owe his position solely to chance; he could plausibly claim no personal title to the throne; and thus, as king he would come to be seen clearly for what he really is, viz., an entity of pure willing. I doubt that Hegel would be very comfortable with such a process, but I do not see that he could have any clear philosophical objection to it. Nor do I see that such a system would present any particular problems; conceptually, at least, it would seem to work pretty well. Of course, certain states in antiquity selected leaders by lot, and we use such a method to pick juries. Thus, there seems to be no very good reason why a king, as defined by Hegel, should not be chosen in this way.

3. *The role of the monarch.* Given Hegel's formulation, one might still wish to say that the monarch is substantively irrelevant

and that he merely symbolizes the unity of the state. But a defense of monarchy along these lines would seem to invoke considerations of expediency rather than conceptual integrity, and Hegel explicitly rejects this approach. Thus, for example, he does indeed suggest that hereditary succession would make for smoother transitions of power and would obviate the development of factions. But he insists that "this aspect . . . is only consequential, and to make it the reason for hereditary succession is to drag down the majesty of the throne into the sphere of argumentation, to ignore its true character as ungrounded immediacy and ultimate inwardness, and to base it not on the Idea of the state immanent within it, but on something external to itself . . . " (281). I think it clear, then, that Hegel intends the monarch literally to make decisions which, as such, will be the decisions of the state. In the light of this, it is hard to see how his role could be merely formal. It is true that the king simply ratifies the general wisdom of the political organism and renders it in the form of a free action. But he must do this of his *own* free will. He cannot be conceived of as merely a heteronomous functionary, for this would belie his autonomy and, hence, the autonomy of the state. He must freely and rationally decide to ratify those policies which the political organism has generated. And again, it is absolutely necessary that this function be performed; for the monarch does not merely symbolize but concretely constitutes—in Copp's sense—both the unity and the freedom of the state. Indeed, without the monarch, the state would not simply lose a symbol; it would lose its very capacity to act in a free and rational manner.

There is, I would suggest, nothing in Hegel's absolutism for a modern liberal to fear. The king, insofar as he fulfills the requirements of his role, will indeed be fully responsive to the needs and judgments of the people. For the monarch willfully to ignore what the rest of the organism provides is to be capricious and unfree, to behave in a despotic manner (286), hence to be something other than a monarch. But what of the king who fails in precisely this respect and indeed becomes a despot? What guarantee is there? It is most instructive to note that Hegel does not speak of a right to revolt. For such a right would redefine the relationship between monarch and people on a legal/contractual, rather than organic, basis. It would see political society in accommodationist terms, as a series of trade-offs between the forces of freedom and those of order, and would emphasize the right of either side to rebel if the accommodation fails. In short, it would define political society as a marriage of convenience between distinct and fundamentally independent units.

Thus, Hegel sees the guarantees against despotism to lie rather in the objective organicism of the state itself (286). What this seems to mean, most simply, is that the rise of despotism necessarily leads to the demise of the organism. When a tyrant accedes to the throne, the organism becomes sick; its various members suffer and, as a single thing, it suffers accordingly. The result is a kind of moral or cultural disintegration and, perhaps, political anarchy. Indeed, it is possible that such a disease would produce what we normally call a revolution. The organism, as constituted, would be fundamentally dead, and its members would of necessity struggle to reconstitute a new organism with, presumably, a new monarch. There is a sense, then, in which something like revolution is implicit and necessary in Hegel's account of the state. A despot must be deposed. But Hegel's avoidance of the word *revolution*, and related words, is again based on a need to distinguish organic disintegration from the violation of a contractual agreement. When the latter occurs, one has a right to revolt; when the former occurs, one is simply plunged into disorder. In both cases, the purely circumstantial result may well be the same—a breakdown of order or, if the tyrant successfully resists, extreme forms of repression. But it seems that Hegel is nonetheless correct to insist on the distinction. For again, to speak of a right to revolt is to deny the organic conception of the state, which, in turn, is to forfeit the opportunity truly to resolve the tension between individual and society. Thus, strictly speaking, there is no right to revolt; there is only a need to reconstitute the political organism, to make it whole and healthy once again.

4

As we have seen, political society is conceived as an organic unity of autonomous and rational agents. Such a conception appears to fulfill—and perhaps alone can fulfill—Hegel's perfectionist goals.

Specifically, by looking at the state in this way, Hegel seeks to demonstrate how the claims of individuality and those of society can each be fully and satisfactorily realized. As an organism, the state operates in terms of rules or patterns, the legitimacy of which is universally accepted. It follows that this will likely be an orderly society, a harmonious coming together of distinct elements, much in the manner described by the theorists of the classical polis and exemplified perhaps best of all by Plato's true or most healthy city, the "city of pigs."[22] But, further, such an organism would also satisfy the claims of individuality insofar as the coming together of distinct elements requires the free and rational choice of each. The organism does not repress but, rather, is in fact dependent upon the mature development of individual autonomy. Without such development, political society would indeed be *nothing more* than a city of pigs, composed not of moral agents but of an inferior species and thereby frustrating the essential demands of the modern subject.

The Hegelian conception of monarchy appears to be fully consistent with, and perhaps even necessitated by, this perfectionist project. But, further, I think much the same can be said for the "inwardly differentiated" constitution as a whole. That is, Hegel's discussion of the other two "moments" of the constitution—the executive and the legislative—and of their interrelationships appears, in many respects, to comport nicely with his organic conception of political society. Indeed, I think some of the most controversial and difficult of Hegel's views can be understood and plausibly defended largely in these terms. Three such views merit some brief attention pertaining, respectively, to Hegel's elitism, his discussion of mixed government, and his separation of civil society and the state.

To insist upon Hegel's distrust of democracy is surely to belabor the obvious. Seen in the light of the organic conception of the state, though, it appears that his elitism may turn out to be rather less unpalatable even for those passionately committed to democratic government. On the one hand, Hegel writes of the masses as follows: "the truth is that if 'people' means a particular section

22. Plato, *Republic*, 372e.

of the citizens, then it means precisely that section which does *not* know what it wills. To know what one wills, and still more to know what the absolute will, Reason, wills, is the fruit of profound apprehension and insight, precisely the things which are *not* popular" (301). In this passage and elsewhere, Hegel is saying—at the least—that people differ in terms of their capacity to apprehend, hence to act on the basis of, that which reason prescribes. To deny this would require affirming something close to the absolute intellectual equality of humans. I know of no major political theorist—left, right, or center—who would make this judgment and, indeed, the notion of unequal abilities is a part of virtually all democratic societies. To say, then, that some people know more than others, and that some have greater capacity for knowledge than others, is not necessarily to offend democratic sensibilities.

It seems, therefore, that we must attend instead to the particular institutional/political implications that Hegel deduces from this presupposed inequality. And in this regard, the organic conception of the state again appears to be consistent with a good deal of democratic practice. Hegel's elitism prompts him to assign important political functions to people of ability; not everyone is capable of public service, and the organism, as a rational, functional whole, must reflect this fact. Nevertheless, he also insists on the importance of public opinion and on the opportunity of the masses to express their views and make their desires known (308 and 318). He envisions a representative system in which deputies are, in some indirect sense, responsive to the views of their constituents (308). And, of course, he insists on a merit system that "guarantees to every citizen the chance of joining the class of civil servants" (291). All of this is justified in terms of the functional necessities of the political organism. Certain parts of the organism are suited to inquiring, deliberating, knowing, and ultimately deciding; others are better suited to opining, reacting impulsively to events, and articulating felt needs and interests. To be sure, we may sense that Hegel somehow prefers the former to the latter. But still, the organism must be defined and understood in terms of its nerve-endings as much as its mind; both are absolutely and, in a sense, equally necessary in order for the organism to be what it is, hence both must be given their due.

Now some democrats will insist that intellectual inequalities are or ought to be, politically and institutionally irrelevant, that the power to deliberate and decide should be equally apportioned. Hegel disagrees, but the extent of the disagreement should not be exaggerated. He finds the idea that everyone is equally "at home" in the business of the state to be a "ridiculous notion" and that the rational constitution needs to reflect important differences among people (308). But again, and in virtually the same breadth, he insists that, in the rational state, public opinion is a field "open to everyone where he can express his purely personal political opinions and make them count."

Thus, Hegel's antipathy to democracy manifests itself essentially in the view that different individuals have different roles to play in a well-ordered polity, that some are suited to—say—political analysis or informed deliberation or, indeed, the technical mastery of a particular policy area, while others are not. In contemporary American politics, we might say that some individuals are better qualified than others to sit on the Council of Economic Advisors; that through temperament, interest, and ability some are particularly adept in the arts of office-seeking and office-holding; that judges should know the law, bureaucrats should know how to administer, environmental analysis should be performed by environmental scientists, and the like. It seems that we can make such judgments without committing ourselves to a retrograde kind of elitism. As democrats, of course, we also insist that the public must have its say, must be permitted to express its views, which, in turn, must be taken seriously by those whose responsbility it is to devise and enact social policy. But, then, so does Hegel. Certainly, Hegel does reject the principle of popular sovereignty, but, again, he locates sovereignty not in some elite group or person but in the organism as a whole. He disapproves of universal suffrage but provides for a functional system of representation similar, in certain respects, to the proposals of Fabian socialists such as G. D. H. Cole. He abjures talk of natural rights but argues for a system of due process based on precedent and written law, for the absolute right to own property, and for quite substantial freedoms of expression. Hegel is no democrat, but it is not clear that his rational state, properly understood, is incompatible with, or subversive of, a number of the most fundamental democratic values.

With reference to the separation of powers, once more Hegel's argument seems quite plausible in the context of his political organicism. As is well known, he insists on a structure of mixed government but rejects the notion of checks and balances. The various powers of government should be seen not as independent and, in some sense, self-interested actors but as essential parts of the political whole. Each, that is, performs a distinctive function and, thus, each contributes something important to the decision-making process. The legislative powers provide the government with general laws and principles—the "universal" element—which reflect the collective wisdom of the state as manifested, at least in part, by the corporate entities that comprise civil society. These corporate entities—municipalities, groups, business concerns, cultural organizations, and the like—are the stuff that social life is made of, and they provide the legislature with the raw materials from which to formulate specific policies. The executive branch, the civil service, is entrusted with the task of applying the laws, of subsuming particular cases under universal principles. It is comprised of persons whose particular traits—training, temperament, commitment, and the like—qualify them for a career in what we now call the public sector. And, of course, the monarch performs the function of deciding, willing for the state as a whole, and lending authority to the particular laws and procedures of the state by stamping them as the actions of the organism as such.

In this sense, then, the doctrine of mixed government need not invoke Madisonian principles of balance, mutual restraint, and political fragmentation. The organic conception of the state simply prescribes a degree of functional specialization in which each power does that work most suited to it. Rather than being opposed to one another, the branches of government pursue different aspects of a single, overriding endeavor, viz., the effort to devise and implement public policies sanctioned by the principles of human reason.

Finally, the controversial split between state and civil society, which has attracted so much attention among scholars, similarly seems to be both plausible and quite appropriate in the context of Hegel's political organicism. Marx himself complained of this split and argued that the state ought to reflect (and, perhaps, must inevitably reflect) the forces of social life.[23] But if our analysis thus

23. Karl Marx, *Critique of Hegel's 'Philosophy of Right'* (Cambridge: Cambridge

far has been correct, then we may conclude that the relationship between state and civil society is, for Hegel, actually quite intimate. The interests, needs, values, and desires that are generated by the institutions of social life are given full expression in the rational state, with the sole provision that they are not necessarily decisive, either singly or even collectively. That is to say, in a rational state the powers of government will take into account and, presumably, heed the demands of social institutions, provided those demands accord with the requirements of human reason. This latter quali- fication is, of course, a substantial one. It amounts to the assertion that rational principles may be different from the mere accumu- lation of particular desires, an assertion itself rooted in the Kantian distinction between the free will of reason and the heteronomous will of desire. For Hegel, as for Kant and, more particularly, Rous- seau, there is a difference between the will of all and the general will. The latter is what reason would prescribe, if only it were known; it is, as a result, motivated not by parochial interests but by an effort in good faith to attend to the public interest.

In marking a distinction between state and civil society, then, Hegel is simply marking the distinction between the human func- tion of rational deliberation and choice and that of desire. Both functions are important for the political organism but, again, they must be properly ordered. The human individual is free only if his will, though *informed* by impulse and desire, is ultimately *per- suaded* by reason and principle. Similarly, the state is free only if the interests of civil society are satisfied in the context of, and on the basis of, more substantial considerations.

Thus, with respect to these issues of democracy, mixed govern- ment, and the relationship of state and society, Hegel adopts views that are by no means unconventional or anachronistic; his positions comport quite well with a great deal of modern political theory and practice. However, his effort is to provide these positions with more substantial philosophical grounds, and those grounds are rooted in an organic conception of political society quite foreign to the characteristic prejudices of modern, liberal political thought. Mixed government, for example, is typically defended on the basis

---

University Press, 1977), especially pp. 76ff. See also Pelczynski, ed., *The State and Civil Society*.

of empirical considerations involving human psychology, the lessons of history, and the requirements of expediency. Ever mindful of these, Hegel still seeks to offer a further and much more substantial justification in which mixed government is shown to comport with, is perhaps even entailed by, our very conception of the political state—a conception which is, in turn, derived from an analysis of the tension between individual and society. We adopt mixed government, therefore, not for instrumental reasons, not to solve some particular, practical problem, but because it is conceptually required.

It is, however, impossible to end this discussion without noting a number of specific formulations in the philosophy of Right that seem to resist this kind of interpretation. They are formulations which, even after considerable scrutiny, do not appear to be entailed by, and indeed seem to be even inconsistent with, the concept of political society that we have reconstructed. It is ultimately hard to know what to make of these formulations, but they do indeed raise the possibility that the rational state, as presented by Hegel, does in fact suffer from some serious structural flaws of a philosophical nature.

We cannot at this point hope to provide a full account or even a listing of these problem passages; but consider the following examples by way of illustration.

1. In certain passages pertaining to the relationship between state and civil society, Hegel speaks not simply of functional distinctness but, indeed, of something that looks suspiciously like a deep-seated opposition: "Just as civil society is the battlefield of everyone's individual private interests against everyone else's, so here we have the struggle of these same private interests against particular matters of common concern, and of both of these together against the higher viewpoint and organization of the state" (289). There is, to be sure, nothing wrong with such "struggle," provided that we understand the basis for its rational resolution. And, indeed, in the very next line Hegel appears to provide such a basis by talking of the patriotism of the citizens that converts the "corporate spirit" into the "spirit of the state." But Hegel never seems to follow up on the consequences of this conversion, and indeed concludes that the corporate realm is a playground [*Tummelplatz*] for "personal knowledge, personal decisions and their execution, petty passions

and conceits" (289). Most importantly, it is not clear to what extent the individuals who are active in this playground ever truly fulfill the requirements of individuality that involve, as we have seen, a free and informed decision to participate in the political organism as reason prescribes. In the present case, the value of society's rules and patterns seems to emerge over against, and without the reasoned acceptance of, many of the individuals who comprise that society. Such a situation would be perfectly compatible with political organicism per se; but is seems not to jibe very well with Hegel's peculiar brand of organicism which, as we have seen, contemplates an organic unity of autonomous and rational agents.

2. Moreover, the struggle of state against individual manifests itself quite clearly as a power struggle, as an opposition of forces rather than a fruitful juxtaposition of distinct capabilities: "In the universal power of the state, public officials performing their duties find protection against the subjective side, against the private passions of the governed whose private interests, etc., are injured through the authoritative imposition of the universal" (294). Again, this kind of power relationship, whereby the good of the whole is forcefully imposed on the individual parts, is consistent with organicism in general but not, it seems, with Hegel's organicism. We can certainly see how the power of the state would be a useful expedient against the centrifugal tendencies of self-interested persons, but it is hard to see how it comports with the fundamental requirements of Hegel's perfectionism.

3. Hegel adds that we also need protection of a coercive nature against the public officials themselves. To wit: "The security of the state and of the governed against the misuses of power by the ministers and their officials lies [also] in the authority of communities and corporations, whereby the [often inadequate] effort to control from above the intrusion of subjective caprice into the behavior and authority of public officials is completed from below" (295; cf. *EG* 539). Indeed, there are a series of devices for checking the potential abuses of official power, including the hierarchical structure of organizations, the principle of bureaucratic accountability, and—in a formulation strikingly reminiscent of Madison's *Federalist no. 10*—the extensive size of the state (296). Further, the Marxian critique of bureaucracy, which was aimed at Hegel above all, is in fact anticipated by Hegel himself: "The control

from above over [the potential abuse of official authority] lies in part in the immediacy and personal nature of the relationship [between bureaucrats and citizens], and also in the common interests of officials who form a clique over against both their inferiors and their superiors. . . . " (295). While Hegel very clearly rejects the notion of checks and balances, of the state as an inorganic concatenation of opposed and only conveniently juxtaposed powers, much of what he actually says in such passages seems very Madisonian indeed.

4. Consider again the degree to which the legislative branch, or public opinion more generally, controls and, in Hegelian terminology, appears opposed to the activities of the bureaucracy:

> The guarantee of the general welfare and public freedom lies in the Estates . . . in the fact that the anticipated censure of the many, especially public censure, has the effect of inducing officials to employ in advance their best judgment [*Einsicht*] with respect to their duties and the plans that they are considering, and to deal with these only in accordance with the purest of motives—a compulsion [*Nötigung*] which is equally effective with respect to the members of the Estates themselves. [301]

Presumably, without such "compulsion," without this kind of external threat, the officials and legislators of the rational state might well act out of other than the purest of motives. That is, it seems, that the correct functioning of at least certain parts of the state depends not exclusively on the free and rational will of those parts but also on the force of various external, heteronomous factors.

5. So the Estates are a barrier against abuse by the executive branch. But again, we should not put too much faith in the legislative powers. For the Estates, "which emerge out of individuality, the private standpoint, and particular interests, are so inclined to devote their activities to these at the expense of the general interest" (301). It looks very much as if the vigilance of the Estates vis-à-vis officialdom might be motivated by self-interest, and vice versa. Ambition is thus made to counteract ambition; the result may be effective in certain ways, but it hardly seems consistent with the fundamental requirements of Hegelian political philosophy as we have described them.

There are countless other cases of apparent checks and balances in the philosophy of Right involving protections against mass society, the usefulness of the agricultural class as a moderating factor owing to its particular empirical circumstances, certain limits on the freedom of expression, and the like. As indicated above, it is hard to know what to make of these. To repeat, Hegel does indeed insist that the opposition among the powers of the state is merely apparent (302), but it is not enough simply to assert this; the overcoming of an apparent contradiction must somehow be demonstrated.

As we have seen, against the modern, external theory of the state there are, in principle, two kinds of organicism. The traditional variety, based on the functionally necessary juxtaposition of parts, seems to be perfectly consistent with all of the apparent oppositions we have discovered; thus, Hegel could claim to resolve them—to show that they are only apparent—on such organicist grounds. The system of checks and balances may be said to serve the larger interests of the whole; hence, there is no "real" opposition among the parts, since all are contributing, in their own distinctive ways, to the health of the organism. But, as we have also seen, Hegel rejects traditional organicism for very important reasons. He insists on an organic unity of otherwise free and rational entities, for only in this way can he fully and decisively solve the problem of individual and society. According to this formulation, the unity of the state must be rooted not simply in some higher principle of organic structure, but in a principle to which the various constituent parts have at least some conscious access so that they are able to recognize and freely affirm it. It is only thus that the individuality of the individual is authentically preserved.

At many points, though, Hegel's solutions seem plainly offensive to this kind of organicism. The unity of the rational state often appears to be based not on free, rational choice but, rather, on propaganda (as in the reliance on patriotic appeals), on outright coercion (using the state's police powers), on political power (as in the system of constitutional checks and balances), or on empirical accident (the fortuitous equilibrium among class interests). Again, the functional requirements of the organism appear to assert themselves despite, or without reference to, the substantial claims of individuality. Hegel does say, and emphasizes the fact, that the rational constitution preserves the "moment of subjectivity." But at many points, subjectivity appears to be preserved only in—by Hegelian standards—an unsatisfying, "abstract" manner, i.e., as private inclination, self-interest, caprice, and the like. The rational constitution most certainly does provide considerable room for the exercise of the "natural" or "arbitrary" will. But, for Hegel, such a will is unfree and irrational; hence, to be responsive to its needs is, in effect, to ignore or even subvert the real claims of individuality and human subjectivity.

We may, of course, decide that the expedients written into the rational constitution are prudent, that the ills they seek to redress are quite real, and that by including them Hegel is introducing a welcome practical dimension to his political philosophy. And, indeed, we could hardly complain about this if Hegel's project were a matter of pragmatic policy analysis. But it seems clear that the philosophy of Right is properly concerned not with this or that expedient designed to scratch this or that particular itch but, rather, with deducing the concept of political society itself. Its goal, that is, is to construct an internally coherent, discursively necessary picture of political society, a standard against which particular societies can be judged and according to which the practice of politics can be prescribed. Thus, the inclusion of such expedients in an account of the concept of the state seems to be, at best, an adulteration. Regardless of their efficacy and attractiveness, they seem to have no place in the philosophy of Right.

But, more strongly, to the degree that they actively contradict certain foundational principles of that philosophy, they suggest rather deeper problems. Throughout the philosophy of Right—in the discussions of crime and punishment, morality, the family, and even civil society—Hegel has painstakingly developed a perfectionist theme, the thesis that the full development of the social order is coincident with, and dependent upon, the equally full development of human freedom and individuality. The claims of political society can be satisfied only through the free, rational, and self-conscious choices of the individuals who comprise that society. Thus, as we have seen, punishment acknowledges the capacity of all humans to attain individuality. The critique of Kantian morality reveals the degree to which individuality is fundamentally a matter of making choices that conform to the dictates of reason. The health of the family is utterly dependent upon the development of individuality in this full sense, upon the capacity of the parties to act on the basis not of the arbitrary will but, rather, the rational will of the "concrete person." In civil society, the encounter with others in a growing web of interdependence demonstrates the need to rewrite the family on a larger scale, to emulate—mutatis mutandis—its example of a freely chosen organic unity at the level of society as a whole. In all of these arguments, and against the dominant theses of modern political thought, Hegel has sought to develop, piece by piece, a new concept of individuality, now seen as involving free and self-conscious membership in a rationally structured community, and also a new concept of society itself, understood as an organic unity of rational and autonomous individuals. With individuality and society thus reconceptualized, the fundamental dialectic of political philosophy is overcome; the apparent contradiction between individual and society simply dissolves.

But the actual account of the rational constitution describes a political society which, at many places, seems to fail in precisely these terms. Organicism survives, but it is no longer clear that it is an organicism rooted in the full development of concrete persons. This may suggest that the culmination of the philosophy of Right is marred only by the inclusion of certain inessential and otherwise intrusive elements, elements that can be dispensed with and that undermine only the presentation, but not the substance, of the concept of the state. More seriously, it may suggest, rather, that Hegel's rational constitution suffers from some deep structural flaws, and that it fails ultimately to fulfill the project of the philosophy of Right as defined and adopted by Hegel himself.

7

Epilogue:
Politics and the Ethical Community

The concept of Right describes an extensive and varied set of institutions or social practices, including the ones we have considered in the preceding chapters. These institutions share several fundamental features. Each is based on a unity of individuals, a rationally justified unity the claims of which must be given a certain priority over other kinds of claims, in particular those of the arbitrary individual will. But, further, unity is in each case dependent upon the individuals themselves recognizing and freely choosing to honor this priority. Thus, the practice of punishment necessarily presupposes the rationality of the criminal; marriage is based on the parties acknowledging and submitting to the discipline of the family; the state is an organic unity of reflective, self-conscious citizenship; and the very idea of ethical life implies the notion of autonomous, rational agency. The complete account of such institutions amounts to a species of what we have called perfectionism. It is a political philosophy that acknowledges and fulfills the legitimate requirements of society while also satisfying, in an equally complete way, the claims of individuality. It achieves this by reconceptualizing each side of the equation, society and individual, in terms of a single, internally consistent set of criteria rooted in human reason.

We have seen, however, that certain of Hegel's particular recommendations appear to controvert the concept of Right understood in this way. In particular, there are features of his account which seem to preserve in the rational state only an attenuated, unsatisfactory sense of individuality, hence to frustrate a basic aim of perfectionism. By way of conclusion, we may make several brief observations in this light that will perhaps more clearly identify the nature of these anomalies and suggest something further about Hegel's importance for the study of political thought.

1. We may begin by wondering exactly what kind of individuality is required by political perfectionism. On the one hand, it seems doubtful that any sensible conception of the state would require that it be filled with philosophers, i.e., persons who have apprehended, as has Hegel, the Idea in all its fullness and complexity. (Indeed, we may well think, with Plato, that a community of philosophers would hardly be a political community at all.) Hegel of course regards the concept of Right as being necessarily consistent with the facts of human nature, and those facts overwhelmingly suggest that very few people indeed will be interested in pursuing a life of speculation. Thus, the citizens of the rational state must be, in some substantial sense, ordinary people.

On the other hand, it also seems clear that the subjectivity or individuality characteristic of the well-ordered community can reside neither in some higher, transpersonal will nor in a playground set aside for the exercise of capricious and arbitrary choice. In each case, the fundamental requirements of perfectionism—as elaborated in discussions of the rational criminal, the reflective moral agent, the responsible partner in marriage—would be seriously compromised. The institutions of ethical life, including the state itself, must be composed of individuals whose membership is a matter of free and reasoned choice; such individuals would be, in Hegel's term, Concrete Persons.

It seems, then, that the Hegelian citizen must have a clear capacity to act in terms of a rational and discernable moral principle, that he be able to appreciate to some degree the sense in which that principle might be legitimate, and that he be situated so as to exercise those capabilities in more or less regular fashion. He must, at a minimum, recognize that the laws of the state, if properly rendered, have a certain moral force, and that his own dignity and individuality importantly rest on his acknowledging and submitting to that force. Such a citizen need hardly be a philosopher. I would suggest that we all know many people who, though lacking any interest in and capacity for philosophy, already fit the bill quite well indeed.

2. Still, it seems certain that most individuals, while perhaps capable of fulfilling the demands of Hegelian citizenship, none-

theless fail to do so in their daily lives, and that we would be hard-pressed to get them to live according to such a standard. Indeed, the anomalies we have found in the philosophy of Right seem to be responsive precisely to this kind of difficulty, the difficulty of approximating in the empirical world the concept of Right. The idea of citizenship implicit in Hegel's perfectionism may be all well and good. But actually putting that idea into practice is quite a different matter; and it is in response to this that Hegel included in his account features designed to accommodate a less-than-perfected citizenry.

As indicated in the previous chapter, I believe that such features cannot be central to Hegel's political thought insofar as the purpose of the philosophy of Right is to derive the concept of Right itself. That concept stands not as a utopia or an ideal to be realized in some distant future; nor can it include practical, "how to" recommendations or specific devices for achieving a "best possible" state. Rather, it presents the underlying truth of political society as we understand it. To analyze Right is to explore a standard which is implicit in our own political practice and against which particular existing institutions may be fruitfully evaluated. Of course, the elucidation of practical remedies or realistic compromises is a perfectly respectable endeavor on its own account. But it cannot be a *philosophical* endeavor, at least in the Hegelian sense of philosophy, hence can play no important role in the "science" of Right. We would do well, then, to identify such elements as secondary and intrusive, and to purge them from our account of Hegel's concept of Right.

3. The problem of translating philosophically derived standards into actual practice is, of course, hardly unique to Hegel. We may, for example, profitably consider some of Rousseau's writings in precisely these terms. Whereas his major works, including the *Social Contract* and the *Emile*, appear to offer a variety of perfectionism, certain of his occasional essays clearly sacrifice perfectionist principles in the interest of practicality. Thus, in *The Government of Poland*, Rousseau devotes rather little attention to the value of individuality or moral liberty and emphasizes, instead, the needs and requirements of the community as a whole. He describes a kind of accommodation, one that happens to be skewed quite decisively in favor of society's rules and patterns.

But, more importantly, it is a solution which, though perhaps informed by the philosophical concept of political society, cannot be said to embody that concept in any adequate way.

Much the same might be said for Kant's political thought. Whereas Kantian ethics seems to be roughly perfectionist in inspiration, insofar as it pictures a "kingdom of ends" composed of free moral agents, his specific political prescriptions often turn out to be far more conventional. Indeed, the problem of translating the ethical philosophy into everyday life is an extremely difficult one for Kant and his admirers; a recent result is the effort to read the Third Critique as containing the source of a Kantian theory of moral and political practice.

4. Along these lines, it may be useful to explore a bit further the comparison between Kant and Hegel. In *Religion within the Limits of Mere Reason*, published rather late in life, Kant distinguishes the concept of a political community from that of an ethical community.[1] The former is understood in accommodationist terms. It is a legal entity, arising contractually out of a state of nature and possessing the legitimate right to coerce individuals: "The freedom of each individual is limited on the basis of those conditions under which the freedom of everyone else can be preserved according to the common law. . . ."[2] As an institution of laws, of legality, the political community is essentially concerned with external behavior; its goal is to regulate the activities of persons so as to achieve an orderly and peaceful society.

On the other hand, an ethical community must be fundamentally noncoercive. Since the very concept of ethics involves freedom from coercion, the notion of an ethical community based on law would be a contradiction in terms. Rather, in Kant's account such a community must be a union of individuals arising out of the freedom and virtue of each and oriented toward a single goal, viz., the idea of a universal republic devoted to moral principles. The focus is not on external behavior, but on the inner morality of actions; and the result is a community of great solidarity composed of free, self-legislating persons.

1. Immanuel Kant, *Die Religion innerhalb der Grenzen der blossen Vernunft* (Hamburg: Felix Meiner, 1956).
2. Ibid., p. 106.

This distinction comports nicely with the categories we have been using, and the comparison with Hegel is instructive. It seems that, for Kant, the concept—the rational essence—of political society is accommodationist; to balance interests is the very nature of the political. Thus, there is a sense in which Kant might well regard practical social remedies not as deviations from, but as efforts to actualize, this concept. I believe that Hegel must disagree. For it seems that, in his account, political society properly understood is rather similar to what Kant calls an ethical community. That is, our underlying view of how humans ought to live together is much closer to the Kantian notion of a universal "church" than it is to a Hobbesian commonwealth. Indeed, it seems that Hegel wishes to subsume all social institutions under a perfectionist ideal; and, as a result, efforts to solve this or that particular problem, to accommodate one set of interests to another, must be deviations from the philosophy of Right. (Again, to say this is not to deny such efforts a perfectly respectable role, but only to rule them out as part of the speculative science of Right.) In this regard, I believe that Hegel's intention to view political society as an ethical community is emblematic of the degree to which his political thought is so very different from the superficially similar views of more orthodox liberals, including Kant himself.

There is a further difference between Kant and Hegel on this general question. For Kant, the laws of an ethical community "cannot be thought of as *originally* emanating merely from the will of some superior. . . . For then they would not be ethical laws and the duty proper to them would not be the free duty of virtue but the coercive duty of law."[3] That is, laws imposed from without would undermine the freedom of individuals, hence undermine the ethical nature of their community. Hegel would fully agree. But Kant's solution is to find the source of such laws in God, understood more or less in the traditional sense; for reasons that are not entirely clear, Kant seems to think that being ruled by God is not really being subject to an external force. In his view, then, an ethical community requires faith in some transcendent and divine entity. Hegel, on the other hand, claims that valid ethical laws can only be discovered through human reason; and while there is cer-

3. Ibid.

tainly a great deal of language in his work pertaining to the notion of a God and relating that notion to reason itself, to *Geist*, it seems that the more traditional, perhaps pietistic view is largely missing from his account.

Thus, while Kant restricts the notion of an ethical community to the nonpolitical sphere and identifies in it a necessary element of faith, Hegel applies a similar notion to political society itself and conceives of it in terms of a rather thoroughgoing rationalism.

5. At this juncture, we may well ask why we should prefer Hegel's account. Kant's derivation of the concept of political society certainly rings a bell. By implication, he seems to be suggesting that the accommodationist view is, in fact, *conceptually*, not just empirically, correct, and that the effort philosophically to derive the concept of political society leads not to an ethical community as Hegel thought but, rather, to a commonwealth along roughly Hobbesian lines.

It seems that Hegel's defense must rest simply on the claim that the accommodationist view, though it perhaps describes something important, cannot express our concept of political society precisely because it fails to solve the problem of individual and society. The presupposition here is that this problem provides the desiderata for identifying a satisfactory theory of the political community; the better the solution, the more adequate the concept. If we accept this, then, as we have seen, a perfectionist approach—similar to what is expressed in Kant's concept of the *ethical* community— must be authoritative for *political* society as well, since an accommodationist concept can do full justice neither to the value of individuality nor to that of society and its rules. The accommodationist concept would, of course, have a stronger case if it could be shown that there is simply no conceptual resolution to the problem of individual and society. But Hegel claims to have demonstrated otherwise, and it may well be that this claim is correct.

6. If it is correct, then the implications for our understanding of post-Hegelian philosophy would be quite dramatic. It would suggest, to begin with, that the perfectionist project does indeed provide the philosophical concept of modern political society, much as Plato had provided the philosophical concept of the polis. The notion of political society qua ethical community, along with a description of the basic features of that society, would amount to

a culmination, so to speak, of modern political philosophy. If, as has been argued, systematic philosophical speculation ends with Hegel, then perhaps so does political philosophy, at least on a grand scale, and for good reason. For to claim that Hegel has indeed derived *the* concept of political society is to claim also that this work no longer needs doing.

I am far from making this claim. Still, even if it were true that Hegel had successfully derived the concept of political society, this would certainly not in itself spell the end of political theory. Rather, it would suggest a certain reorientation of the goals of political thought. To begin with, theorists would presumably concern themselves with the periodic task of rearticulating the perfectionist concept of the community, exploring its dimensions in the light of history and giving it thereby a new kind of vitality and urgency. The language of politics changes, as do certain intellectual habits; the political philosopher would have the role, then, not of discovering but of reappropriating the concept of political society so as to renew and reestablish its authority.

Beyond this, we might well wonder if the concept of political society could ever be truly complete. As we have seen, such a concept may have numerous specific implications pertaining to diverse issues, including punishment, the role of family, the structure of government, and the like. Presumably, the task of a post-Hegelian political philosophy might be to explore such various implications. Given the concept of political society, what should the law of property be? how should representatives be judged? what are the implications for distributive justice? can political society take a life? are there any "natural" rights? It may be that answers to such questions are implicit in the perfectionist project itself, and that deriving those answers would be a basic task of a post-Hegelian philosophy. In this way, the aim of such a philosophy would be not to discover but to flesh out the concept of political society.

Finally, political theorists would presumably also be concerned with those more practical considerations which we have distinguished from the concept of Right itself. These considerations might involve evaluating existing communities in the light of the perfectionist standard and suggesting remedies designed to change communities in appropriate ways. As we have seen, this would not be a philosophical endeavor, at least in the Hegelian sense, but there is no reason why it could not be part of a quite serious and rigorous science or theory of politics informed by philosophical considerations. Thus, Rousseau's prescriptions for Poland take on added force when viewed in the light of the concept of the general will; similarly, a discussion of, say, the American electoral system would surely be strengthened by considering the underlying nature of political society as we understand it.

Again, I am far from claiming that Hegel has indeed discovered the concept of Right. Still, it is worth remarking that the history of post-Hegelian political thought has followed roughly along the lines I have suggested. There have been few if any "grand systems" of political philosophy. Rather, philosophers have been concerned to reappropriate the very concept of political society; they have examined particular issues of political philosophy and have explored them more or less consciously in the light of either an accommodationist or perfectionist perspective; most importantly, they have examined particular societies and have evaluated them with the concept of political society in mind.

Surely the clearest case of political thought in these terms is that of Marx. Indeed, we see in Marx's work each of the basic tasks characteristic of a post-Hegelian philosophy. There is, to begin with, a quite powerful restatement of the perfectionist concept of political society. This is most apparent, I think, in the brief discussion of communism that occurs in the Paris Manuscripts. There Marx describes a deeply unified social system composed of utterly free and fully developed individuals, an anarchist or "nonpolitical" community in which social patterns arise out of and nurture the autonomy of its citizens. He tells us that in communist society "[a]ctivity and mind are social in their content as well as in their *origin*; they are *social* activity and social mind. . . . My *own existence* is a social activity . . . the individual *is* the *social being*."[4] Thus, to be a human, properly understood, is to participate in a web of social relationships or patterns, to be a member of society. Indeed, "[i]ndividual human life and species-life are not different things, even though the mode of existence of individual life is necessarily

4. Karl Marx, *Early Writings*, trans. and ed. T. B. Bottomore (New York: McGraw-Hill, 1964), pp. 157–58.

either a more *specific* or a more *general* mode of species-life. . . . "[5] But further, for Marx, as for Hegel, this social membership must be freely and reflectively chosen by the individual, for the whole development of communism involves a "comprehended and conscious process of becoming."[6] As a result, each individual remains an individual in the truest sense; he is, at one and the same time, a member of a larger organization and a distinctive creature unto himself: "Though man is a unique individual—and it is just his particularity which makes him an individual, a really *individual* communal being—he is equally the *whole*, the ideal whole, the subjective existence of society as thought and experienced."[7] We would certainly not want to conflate the basics of Marx's political thought with those of Hegel. But with this notion of a "really individual communal being," Marx seems to be appropriating and rearticulating something quite akin to the perfectionist idea of citizenship and community; and this idea appears to animate the entire Marxist project.

Of course, Marx also provides a philosophical analysis of numerous conceptual issues emanating from such a view of political society. Thus, we have accounts of alienation and the nature of work, the "metaphysics" of commodity exchange, ideology and the nature of political consciousness, the essence of the family, the relationship between free individuals and the physical world, and the like. When, for example, Marx pursues a theme such as alienation, we may say that he is developing certain of the premises upon which his conception of political society is also based.

Finally, the bulk of Marx's writings are of course concerned with evaluating existing political societies in the light of his concept of the community. His analyses in this respect are broadly empirical and, as such, have a special relationship to the themes we have been pursuing here. Throughout this book we have distinguished two kinds of approaches to the problem of individual and society. One of these involves an effort to accommodate the interests of individuality to those of the social realm, and vice versa; the second contemplates the complete fulfillment of those interests, based on

5. Ibid.
6. Ibid., p. 155.
7. Ibid., p. 158.

a deeper understanding of the concepts involved. As mentioned briefly in chapter 1, though, there is a third approach. The problem of individual and society manifests itself as a contradiction only in certain empirical circumstances. We normally think of such circumstances as being so regular and unavoidable as to be unworthy of critical inspection; but in principle, if those circumstances could be eliminated, then perhaps the contradiction itself would never actually arise.

I would suggest that Marx's approach to the problem of individual and society develops along these general lines. It seems certain that his conceptions of individuality and society are such as to show how the value of each may be maximized without undermining that of the other. Thus, he does indeed pursue a perfectionist strategy. But to this he appends an empirical account of those circumstances in which such a strategy might actually bear fruit, not simply in thought but in practice. Above all, these circumstances involve the suppression of private property. Marx surmises that if the world of affairs were ordered so that (among other things) the accumulation of private wealth were impossible, then conditions would be ripe for the end of alienation. As a result, we might witness the appearance of that "really individual communal being" who, by consciously adopting the standpoint of society as his own, would be affirming his uniqueness and individuality.

The hypothesis, then, is that a perfectionist conception of political society—emerging from Rousseau and philosophically elaborated by Hegel—is adopted by Marx himself; that this conception does indeed describe the essence of modern politics as we understand it; and that Marx begins systematically to explore the philosophically informed but fundamentally nonphilosophical project of asking how circumstances might be changed so as to better approximate that conception in the empirical world. The basic philosophical task, then, culminates in Hegel's philosophy of Right; and the new task, the task of empirical political theory, commences with Marx.

One cannot, perhaps, be very comfortable with such broad hypotheses expressed in so brief a span; they seem, at once, all too obvious and all too obscure. I present them not as claims to be defended, but merely as hypothetical speculations that may suggest at least some of the stakes involved in my account of the philosophy of Right. But there is here a further qualification to be made. For these speculations assume not only that Hegel was concerned with "modern" politics but that post-Hegelian political thought continues to be involved with, and influenced by, this same historical phenomenon, the phenomenon we call modernity. If this assumption is correct, then the attempt to reappropriate and put into practice Hegel's concept of Right would be entirely apt. We must recall, though, that according to Hegel himself philosophy comes on the scene too late and that it can only uncover the essence of a world already beginning to decay, a world being brushed aside by a new order, vigorous, inexorable, yet still opaque to philosophical reason. If in fact we find Hegel's political philosophy persuasive, if we come to regard his system as authoritative, we must nevertheless consider the possibility that it is so only for yesterday, that it is in some deep sense an anachronism, and that the emergent world of politics awaits a new "grand theory" the outlines of which cannot be even dimly perceived. To be sure, it is hard to imagine what might come after modernity; the notion of a "post- modernism" seems altogether too parasitic. But if some such era is indeed looming somewhere on the horizon, then we can only presume that Hegel will be related to a new philosopher of politics in much the same way that Plato is related to Hegel— a relationship of sublation, of preservation yet annullment, resulting in a new, dramatically different account of political society which may, at first blush, seem entirely conventional and plain.

Index

251